TERRORISM IN INDIA AND ABROAD

TERRORISM IN INDIA AND ABROAD

Solutions to Prevent it

Smita Sahebrao Sonavane

KALPAZ

Terrorism in India and Abroad: Solutions to Prevent it

ISBN: 978-81-7835-882-6

Published in 2011 in India by
Kalpaz Publications
C-30 Satyawati Nagar Delhi-110052
E-mail: kalpaz@hotmail.com
Phone: 9212729499

Leser Type Setting by: Square Vision, Delhi

Printed at : Chawla Offset Press, Delhi

CONTENTS

In her aspiration
By our inspiration
This research work is dedicated
to my beloved caring and concerned
mother Late Smt. Vijaya Devi
Sahebrao Sonavane who died on
17th August 2000

PREFACE

I am very thankful to my guide Dr. B. S. Bharaswadkar, due to able and competent Guidance of Dr. Bharaswadkar I could complete my research work. I also express my thanks to the libraries of university and colleges of different areas of India i.e., Delhi, Mumbai, Bangalore, Hyderabad and also High Court of Mumbai and Andhra Pradesh and also Indian Institute of Law Delhi. I also express my thanks to the Nagpur High Court, Aurangabad High Court and Nagpur University. I also express my thanks to Ambassadors of America, Russia and Indonesia etc. for giving necessary information.

During completion of this difficult work, my husband, my father, mother and brother sister and in-laws etc. assisted me and also encouraged me to do this work. Jail officers, Justices and Judges and also brother Advocates and Principals of Law Colleges also had given co-operation for completion of this work.

I sincerely acknowledge all these above mentioned persons and also express my sincere gratitude towards them.

Smita Sahebrao Sonavane

INTRODUCTION

September 11, 2001, World Trade Centre, October 1, 2001, J & K Assembly, Srinagar, December 13, 2001, Parliament House, New Delhi, September 24, 2004 Swaminarain Temple, Gandhi Nagar. These are the few examples of sheer madness committed by the terrorists on Government buildings and innocent people, due to which several precious lives have been lost.

This method of madness is adopted by various terrorist organizations to attack the symbol of power to destabilize sovereign nations. If it does not work, terrorists change strategy to attack religious symbols. Their sinister plan is to provoke the sectarian and communal violence. These are not fanatics on the loose but pawns of mastermind bent upon to destabilize the whole world, especially India.

Terrorists always have the advantage of surprise attack combined with suicidal zeal. This makes the job of security personnel extremely difficult, especially if the strategy is focused to it soft targets like temples.

To curb these terrorist violence a new enactment, namely, "THE PREVENTION OF TERRORISM ACT, 2002" (POTA) has been enacted. The object of enacting this new Act will be clear from the statement and objects and reasons appended to the "Prevention of Terrorism Bill, 2002".

"The country faces multifarious challenges in the management of its internal security. There is an upsurge of terrorist activities, intensification of cross-border terrorist activities and insurgent groups in different parts of the country. Very often, organized crime and terrorist activities are closely inter-linked. Terrorism has now acquired global dimensions and has become a challenge for the entire world. The reach and methods adopted by terrorist groups and organizations take advantage of modern means of communication and technology using high teach facilities available in the form of communication systems, transport, sophisticated arms and various other means. This has enabled them to strike and create terror among people at will. The existing criminal justice system is not designed to deal with the type of heinous crimes with which the proposed law deals with.

In view of the situations, as stated above, it was felt necessary to enact legislation for the prevention of, and for dealing with, terrorist activities. However, sufficient safeguards are sought to be provided in the proposed law to prevent the possibility of its misuse. Parliament was not in session and the circumstances existed which rendered it necessary for the President to promulgate the Prevention of Terrorism Ordinance, 2001 on 24th October 2001. During the Winter Session of Parliament in December, 2001 steps were taken for the introduction of the Prevention of Terrorism Bill, 2001 in the Lok Sabha. However, the Bill could not be introduced and considered in the Lok Sabha as Parliament adjourned Sine Die on 19th December, 2001. The terrorist attack on Parliament House on 13th December, 2001 and the prevailing circumstances rendered it necessary for the President to promulgate Prevention of Terrorism (Second) Ordinance, 2001 on 30th December, 2001 with a view to give continuity to the Prevention of Terrorism Ordinance, 2001 promulgated on 24th October, 2001."

The Prevention of Terrorism Bill, 2002 seeks to replace the Prevention of Terrorism (Second) Ordinance, 2001.

In Simranjit Singh Mann v. Union of India, 2002 Cr LJ 3368 at paras 6 to 11, Jawahar Lal Gupta, J. of Punjab & Haryana High Court has evaluated the summary of the Prevention of Terrorism Act, 2002 as under:

"It has six chapters. The First one gives the short title, extent, application, commencement and duration of the Act. Section 2 defines various expressions used in the Act. Chapter II consists of Sections 3 to 17. Section 3 has seven clauses. Sub-section (1) defines a "terrorist act". Clause 2 prescribes the penalty. Clause 3 provides for punishment of persons who conspire or attempt to commit or advocate, abet, advise or knowingly facilitate "the commission of a terrorist act or any act preparatory to terrorist act". Clause 4 provides for penalty to the persons who voluntarily harbour or conceal or attempt to harbour or conceal "any person knowing that such person is a terrorist". This provision does not apply "to any case in which the harbour or concealment is made by the husband or wife of the offender". Clause 5 provides for punishment "which may extend to imprisonment for life or with fine which may extend to Rs. 10 lacs or with both" to any person "who is a member of the terrorist gang or a terrorist organization........." The holding of the proceeds of any terrorist act is made punishable under Clause 6. Sub-section (7) is intended to ensure a free and fair trial. It provides for the award of penalty to a person who threatens a witness or any other persons in whom such witness may be interested, with violence or wrongfully restrains or confines such person. Unauthorized possession of arms or ammunitions in a notified area, or bombs, dynamite or hazardous explosive substances or other lethal weapons capable of mass destruction or a biological or chemical substance of warfare is made punishable under Section 4. Contravention of the Provisions of the Explosive Act, 1884, the Explosive Substances Act, 1908, the Inflammable Substances Act, 1954, the Arms Act, 1959 with an "intent to aid any terrorist" is made punishable with imprisonment for a term which may extend to imprisonment for life" and also fine under Section 5. Holding of proceeds of terrorism has been made illegal and these are made liable to forfeited under Section 6. Section 7 gives the powers of the Investigating Officers and provides for appeal against the orders of the designated authority. Section 8 provides for the forfeiture of proceedings of terrorism. Under Section 9, provision for issue of show cause notice before an order for proceeds of terrorism is passed, has been made. Section10 provides for an appeal to the High Court against an order of the Special Court, which passes the order for forfeiture. Under Section 11, it has been provided that the order of forfeiture shall not debar the award of any other punishment. Section 12 deals with the claims of third parties. Section 13 confers the powers of a Civil Court on the designated authority for the purpose of "making a full and fair enquiry into the matter before it". Section 14 makes it obligatory for the named authority to furnish the information sought by an investigating officer.

Section 15 provides that transfer of property after the issue of an order under section 7 or notice under section 9 is liable to be ignored. Section 16 authorizes attachment and forfeiture of property belonging to a person who has been convicted of an offence punishable under the Act. Under Section 17, it has been made incumbent upon a company to transfer shares to the Central or State Government.

Chapter III consists of Sections 18 to 22. It deals with terrorist organizations. Chapter IV (Sections 23 to 35) provides for the constitution of Special Courts, the place of sitting, jurisdiction, powers, the public prosecutors, procedure, protection of witnesses, admissibility of confessions made to police officers, transfer of cases to regular Courts, appeal and transfer of pending proceedings etc.

Chapter V (Section 36 to 48) arms the authority with power of interception of electronic communication etc. Chapter VI consists of 47 to 64. It contains miscellaneous provision in regard to procedure, cognizance of offences, officers competent to investigate, arrest permissible presumptions bar of jurisdiction of Civil Courts, exclusion of proceedings before Courts or other authority under any law relating to naval, military, air force and other armed forces of the Union. Section 56 gives over riding effect to the provisions of the Act. Section 57 protects the Government and its officers in respect of action taken in good faith. Section 58 provides for punishment and compensation for malicious action. The passport and arms license of a person charge-sheeted under the Act is "deemed to have been impounded for such period as the Special Court may deem fit under Section 59". Section 60 provides for the constitution of review committees. The High Courts have been empowered to frame rules by notification in the Official Gazette for carrying out the provisions of the Act relating to Special Courts within their territories. A similar power to frame rules for carrying out the purposes of the Act has also been conferred on the Central Government. Under Section 63, the orders and rules made by the Central Government have to be placed before Parliament. Section 64 repeals the Ordinance and saves any action taken there under.

The Schedule to the Act enlists the Terrorist Organizations. The qualifications for appointment etc. of the Chairperson and the Members of the Review Committee have been prescribed under the "Review Committee (Qualifications for Appointment and other Conditions of Service of the Chairperson and Members) Rules, 2002".

About the rationale for the Prevention of Terrorism Act, 2002, Punjab and Haryana High Court in Simranjit Singh Mann v. Union of India, 2002 Cr LJ 3368 at pp. 3373-76 in paras 17 to 25 and 29 to 30 observed as under:

"Terror', 'Terrorism' or 'Terrorist' have not been defined in the impugned legislation. But these are not terms of art. The plain meaning as given in the dictionary should suffice. In this sense, "terror" means : a state of intense fright or apprehension, stark fear". Similarly, 'terrorism' means "the systematic use of terror as a means of coercion; an atmosphere of threat or violence". A 'terrorist' is "an advocate or practitioner of terror as a means of coercion, one who panics or causes anxiety". However, this term was duly defined in Section 2 (1) (h) of the Terrorist Affected Areas (Special Courts) Act, 1984.

Terrorism and violence are not a recent phenomenon. We live in a world that has crucified Christ, assassinated Abraham Lincoln, killed Kennedy and murdered Mahatma Gandhi. Today, as noticed by their Lordships of the Supreme Court in Kartar Singh v. State of Punjab, 1994 (2) JT (SC) 423: (1994 Cri LJ 3139) the terrorists "are waging a domestic war against the sovereignty of their respective nations or against a race or community in order to create an embryonic imbalance and nervous disorder in the society either on being stimulated or instigated by the national, transnational or international hardcore criminals or secessionists etc. Resultantly, the security and integrity of the countries concerned are at peril and the law and order in many countries is disrupted......... The cult of the bullet is hovering the globe completely robbing off the reasons and rhymes."

In India, different parts of the country have continued to remain disturbed for a long time. The States in the North, Northeast and South are still witnessing violence against men and materials. Thousands of innocent men and women have been murdered. Tons of arms and ammunition have been recovered. The States and the Centre have periodically, promulgated various statutes. Yet, the evil has not been eradicated. The situation continues to be bad. It is a matter of coercion for the citizen and the society.

In view of the prevailing security situation in the country, it is not surprising that the Government of India had requested the Law Commission to "undertake a fresh examination of the issue of a suitable legislation for combating terrorism and other anti-national activities.......". In pursuance to this request from the Government, the Commission had undertaken a study. A working paper was prepared and circulated. While dealing with the security situation in difficult parts of the country, it was inter alia noticed by the Commission that:

(i) There have been 45182 incidents of terrorist violence in the State of Jammu and Kashmir during the period from 1988 to March, 1999. In this violence, 20506 persons had lost their lives. There were numerous cases of abductions, robberies, extortions, explosions, arson and killing. Security forces personnel, friendly militants and political activists were the priority targets of the militants. Most of the militants were of foreign origin. Mercenaries and fanatic fundamentalist terrorists from Afghanistan, Sudan, Pakistan and other countries are being inducted increasingly into its movement. The terrorism of India has become a part of international terrorism and India one of its prime targets.

(ii) The State of Punjab remains vulnerable to sporadic terrorist actions by the remnants of the militants who appear to be under pressure to revive the separatist movement. The militant bodies are funded and equipped mainly by the overseas activists.

(iii) North East Region : Militant activities of various insurgent and extremist groups and ethnic tensions have kept the conditions disturbed in large areas of the North East. Details regarding the role of specific groups in different areas were noticed.

(iv) The religious militancy which had first raised its head in 1993 with bomb explosions in Mumbai, continues to make its presence felt. In 1997, there were 23 blasts in Delhi. In the year 1998 , Mumbai witnessed three explosions just before the Parliamentary elections. Al-Ummah, the fundamentalist militant outfit of Southern India was responsible for 17 blasts in different areas of Coimbatore.

(v) The ISI sponsored terrorism and proxy war has resulted in deaths of 29151 civilians, 5101 security personnel and 2730 explosions. Property worth Rs. 2000 cores is reported to have been damaged. Almost 437600 Kg. of explosives, mostly RDX, had been inducted and 61900 sophisticated weapons had been smuggled into India. It is estimated that the security related costs in countering ISI's activities have totaled an amount of Rs. 64,000 crores.

In view of these reasons (which have been culled out from the report) the Commission had agreed with the opinion of the Government that Indian requires "a permanent anti-terrorist law". Thus, the paper was prepared and circulated by the Law Commission.

The release of the Working Paper was followed by "the hijacking of the Indian Airlines Flight IC-814, the release of three notorious terrorists by the Government of India to save the lives of innocent civilians and the crew of the said flight". The Commission conducted seminars. Divergent views were expressed during discussions. The representatives of Human Rights Organizations had "questioned the very necessity" of a "legislation to combat terrorism". It was contended that "TADA was widely abused and misused by the police authorities.......... It had not succeeded in checking terrorism............. if TADA could not successfully counter terrorism.............. how could the present legislation succeed". The existing laws like the Indian Penal Court were enough to effectively deal with even the prevailing situation.

On the other hand, supporters of the law "pointed out that today India was threatened not only with external terrorism but also with internal terrorism. The Indian Penal Court was not conceived and not meant for fighting organized crimes, it was designed only to check individual crimes and occasional riots at local level. Crime perpetrated by highly trained and armed fanatical elements who are trained, finance, armed and supported by the hostile foreign countries and agencies had to be fought at a different level than as an ordinary law and order crime.

The Law Commission considered the matter. Even the views expressed on behalf of the National Human Rights Commission were noticed. On a detailed examination of the views, the Law commission in its 173rd report concluded that "a legislation to fight terrorism is today a necessity in India". This report was submitted to the Government in April, 2000.

The Government did not rush. The Act was not promulgated in haste. However, the situation in the country showed no signs of improvemente. In fact, the acts of violence were on the increase. The attack on the World Trade Centre on the morning of September 11, 2001, bears testimony to the fears expressed by the protagonists of a law for prevention of terrorism. The senseless attack on the Indian Parliament could have reinforced the view. Organized acts of terrorism are no longer confined to a particular place or country. The threat is global. And it is on the increase. Despite, the fact that America has attacked Afghanistan with the most effective means of destruction. Thus, the need for the impugned Act.

The 'upsurge of terrorist activities', 'intensification of cross border terrorism', the violence perpetrated by the 'insurgent groups' are an existing reality and a global phenomenon. The 'modern means of communication' and other facilities enables the terrorists 'to strike and create terror at will'. The existing justice delivery system was not equipped to deal with the 'heinous crimes'. Thus, the imperative need 'to make provisions for the prevention of and for dealing with terrorist activities and for matters connected therewith'. The aims and objects disclosed at the time of introduction of the Bill and the 'preamble' provide a clear answer and the real rationale for the promulgation of the Act by the Parliament.

The promulgation of a statute is primarily a question of policy. It has to be decided by the legislature. Defense of India is a matter of national concern. It is not an issue for debate. The present matter lay clearly within the province of the Parliament. It has promulgated the Act. And we are not the only people to have felt the need for such a law. The United States of America had promulgated the "Anti- terrorism and Effective Death Penalty Act, 1996". Similarly, in the United Kingdom, different Acts have been periodically promulgated. One of these being "The Criminal Justice (Terrorism and Conspiracy) Act, 1998". If various countries have felt a need for statutes to combat terrorism, there appears to be no reasons to accept the contention that India could have done without it. There is a clear rationale for the Act.

About the constitutionality of the Act observation of Punjab and Haryana High Court at paras 36 to 38 in Simranjit Singh Mann v. Union of India, 2002 Cr.LJ 3368 at pp. 3375-76 is quote worthy as under:

The State is under a duty to protect the people, their person and property. This duty is as sacred and sacrosanct as the guarantee of a person's right to equality, life and liberty. And then, every right carries with it a duty. The need to synthesis right with duty so as to achieve the objective of a cohesive community, has been historically recognized. The French Convention of 1793 records that "common happiness" is the aim of society. The basic purpose of law is to ensure "the greatest happiness of the greatest number." In this context W. Friedman in 'Legal Theory' (5th Ed.) has said that:

"The relation of the rights of the individual to those of his fellow individuals in the community has gradually led to a profound modification of the legal values of the modern democracy. It has increasingly tempered individual right by social duty……. Democratic communities have universally, though with varying speed and intensity, accepted the principle of social obligation as limiting individual right".

Every right rests upon some degree of restriction. Social obligation limits the individual's liberty. The society has its own science. Liberty can never mean license. It does not mean doing what one likes. Nor can it lie in destroying the rights of others. In a civilized society, liberty should only insure that a person is able to do what he ought to be doing. Every man has to respect the rights of other before he can justifiably assert his own. Liberty has to be earned before it can be enjoyed. Men of "intemperate habits" cannot be free. Their passions forge their fetters." While advocating the cause of 'Human Rights', this basic truth has to be remembered.

The terrorist causes a terrible trauma to the innocent. His acts pose a threat to the human society. A person who "with intent to threaten the integrity, security or sovereignty of India or to strike terror in the people or any section of people does any act or thing by using bombs. Dynamite or other explosive substances………. of a hazardous nature or by any other means whatsoever…….. "or is and continues to be a member of an association declared unlawful under" a statue cannot justifiably complain of discrimination when he is treated differently from another who commits a bridge of law under totally different circumstances. A person who threatened the sovereignty and integrity of the country is certainly different from a person who merely threatens an individual. The two are not similarly situate. Unequal cannot complain of inequality. In the present case, the differential resentment rests upon a valid foundation. The provisions of the Act do not suffer from the vice of discrimination as envisaged under Art.14 of the Constitution. In fact, a similar argument was categorically negatived in Kartar Singh v. State of Punjab, 1994 Cri LJ 3139 : 1994 (3) SCC 569 1994 (2) JT 423".

About the right and liberty of an individual under the Act, the Punjab and Haryana High Court in Simranjit Mann v. Union of India, 2002 Cr LJ 3368 at pp. 3368 at pp. 3376-77 at paras 42 to 47 observed :

"At perusal of the provisions of the Act shows that at every stage the powers under the Act have been conferred on high authorities. The Act contemplates a 'designated authority'. It is defined under section 2 (b) to mean an officer 'of the Central Government not below the rank of Joint Secretary to Government or........ of the State Government not below the rank of Secretary' as may be specified "by a notification published in the Official Gazette. The 'authority' has to make an enquiry. Under Section 13 of the Act, the authority has been armed with "all the powers of a Civil Court required for making a full and fair enquiry into the matter before it." Under Section 18, provision in respect of terrorist organizations has been made. These are listed in the Schedule. The Central Government has the power to add to or remove an organization from the Schedule. Even an application can be filed to the Central Government for the removal of an organization from the Schedule. The order of the Central Government can be reviewed by the Review Committee in exercise of the powers under Sections 19(5) and 19(6). Provision for the constitution of Review Committee has been made in Section 62. Not only that. Even rules governing the appointment etc. of the Chairperson and Members of the 'Review Committee' have been duly promulgated. Under Rule 3, a person who has been or is a sitting Judge of the High Court can be the Chairperson. The Member has to be of the rank of a Secretary in the Government.

Then, there is a complete machinery for the judicial process. Section 23 of the Act provides for the Constitution etc. of the Special Courts. Clause 4 provides that "a special Court shall be presided over by a Judge to be appointed by the Central Government or as the case may be, the State Government, with the concurrence of the Chief Justice of the High Court." By virtue of Clause 6, a person "shall not be qualified for appointment as a Judge or an Additional Judge of a Special Court unless he is immediately before such appointment, a Sessions Judge or an Additional Sessions Judge in any State." Every offence punishable under the Act can be tried" only by the Special Court........ constituted for trying such offence under Section 23. "The case pending before a Special Court can be transferred to any other Special Court within the State by the High Court. The Supreme Court can transfer a case even outside a State. Such order of transfer can be passed in cases where it is" not possible to have a fair, impartial or speedy trial, or it is not feasible to have the trail without occasioning the breach of peace or grave risk to the safety of the accuse: the witnesses, the Public Prosecutor and a Judge of the Special Court or any of them" or in the interest of justice. Section 29 provides the procedure and powers of Special Courts. It ensures the grant of a reasonable opportunity to the accused.

Section 34 provides that an appeal shall lie from "any judgment sentence or order, not being an interlocutory order of a special Court to the High Court both on facts and on law. "Such appeals have to be "heard by a Bench of two Judges of the High Court." Even when the special Court grants or refuses bail, a provision for appeal to the High Court has been made.

Even investigation has been entrusted to senior officers. Section 51 inter alia provides that an officer investigating the case under the Act shall not be below the rank of Deputy Superintendent of Police.

The Act makes a clear provision to ensure that the procedure is fair. Under Section 52, it is obligatory for police officer who arrests a person to inform him "of his right to consult a legal practitioner as soon as he is brought to the Police Station". Information of his arrest has to be "immediately communicated by the police officer to a family member or in his absence to a relative of such person, by telegram, telephone or by any other members and this fact" has to be "recorded by the police officer under signature of the person arrested." During the course of interrogation, the person arrested has to be "permitted to meet the legal practitioner representing him".

A perusal of the provisions shows that keeping in view the seriousness of the offence involved and the rights of the individual, provisions for investigation by Senior Officers, trial by persons of the rank of Sessions Judge and appeal to the High Court have been made. Safeguards have been provided at every stage".

About the safeguards for the accused under the Act, paras 48 to 54 in Simranjit Singh Mann v. Union of India, 2002 Cr LJ 3368 at pp. 3377-78 are noteworthy:

"The Statue takes within its fold the terrorists as well as the terrorist organizations. It provides for penalty not only to the persons indulging in a terrorist act but also for the forfeiture of the property. Section 7 empowers the Investigating Officer not below the rank of a Superintendent of Police to make an order for attachment or seizure of the property. However, even this provision has in-built safeguards. Firstly, the Investigation Officer should have "reason to believe". Secondly, he has to seek prior approval in writing of the Director General of Police of the State in which the property is situated. Thirdly, the Investigating Officer has to "inform the designated authority as defined under Section 2 (i) (b) within 48 hours of the seizure or attachment of the property". Thereafter, the designated authority has to give an "opportunity of making a representation" to the "person whose property is being attached". The designated authority can confirm or revoke the order of attachment. Thereafter, a person aggrieved by the order of the designated authority has the right to file an appeal before the Special Court. Similarly, under Section 8, the property that "constitutes proceeds of terrorism can be ordered to be forfeited by the Special Court." Even in this behalf, Section 9 provides for the issue of a show cause notice before passing any adverse order for the forfeiture of property. Under Section 10, an appeal lies against the order of the Special Court to the High Court.

The obvious objects is to reach the property of the terrorist who often finds a safe haven abroad and eludes the process of law. In any event the provisions embody a fair procedure and ensure an adequate opportunity.

A 'terrorist act' is defined in Section 3. The penalties vary from fine forfeiture of property, and life imprisonment to death sentence. However, there are adequate safeguards. The power is vested in high authorities. There is provision for grant of adequate opportunity at every stage. The Act postulates a fair trial. The order passed by the 'Designated Authority' or the 'Special Court' can be questioned by way of an appeal. The appeal against an order of conviction passed by the Special Court lies to the High Court. Still further, the safeguard as envisaged by their Lordships of the Supreme Court in Kartar Singh's case (supra) while considering the constitutional validity of TADA have been clearly provided.

A perusal of Section 3 shows that a person who threatens the unity, integrity, security or sovereignty of India or continues to be member of an unlawful association can be awarded the punishment of death or imprisonment for life. The members of organizations, which are involved in the terrorist act, are also considered guilty of the offence. For that too, a deterrent punishment of imprisonment which may extend to a term for life or/and fine, which may extend to Rs. 10 lakhs, has been provided.

The quantum of punishment is primarily a question of policy. It is for the Parliament to prescribe it. The Court can interfere only if the provision is arbitrary and, thus, unconstitutional. A perusal of the provision shows that the punishment can "extend of imprisonment for life." The statue does not provide the minimum. It cannot be said to be arbitrary. It vests a clear discretion in the Court. This is all the more so in view of the fact the offence under the Act is heinous and the power has been vested in Special Courts. Still further, the remedy of appeal etc. before a Division Bench of the High Court provides for judicial review of the decision. And then the constitutional remedies before the Apex Court are also there. In this context, the observations of Krishna Aiyar, J. in Sunil Batra v. Delhi Administration, (1980) 3 SCC 488 ; (1980 Cri LJ 1099) may be noticed-

'A prisoner wears the amour of basic freedom even behind bars and that on breach thereof by lawless officials, the law will respond to his distress signals through writ aid. The Indian Human has a constant companion—the Court armed with the Constitution'.

"Resultantly, it is clear that there are adequate safeguards for the accused".

With regard to protection of witnesses under Section 30 of the prevention of Terrorism Act, 2002 the Punjab and Haryana High Court at paras 55 to 58 in Simranjit Singh Mann v. Union of India, 2002 Cr LJ 3368 at 3378-79 observed as under:

"The provision provides as under:

"30. Protection of witnesses: (1) Notwithstanding anything contained in the Code, the proceeding under this Act may, or reason to be recorded in writing, be held in camera if the Special Court so desires.

(2) A Special Court, if on an application made by a witness in any proceeding before it or by the Public Prosecutor in relation to such witness or on its own motion, is satisfied that the life of such witness is in danger, it may, for reasons to be recorded in writing, take such measures as it deems fit for keeping the identity and address of such witness secret.

(3) In particular, and without prejudice to the generality of the provisions of sub-section (2) the measures which a Special Court may take under that sub-section may include-

(a) The holding of the proceeding at a place to be decided by the Special Court.

(b) The avoiding of the mention of the names and addresses of the witness in its orders or judgment or in any records of the case accessible to public;

(c) The issuing of any directions for securing that the identity and address of the witness are not disclosed;

(d) A decision that it is in the public interest to order that all or any of the proceedings pending before such a Court shall not be published in any manner.

(4) Any person who contravenes any decision or direction issued under sub-section (3) shall be punishable with imprisonment for a term which may extend to one year and with fine which may extend to one thousand rupees."

The provision does not in terms say that the identity of the witness shall not be disclosed to the accused in any case. Thus, the claim as made by the counsel that the provision denies fair trial cannot be sustained. Still further, the provision is primarily meant to protect the witness. That too, when it is satisfied that there is a good reason for it. Nothing more.

A perusal of the provisions of Section 30 shows that the Special Court can, for reasons to be recorded in writing, order that the proceedings be held in camera. Under Clause 2, a witness or the Public Prosecutor can take an application. The Court can proceed even suo motu. If it finds "reasons to be recorded in writing" that "the life of such witness is in danger" then it can take "such measures as it deems fit for keeping the identity and address of such witness secret." Clearly, the provision is only intended to provide a sense of security to the witness. Not to deny a just and fair opportunity to the accused. It is only in a case where the Court is satisfied that there is danger to the life of the witness that his identity and address can be kept secret. The provision only promotes the interest of justice. It is meant to guarantee that the witnesses are able to appear and depose without fear of retribution at the hands of terrorists or the other members of their gangs. The legislative intent is clear. The real purpose of the provision becomes obvious on a perusal of the provision in Clause 3 whereby the Special Court is empowered to hold the proceedings at a place it considers appropriate. The names and addresses of the witnesses may not be recorded in the orders, judgments or placed on record of the case, which may be accessible to public. The Court is empowered to issue directions to ensure that the identity and address of the witnesses are not disclosed. In the larger interest of public, the publication of the proceedings can be regulated. Violation of an order of the Court has been made punishable with imprisonment.

The provision is not arbitrary or unfair. It has a purpose to serve. It seeks to ensure a fair trial for the accused and to protect the life of witness. The existing circumstances and the past experience justify it. There is no infraction of any right or law."

About the role of police under the Prevention of Terrorism Act, 2002 the Punjab and Haryana High Court in Simranjit Singh Mann v. Union of India, 2002 Cr. LJ 3368 at paras 60 to 65 observed:

Firstly, A word about the police.

In a society governed by the rule of law, the policeman plays important role. The car driver does not see the red light till there is a cop. Nobody observes any speed limit when there is no patrol car. The burglar is kept at bay, even if there is a retired old man in uniform. The policeman is the guardian of the individual's person and property. He is the guarantor of the citizen's freedom. The presence of the policeman is essential to maintain law and order.

Today, the human society faces a devaluation of values. A Spiritual impoverishment. A social collapse. Criminality. Whatever be the cause, we are all a part of the system. Every one of us is a product of the society that we live in. When the 'wood is crooked, the furniture cannot be straight.'

People criticizes the police everyday. In one voice. At all levels. The chorus is-It does not have "a License to kill. Police needs paradigm-shift." The Bench and the Bar, the Citizen and the Criminal, the Press and the politician, the Rogue and the Reformist' denounce the police. The cant of criticism is continuous. It is fair?

No one can please every one. Such an attempt shall spell a formula for failure. No one can be perfect. Perfection is still an enigma. A new aberrations shall occur everywhere. But a few black sheep, who may exist in all sections of society, cannot blacken the face of the whole force. Nor can individual errors justify a generalization. The criticism of the police may be justified. But there is also a need to notice the difficulties that the policemen face. We have to develop a respect for the man in uniform. He is the symbol of State's authority. He has to discharge onerous duties. He must be supported and trusted. Only then he would gain in confidence and have a proper sense of responsibility. Distrust of the policeman can only destroy the fading morale of the force. We need to change our perception. The present provision appears to be a step in that direction."

About the admissibility of confession before the police officer as provided under the Section 32 of the Prevention of Terrorism Act, 2002, the Punjab and Haryana High Court in Simranjit Singh Mann v. Union of India, 2002 Cr LJ 3368 at p. 3380 visualized certain safeguards as to confession by accused before the police officer and observed:

"What are the safeguards?

Only an officer who is not below the rank of a Superintendent of Police can record the confession. It has to be recorded in writing or on any mechanical or electronic device like cassette, tape or sound track. Before recording the confession, the accused person has to be warned. The concerned officer has to explain to the accused in writing that "he is not bound to make a confession and that if he does so it may be used against him." The accused has the option to remain silent. The police officer cannot compel him to make any confession has to be recorded "in an atmosphere free from threat or inducement and" has to be "in the same language in which the person makes it". The matter does not end here. There is a further safeguard. The person making confession has to be "produced before the Court of a Chief Metropolitan Magistrate or the Court of a Chief Judicial Magistrate along with the original statement of confession written or recorded on mechanical or electronic device within 48 hours". The Magistrate has to "record the statement made by the person so produced and get his signature or thumb impression." In case of "any complaint of torture", the person has to be produced "for medical examination before a Medical Officer not lower in rank than an Assistant Civil Surgeon". The person has then to be sent to the judicial custody. If is clear that the provision enough protection to the person.

The impugned section does not embody anything unknown to the civilized society. Various countries accept confession made before a police officer. It has various safeguards. It is not arbitrary. The accused in case of complaint has the right to inform the Chief Judicial Magistrate etc. Medical examination eliminates chances of extraction of confession by inducing fear or inflicting torture etc.

It is undoubtedly true that under the Evidence Act, 1872, the statement made before a police officer is not treated as substantive evidence. However, the departure from the provision under the Indian Evidence Act does not vitiate the provision. In fact, the issue has to be considered in the context of the problem that confronts the country. If the innocent people have to be saved from the terrible trauma caused by terrorists, a departure from the archaic rules of evidence is essential.

And then a similar provision had been made TADA. It was upheld in Kartar Singh's case. It was invoked. The petitioner has referred to the case of Devinder Pal Singh. The death sentence based on confession made by the accused before a police was sustained by their Lordships of the Supreme Court in Devinder Pal Singh v. State N.C.T. of Delhi, JT 2002 (3) SC 264. By majority, the Court had held that "justice cannot be made sterile on the plea that it is better to let hundred guilty escape than punish an innocent. Letting guilty escape is not doing justice according to law. "Thus, the provision is not unknown to law or the Courts."

Regarding the bail of accused under the POTA, 2002 it is observed in Simranjit Singh Mann v. Union India, 2002 Cr JT 3368 at para 76 as under.

It is undoubtedly true that in cases of ordinary crime, 'bail and not jail' is the normal rule. Liberty of the citizen is important. However, as already stated, the terrorist belongs to a totally different class. A stringent provision regarding grant of bail is only intended to preserve public peace. It is to ensure that there is no recurrence of the crime. Thus, the Court been empowered to deny bail unless it is "satisfied that there are grounds for believing that he is not guilty." Grant of bail is always a matter of discretion with the Court. Guidance for the exercise of the undoubted discretion cannot be said to be arbitrary or unreasonable. This is all the more so in the context of the malaise that the statute aims to check.

With regard to constitutional validity of the Prevention of Terrorism Act, 2002, the Punjab and Haryana High Court in need to arm itself with adequate authority to protect the liberty of the law abiding. The existing laws were not enough to fulfill the desired objective. Thus, the impugned Act was made. This is a good man's shield. Also his sword. There is a clear basis for granting protection to the witnesses varying the normal procedure to a limited extent : permitting the confession recorded by an officer not below the rank of a Superintendent of Police to be used against the accused and in placing a restriction on the grant of a bail to a person charged with an offence under the Act. It does not violate the constitutional mandate. There are definite safeguards in the statue. The mere possibility of the power being abused is not enough to annul the Act. The door has to be kept open for trial and error. In any event, even if sum authority acts arbitrarily the law's arms are long enough to reach it. The Act provides adequate remedy against the acts of arbitrariness.

The Act contains a detailed mechanism for investigation by senior officers. It ensures a fair and speedy trial by an officer not below the rank of a Sessions Judge. The aggrieved person has the remedy of appeal to a Division Bench of the High Court. There are adequate safeguards at every stage. In any event, the provision for judicial review ensures justice.

The crime punishment comes out of the same stem. The criminal should have no cause for complaint against the punishment. His sin is the seed. Punishment is for prevention. The terrible terror created by the terrorist is a cause for concern to the society. Certainty and speed are essential for ensuring the efficacy of a punishment. Crime is reduced not by making punishment familiar but formidable. Death penalty may not correct the man who is hanged. But it provides a deterrent for others like him. And for the unjust, strict punishment is the justice. The Act rightly aims at reducing the procedural tangles and arms the Court with the power to impose effective penalties on the terrorist as well as even on those who are his partners in the commitment of the heinous crime against man and his kind. Danger of losing ill-gotten property can also be a definite deterrent."

In view of the above conclusions their Lordships of Punjab and Haryana High Court find that there is no constitutional or legal infirmity in the impugned provisions. Thus, these cannot be invalidated by the issue of a writ, order or direction.

Recently Russia's Parliament have overwhelmingly passed a tough new law against terrorism aiming to curb the recent explosive rise of racist skinheads fascists and Islamic fundamentalists. A spate of violent attacks of non-white foreigners by skinheads, an anti-Semitic bombing and a downtown Moscow rampage by flag-waving soccer fans in the past months have focused public attention on the threat. At the Kremlin's order, the extremism law was rushed through the required three readings in less than three weeks.

This book has been planned in nine parts, apart from POTA, 2002 other laws regarding unlawful activities and international terrorism have been also included in this book. In fact this Book is an 'encyclopedia on Anti-terrorism Law in the world'. In spite of due care having taken to avoid omission and errors, some errors might have crept in. While regretting for such errors, suggestions to improve the book are most welcome from our revered readers which will be given effect in our next edition.

Analogous Law- Section 15 of TADA Act, 1987, is analogous to be sub sections (1) and (2) of Section 32 of POTA, 2002, which reads as under:

"Certain confessions made to police officers to be taken into consideration.—(1) Notwithstanding anything in the Code or in the Indian Evidence Act, 1872, but subject to the provisions of this section, a confession made by a person before a police officer not lower in rank than a superintendent of police and recorded by such police officer either in writing or on any mechanical device like cassettes, tapes or sound tracks from out of which sounds or images can be reproduced, shall be admissible in the trial or such person or co-accused, abettor or conspirator for an offence under this Act or rules made there under :

Provided that co-accused, abettor or conspirator is charged and tried in the same case together with the accused.

The police officer shall, before recording any confession under sub-section (1), Explain to the person making it that he is not bound to make a confession and that, if he does so, it may be used as evidence against him and such police officer shall not record any such confession unless upon questioning the person making it, he has reason to believe that it is being made voluntarily."

Note: Main point of distinction between two provisions is that under sub-section (i) of Section 15 of POTA Act, 1987 confession was admissible not only against the maker of confession but also against co-accused, abettor or conspirator. But now under sub-section (1) of Section

32 of POTA, 2002, confession shall be admissible only in the trial of maker.

Rules relating to confession under the Indian Evidence Act, 1987- Sections 24 to 27 runs as under :

"Confession caused by inducement, threat or promise, when irrelevant in criminal proceeding. A confession made by an accused person is irrelevant in a criminal proceeding, if the making of the confession appears to the Court to have been caused by any inducement, threat or promise, having reference to the charge against the accused person, proceeding from a person in authority and sufficient, in the opinion of the Court, to give the accused person grounds, which would appear to him reasonable, for supposing that by making it he would gain any advantage or avoid any evil of temporal nature in reference to the proceeding against him.

Confession to police officer not be proved: No confession made to a police officer, shall be proved as against a person accused of any offence.

Confession by accused while in custody of police not to be proved against him. No confession made by any person while he is in the custody of a police officer, unless it be made in the immediate presence of a Magistrate[1] shall be proved as against such person.

[2]*(Explanation.*— In this section "Magistrate" does not include the head of a village discharging magisterial functions in the Presidency of Fort St. George[3] (***) or elsewhere, unless such head man is a Magistrate exercising the powers of a Magistrate under the Code of Criminal Procedure, 1882 (10 of 1882)[4]

How much of information received from accused may be prove. Provided that when any fact is deposed to as discovered inconsequence of formation received from a person accused of any offence, in the custody of a police officer, so much of such information, whether it amounts to a confession or not, as relates distinctly to the fact thereby discovered, may be proved."

Confessional statements includes admission of incriminating fact also.—Supreme Court in Aghnoo Nagesia v. State of Bihar[5], held that confessional statement includes not only admission of the offence but also other admissions of incriminating facts relevant to the offence such as motive, preparation, absence of provocation, concealment of weapon, and subsequent conduct which throw light upon the gravity of the offence and the intention and knowledge of the accused. It was also observed by the Court that each and every admission of incriminating fact contained in the confessional statement is part of the confession.[6]

Confession recorded under Section 15 of TADA Act,1987.— Section 15 of the TADA Act makes certain confessions made to police officer admissible in the trial of such person or co-accused, abettor or conspirator for an offence under the Act or rules made there under. Supreme Court considering its constitutionality in Kartar Singh's Case[7], observed that "having regard to the legal competence of the legislature to make the law prescribing a different mode of proof, the meaningful purpose and object of the legislation, the gravity of terrorism unleashed by the terrorists and destructionists endangering not only the sovereignty and integrity of the country but also the normal life of the citizens, and the reluctance of even the victims as well as the public in coming forward, at the risk of their life, to give evidence"- held that the impugned section cannot be said to be suffering from any vice of unconstitutionality. Section 15 is thus an important departure from the ordinary law and must receive the interpretation which would achieve the object of that provision and not frustrate or truncate it. Interpreting the said provision Supreme Court in State' Case[8] has held that a confession recorded under Section 15 of the TADA Act is to be considered as a substantive piece of evidence not only against the maker of it but also against its co-accused. There was difference of opinion amongst the three learned Judges who decided that case regarding the evidentiary value of such a confession against the co-accused is tried in the same case. Wadhwa J. observed that what weight should be attached to such a confession is a matter of discretion of the Court and as a matter of prudence of the Court may look for some corroboration before relying upon such confession against the co-accused.[9]

The term '—Meaning of.—when Section 15, TADA says that confession of an accused is admissible against co-accused as well it would be substantive evidence against the co-accused. It is a different matter as to what value is to be attached to the confession with regard to the co-accused as that would fall in the realm of appreciation of evidence.

The term 'admissible' Under Section 15 has to be given a meaning. When it says that confession is admissible against a co-accused it can only mean that it is substantive evidence against him as well as against the maker of the confession.

'Admissible' according to Black's Law Dictionary means, "pertinent and proper to be considered in reaching a decision. Used with reference to the issues to be decided in any judicial proceeding."

It defines 'Admissible evidence' as, "As applied to evidence, the term means that the evidence introduced is of such a character that the Court or Judge is bound to receive it, that is, allow it to be introduced at trial. To be "admissible" evidence must be relevant, and, inter alia, to be "relevant" it must tend to establish material proposition........." If we again refer to Black's Law Dictionary 'substantive evidence' means "that adduced for the purpose of proving a fact in issue, as opposed to evidence given for the purpose of discrediting a witness (i.e. showing that he is unworthy of belief), of corroborating his testimony."[10]

Though it is entirely for the Court trying the offence to decide the question of admissibility or reliability of a confession in its judicial wisdom strictly adhering to the law, it must, while so deciding the question should satisfy itself that there was no trap no track and no importance seeking of evidence during the custodial interrogation and all the conditions required are fulfilled.[11]

When there is no statutory inhibition for using such confession on the premise that it was not recorded during the investigation of the particular offence which is under trial there is no need or reason for the Court to introduce a further fetter against the admissibility of the confessional statement. It often happens that a confessor would disclose very many acts and events including different facets of his involvement in the preparation, attempt and commission of crimes including the acts of his co-participators therein. But to expel every other incriminating disclosures than those under investigation of a particular crime from the ambit of admissibility is not mandated by any provision of law.[12]

Confession—Recording of.—An analysis of sub-section (1) of Section 15 of the TADA shows that it has two limbs. The first limb bars application of provisions of the Code of Criminal Procedure and the Indian Evidence Act to a confession made by a person before a police officer not lower in rank than a Superintendent of Police and recorded by him in any of the modes noted in the Section. The second limb makes such a confession admissible, de hors the provisions of the Evidence Act in the trial of such person or co-accused, abettor or conspirator for an offence under the TADA Act or rules made there under provided the co-accused, or conspirator is charged and tried in the same abettor or case together with the accused. The import of Section 15 (1) is that insofar as the provisions of the Criminal Procedure Code and the Evidence Act come in conflict with either recording of a confession of a person by a police officer of the rank mentioned therein, in any of the modes specified in the Section, or its admissibility at the trial, they will have to yield to the provisions of Section 15 (1) of the TADA Act as it is given overriding effect.

Thus, Section 162, 164, 281 and 463 of Criminal Procedure Code which have a bearing on the question of recording of statement/confession of a person and Sections 24 to 30 of the Evidence Act which deal with various aspects of confession of an accused stand excluded vis-à-vis Section 15 (1) of the TADA Act and cannot be called in aid to invalidate recording of confession of an accused by a police officer of the specified rank and/or its admissibility in the trial of the co-accused, abettor or conspirator charged and tried in the same case together with the accused for an offence under the TADA Act or rules made there under. It must be made clear that the non obstante clause in Section 15 (1) of the TADA, Act does not exclude the application of all the provision of the Criminal Procedure Code and the Indian Evidence. Act in the trial of offences under TADA Act.[13]

When accused making confessions were made aware of fact that those confessions recorded under Tada Act, then exercise of power under Section 15 by Police Inspector cannot be mala fide.[14]

Where the Police Inspector had made attempts to find out if any Superintendent of Police was available for recording confessions and others had declined to oblige him then no illegality in Police Inspector recording confessions even though he was supervising the investigation.[15]

The obligation to explain and ascertain is to be performed while recording real confessional part and doing so earlier when preliminary part is recorded cannot be proper compliance of Rule 15 (2).[16]

The Rules or guidelines framed by Bombay High Court for recording a confession by a Magistrate under Section 164, Criminal Procedure Code do not by themselves apply to recording of a confession under Section 15 of TADA Act.[17]

Recording of confession- Certificate and memorandum— No Public purpose is likely to be achieved by holding that the certificate and memorandum should be in same form and also in same terms as are to be found in Rule 15(3)(b).[18]

Rejection of confessional statement—The plea that confessional statement was not recorded on the date mentioned in record, held that rejection of confessions on that basis by the Court by adopting hyper-technical approach without considering actual evidence on record particularly evidence of investigating officer was not proper.[19]

Admissibility of confessional statement- Where the confessional statement was recorded in devnagari scrip, script, statements were typed wherein some names and dates have been shown in bold letters. Held that use of bold letters does not make the confession doubtful justifying the conclusion that there had been interpolations as bold letters were intended to highlight importance of names and words. The police officer recording confession categorically stated that "it is not true to say that the confessional statements were already typed by leaving the above stated places blank and subsequently my office did the job of only filling the blanks under my direction". In view of said specific denial and in the absence of evidence to the contrary not relying upon said confessional statements of accused which were voluntarily made, was held to be not proper".[20]

Conviction of accused on confessional statement.........The judicial confessions are usually retracted. Retracted confessions are good confessions if held to have been made voluntarily and in accordance with the provisions of law. Corroboration of the confessional statement is not a rule of law but a rule of prudence. Whether the corroboration is sufficient in a given case would depend upon the facts and circumstances of that case. In the instant case the cause which provoked one of the accused to kill the deceased by the testimony of the widow of the accused. Hence, conviction of accused on basis of said confession could not be said to be not proper because it was retracted.[21]

Recording of confessional statement.—There was a caution envisaged in the Terrorist and Disruptive Activities (Prevention), Rules (1986), Rule 15 (3), that the confessor accused was not bound to make confession and that if he did so the confession could be used against him. There is no legal requirement that the confessor should be administered with such caution every day the officer meets him. While the Police Officer was recording the confession he asked him the question whether he was aware that he was not bound to make the confession to which held that the requirements of Rule had been complied with. There was no complaint that accused confessor was physically or even mentally tortured by the Police at any time. Such confession can be said to have been voluntarily made. The stickers and other materials was also seized from the accused's house, it further proves that the confession contained only truth, hence conviction was not liable to be set aside.[22]

Constitutional validity of Section 15 of TADA (Corresponding to Section 32 of POTA).— In Kartar Singh's case[23] a Constitution Bench of Supreme Court was considering the Constitutional validity of Section 15 of the TADA and learned Judges of the Bench upheld its validity in the aforesaid decision. However, certain guidelines were formulated for compliance by the officers to ensure that confession is not tainted with any vice. Guideline No. 2 to which focus is made by the senior counsel, reads thus : "The person from whom a confession has been recorded under section 15 (1) of the Act, should be produced before the Chief Metropolitan Magistrate or the Chief Judicial Magistrate to whom the confession is required to be sent under Rule 15 (5) along with the original statement of confession, written or recorded on mechanical device without unreasonable delay."[24]

In the instant case it was held that the material on record should show that the confessor was produced before the Additional Chief Metropolitan Magistrate for the purpose of verification of the statement attributed to the appellant.[25]

Voluntariness of confession Validity of— Conviction based on confession without corroboration— Confessional statement before the Police Officer under Section 15 of the TADA was substantive evidence and it could be relied upon in the trial of such person or co-accused abettor or conspirator for an offence punishable under the Act or the Rules.[26]

There is one common feature, both in Section 15 of the TADA Act and Section 24 of the Indian Evidence Act that the confession has to be voluntary. Section 24 of Evidence Act interdicts a confession, if it appears to the Court to be the result of any inducement, threat or promise in certain conditions. The principle therein is that confession must be voluntary. Section 15 of the TADA Act also requires the confession to be voluntary. Voluntary means that one who makes it out of his own free will inspired by the sound of his own conscience to speak nothing but the truth. As per Stroud's Judicial Dictionary, 5th Ed., at p. 2633, threat means :

"It is the essence of a threat that it be made for the purpose of intimidating, or overcoming, the will of the person to whom it is addressed (per Lush J.)[27]

Words and Phrases—Permanent Edition, Vol. 44 622, voluntary defines :

"Voluntary" means a statement made of the free will and accord of accused, without coercion, whether from fear of any threat of harm, promise, or inducement or any hope of reward"[28].

At page 629—'confession' defines :

"Where used in connection with statements by accused, words "voluntary" and "involuntary" import statement made without constraint or compulsion by others and the contrary.[29]

Validity of confessional statement recorded in computer. Merely because the confessional statement was recorded in a computer, it cannot be a ground for holding that the confessional statement was not voluntary. Similarly, a DCP had given a certificate in typing when the requirement was that certificate had to be : "under his own hand". That was urged to be illegal. Held that it would be too technical to discard the confessional statement or doubt its authenticity on that score. This was merely a procedural requirement. The non-observance does not cause any prejudice to the accused. It had not been shown as to how the accused was prejudiced by the certificate having been typed. Procedure is handmade and not the mistress of law intended to sub serve and facilitate the cause of justice and not to govern or obstruct it. Like all rules of procedure, the requirement of recording "under his own hand" demands an approach which would be rational and practical and not otherwise. Such minor deficiency, if any, cannot be considered to be a fatal factor so far as prosecution case was concerned.[30]

Voluntary and truthful confessional statement recorded under Section 15 of the TADA— No corroboration required.—Where the confessional statement of accused was free and voluntary, which was also found sufficient corroboration from testimony of PW 33. Evidence of approver was not trustworthy buy there was no reason to discard the confessional statement of co-accused. Identification made by PW 3 cannot be faulted on ground of delay of few months. Hence, conviction of the appellant did not deserve to be disturbed.[31]

Guidelines to ensure un-tainted confession obtained in the pre-indictment interrogation by a police officer—in Kartar Singh's Case[32] a Constitutional Bench of Supreme Court laid down the following guidelines to ensure that the confession obtained in the pre-indictment interrogation by a police officer was not tainted with any vice but was in the strict conformity with the well recognized and established aesthetic principles of fundamental fairness :

(1) The confession should be recorded in a free atmosphere in the same language in which the person is examined and as narrated by him.

(2) The person from whom a confession has been recorded under Section 15 (1) of the Act, should be produced before the Chief Metropolitan Magistrate or the Chief Judicial Magistrate to whom the confession is required to be sent under Rule 15 (5) along with the original statement of confession, written or recorded on mechanical device without unreasonable delay;

(3) The Chief Metropolitan Magistrate or the Chief Magistrate should scrupulously record the statement, if any, made by the accused so produced and get his signature and in case of any complaint of torture, the person should be directed to be produced for medical examination before a Medical Officer not lower in rank than of an Assistant Civil Surgeon;

(4) Notwithstanding anything contained in the Code of Criminal Procedure, 1973, no police officer, below the rank of an Assistant

Commissioner of Police in the Metropolitan cities and elsewhere of a Deputy Superintendent of Police or a police officer of equivalent rank, should investigate any office punishable under Terrorist and Disruptive (Preventive) Act 1987.

This is necessary in view of the drastic provisions of TADA Act. More so when the Prevention of Corruption Act, 1988 under Section 17 and the Immoral Traffic Act, 1956 under Section 13, authorize only a police office of a specified rank to investigate the offences under those specified Acts.

(5) The police officer if he is seeking the custody of any person for pre-indictment or pre-trial interrogation from the judicial custody, must file an affidavit sworn by him explaining the reason not only for such custody but also for the delay, if any, in seeking the police custody.

(6) In case, the person, taken for interrogation, on receipt of the statutory warning that he as not bound to make a confession and that if he does so, the said statement may be used against him as evidence, asserts his right to silence, the police officer must respect his right of assertion without making any compulsion to give statement of disclosure."

Guideline (3) mandated the concerned Magistrate to scrupulously record the statement if any made by the accused so produced and get his signature. In the event of any complaint of torture, the person should be directed to be produced for medical examination before a medical officer not lower in rank than the Assistant Civil Surgeon. No duty is cast upon concerned Magistrate to record the confessional statement afresh or himself/herself ascertain the nature of and the circumstances under which the confessional statement was made unless a complaint is made by the accused regarding torture; etc.[33]

Confessional Statement of the accused—When admissible:—

The confessional statement recorded under Section 15 of the TADA is admissible against the co-accused or abettor or conspirator provided an accused is tried with other co-accused abettor or conspirator in the same trial in respect of offence under TADA. Such confessional statement of the co-accused or by the co-accused is not admissible against the accused if he is not tried for any offence under TADA.[34]

Section 30 of the Indian Evidence Act and Section 15 of the TADA Act—Distinction.—The difference between Section 30 of the Indian Evidence Act and Section 15 of the TADA Act may also be noticed here. Whereas the former provision requires that the maker of the confession and others should be tried jointly for the same offence. Another point of distinction is that under Section 30 of the Evidence Act, the Court is given discretion to take into consideration the confession against the maker as well as against those who are being tried jointly for the same offence, but Section 15 (1) of TADA Act mandates that confession of an accused recorded there under shall be admissible in the trial of the maker of confession or co-accused, abettor or conspirator, Provided the co-accused, abettor or conspirator is charged and tried in with the accused in the same case. Both Section 30 of the Evidence Act as well as Section 15 of the TADA Act require joint trial of the accused making confession and co-accused, abettor or conspirator.

Having excluded the application of Section 24 to 30 of the Evidence Act a confession recorded under Section 15 (1) of the TADA Act, a self-contained scheme is incorporated therein for recording confession of an accused and its admissibility in his trial with co-accused, abettor or conspirator for offences under the TADA Act or the rules made there under or any other offence under any other law which can jointly be tried with the offence with which he is charged at the same trial. There is thus no room to import the requirements of Section 30 of the Evidence Act in Section 15 of the TADA Act.

Under Section 15 (1) of the TADA Act the position is much stronger for it says, "confession made by a person before a police officer not lower in rank than a Superintendent of Police and recorded by such police officer either in writing or on any mechanical device like cassettes, tapes or sound tracks from out of which sounds or images can be reproduced, shall be admissible in the trial of such person or co-accused, either abettor or conspirator for an offence under this Act or rules made thereunder. Provided that the co-accused, abettor or conspirator is charges and tried in the same case together with the accused." On the language of sub-section (1) of Section 15 a confession of an accused is made admissible evidence as against all those tried together. In this view of the matter also, Section 30 of the Evidence Act need not be invoked for consideration of confession of an accused against a co-accused, abettor or conspirator charged and tried in the same case along with the accused.[35]

Reliability of confessional statement.—In the instant case it was held that there are stringent provisions in the TADA Act and in the Government Order, it is stated that the Government after proper discussion on the facts of the case and the evidence/reports/letters on the record decided to waive the TADA Sections in the cases recorded in the enclosed list. When the Order itself states that all records were perused and considered, we do not think that the learned Designated Judge was justified in rejecting the application. It cannot be said that the Senior Prosecuting Officer had filed the application without consideration of the relevant facts. It cannot also be said that application was filed with any mala fide intention to save some of the culprits from the clutches of law. The request was made only to withdraw from prosecution as against the offences punishable under the TADA Act. Charges in respect the other offences punishable under Indian Penal Code remained and the accused had to face trial for that. Government must have though that the stringent and harsh provisions of TADA Act were not necessary to deal with such situation.

The Court was of the view that the learned designated Judge should have accepted the application for withdrawal from prosecution as against the offences charged against the appellants under the TADA Act. Therefore, that application was allowed and the appellants stand acquitted under Section 321 (b) of Criminal Procedure Code of all the charges framed against them under the TADA Act.[36]

Confessional statement before the police officer under Section 15 of the TADA (corresponding to Section 32 of the POTA) is substantive evidence—Confessional statement before the police officer under Section 15 of the TADA is substantive evidence and it can be relied upon in the trial of such person or co-accused, abettor or conspirator for an offence punishable under the Act or the rules. The police officer before recording the confession has to observe the requirement of sub-section 2 of Section 15. Irregularities here and there would not make such confessional statement. If the Legislature in its wisdom has provided after considering the situation prevailing in the society that such confessional statement can be used as evidence, it would not be just, reasonable and prudent to water down the scheme of the Act on the assumption that the said statement was recorded under duress or was not recorded truly by the concerned officer in whom faith is reposed. It is true that there may be some cases where the power is misused by the concerned authority. But such contention can be raised in almost all cases and it would be for the Court to decide to what extent the said statement is to be used. Ideal goal may be: confessional statement is made by the accused as repentance for his crime but for achieving such ideal goal there must be altogether different atmosphere in the society. Hence, unless a fool-proof method is evolved by the society or such atmosphere is created, there is no alternative, but to implement the law as it is.[37]

Confession under Section 15 of TADA (corresponding to Section 32 of POTA) is a substantive piece of evidence against co-accused also.—Dealing with the scope of Section 15 of the TADA Act and referring to the earlier judgments of Supreme Court in S.N. Dube's case[38] it is held that confession of the accused recorded under Section 15 of the TADA Act is a substantive piece which can be used even against the co-accused if held to be admissible voluntarily and believe. Explaining the position of law the Court held:

"Section 15 of the TADA Act makes certain confessions made to police officers admissible in the trial of such persons or co-accused, abettor or conspirator for an offence under the Act or rules made there under. Considering its constitutionality in Kartar Singh's Case[39] Supreme Court observed that:

"Having regard to the legal competence of the legislature to make the law prescribing a different mode of proof, the meaningful purpose and object of the legislation, the gravity of terrorism unleashed by the terrorists and destructionists endangering not only the sovereignty and integrity of the country but also the normal life of the citizens, and the reluctance of even the victims as well as the public in coming forward, at the risk of their life, to give evidence."

And held that the impugned section cannot be said suffering from any vice of constitutionality. Section 15 is thus an important departure from the ordinary law and must receive that interpretation which would achieve the object of that provision and not frustrate or truncate it. Interpreting the said provision in Rajiv Gandhi's Case[40] Supreme Court has held that a confession recorded under Section 15 of the TADA Act is to be considered as a substantive piece of evidence not only against the maker of it but also against its co-accused.[41]

Recording of confessional statement doubtful-Conviction held improper.—In the facts of the present case, it would be difficult to hold that the confessional statement recorded by Police Inspector, who went there for apprehending the accused, can be considered to be confessional statement recorded under Section 15 of the TADA Act even though it was recorded in presence of superintendent of police. So-called statement was recorded by the police officers in presence of the police party at night time at about 2.30 a.m. between 26th and 27th February, 1992 in the light of the jeep as there was no other light available.

Further, admittedly, the statement was not sent to the Chief Judicial Magistrate as required under Rule 15 of the TADA Rules. The Statement was produced for the first time before the Designated Court on 21.3.1997 Which was allegedly kept in the police diary. Dealing with this contention, the Designated Court held that the procedure prescribed under the Rules was directory.

Even though Supreme Court has held the procedure prescribed under Rule 15 as directory that would not mean that Investigate Officer is not required to follow the said procedure. He has to follow the said procedure. If there is delay in sending the statement the Court would consider its evidentiary value by weighing other evidence brought on record by the prosecution. It is to be stated that in our country under

Constitution, there is separation of judiciary from executive and if lapses on the part of the Investigating Officer are condoned and such statements are used for convicting the accused then the liberty of the citizens would not be safe. If appears that instead of collecting any material or evidence for connecting these accused with the crime, investigating agency has adopted unjustified method.[42]

Confessions made to police officers viz-a-viz, custodial investigations.—In Kartar Singh's Case[43] Supreme Court visualized the above topic (in paras 383 to 396) as under :

"383. The Criminal Procedure Code, 1973 for short 'the Code' and its predecessor occupied the field. Police have been empowered to carry out thorough investigation, as is practicable and reasonable in a cognizable offence, in order that all relevant information and facts about the allegations of the crime are collected and placed for the trial of the offender within the limits set down by law. A suspect, if under arrest, is placed as expeditiously as possible before the Magistrate within 24 hours after excluding the time taken for journey.

References

1. A Coroner has been declared to be Magistrate for the purposes of this section, see the Coroners act, 1871 (4 of 1871) section 10.
2. Ins. By Act 3 of 1981, Section 3.
3. The words "or in Burma" omitted by the A.O. 1937.
4. See now the Code of Criminal Procedure, 1973 (2 of 1974).
5. Aghnoo Nagesh v. State of Bihar, 1966 1 SCR 134.
6. Prakash Dhawal Khairnar v. State of Maharashtra, 2002, Cri LJ 928 at 936 (SC).
7. Kartar Singh v. State of Punjab. (1994) 3 SCC 569 : 1994 Cri LJ 3139.
8. State through Superintendent of Police, CBI/SIT etc., v. Nalini (Popularly known as Rajiv Gandhi Murder case), 1999 AIR SCW 1889 : AIR 1999 SC 2640 : 1999 Cri. LJ 3124.
9. S.N. Dube v. N.B. Bhoir, 2000 Cri LJ 830 at 847 (SC).
10. State of Tamil Nadu through Superintendent of Police CBI/SIT v. Nalini, 1999 Cri LJ 3124 at 3214-3215 (SC).
11. Kartar Singh v. State of Punjab, (1994) 3 SCC. 569 : 1994 Cri LJ 3139 : AIR 1995 SC 1726 : referred in Devender Pal Singh v. State N.C.T. of Delhi, 2002 Cri LJ 2034 at 2052 (SC).
12. State of Gajarat v. Mohammed Atik, 1998 Cri LJ 2551 at 2252-2253 (SC).

13. State of Tamil Nadu v. Nalini, 1999 Cr LJ 3324 at pp. 3327, 3328 (SC).
14. S.N. Dube v. N.B. Bhoir, 2000 Cr LJ 830 (SC).
15. S.N. Dude v. N.B. Bhoir, 2000 Cr LJ 830 (SC).
16. S.N. Dude v. N.B. Bhoir, 2000 Cr LJ 830 (SC).
17. S.N. Dube v. N.B. Bhoir, 2000 Cr LJ 830 (SC).
18. S.N. Dube v. N.B. Bhoir, 2000 Cr LJ 830 (SC).
19. State of Maharashtra v. Bharat Chaganlal Raghani, 2002 Cri LJ 944 (SC) : AIR 2002 SC 409.
20. State of Maharashtra v. Bharat Chaganlal Raghani, 2002 Cri LJ 944 (SC) : AIR 2002 SC 409.
21. State of Maharashtra v. Bharat Chaganlal Raghani, 2002 Cri LJ 944 (SC) : AIR 2002 SC 409.
22. Nazir Ahmed Bhatt v. State of Delhi, 2002 Cri LJ 213 (SC).
23. Kartar Singh v. State of Punjab, 1994 (3) SCC 569 : 1994 Cri LJ 3139.
24. Nazir Ahmed Bhatt v. State of Delhi, 2002 Cri LJ 213 at 216 (SC).
25. Nazir Ahmed Bhatt v. State of Delhi, 2002 Cri LJ 213 at 216 (SC).
26. Devender Pal Singh v. State of N.C.T., 2002 (1) Supreme (Cr.) : II (2002) SLT 702.
27. Wood v. Bowron, 1866 LR 2 QB 21, cited Intimidate.
28. State v. Mullin, 85 N.W. 2d 598, 600, 249, Lown 10.
29. Commonwealth v. Chin Kee, 186, N.E. 253, 260, 283, Mass 248". (Gurdeep Singh v. State (Delhi Admn.) 1999 Cri LJ 4573 at 4580 (SC).
30. Devender Pal Singh v. State of N.C.T. 2002 (1) Supreme (Cri.) 1209 : II (2002) SLT 702.
31. Ravinder Singh @ Bittu v. State of Maharashtra, II (2002) CCR 164 (SC).
32. Kartar Singh v. State of Punjab, 1994 (3) SCC 569.
33. State of Maharashtra v. Bharat Chaganlal Raghani, 2002 Cri LJ at 956-957 (SC) : AIR 2002 SC 409.
34. Baba Peer Paras Nath v. State of Haryana, 1996 Cri LJ 4139 at 4141 (SC) : 1996 (3) All India Cr LR 33 (SC).
35. State of Tamil Nandu through Superintendent of Police CBI/SIT v. Nalini, 1999 Cri LJ 3124 at 3330 (SC).
36. Ayyub v. State of U.P. AIR 2002 SC 1192.
37. Jayawant Dattatraya Suryarao v. State of Maharashtra, 2002 Cr LJ 226 at 251 (SC).

38. S.N. Dube v. N.B. Bhoir, (2000) 2 SCC 254.
39. Kartar Singh v. State of Punjab, (1994) 3 SCC 569 Page 680, Para 253.
40. State v. Nalini, (1999) 5 SCC 253.
41. State of Maharashtra v. Bharat Chaganlal Raghani, 2002 Cri LJ 944 at 963-964 (SC).
42. Bihari Manjhi v. State of Bihar, 2002 Cri LJ 2539 At 2540-2551 (SC).
43. Kartar Singh v. State of Punjab, 1994 Cri LJ (at pages 3233 to 3240).

1

PUNISHMENTS FOR AND MEASURES FOR COPING WITH TERRORIST AND DISRUPTIVE ACTIVITIES

Desigested Court : Conferment of inrisdiction to another Court—The Session Judge, Kamrup, Gauhati was the Designated Court under the provision of Section 9 of the Terrorist and Disruptive Activities (Prevention) Act, 1987. The Designated Court was out of station on the 3 relevant dates on which the Additional Sessions Judge passed the orders.

Admittedly, the Additional Sessions Judge was not a Designated Court under Section 9 of the above Act when the impugned orders were passed. An amount of Rs. 2 lakhs cash was seized from the accused person of the case. The addl. Sessions Judge vide impugned orders particularly dated 10.9.1990 released the seized money to the accused on executing a bond before the Investigating Officer of the case. Perused all the 3 impugned orders particularly dated 10.9.1990.

The Public Prosecutor Mr. "K" submits that the Additional Sessions Judge, not being a Designated Court, has no jurisdiction to pass the impugned orders releasing the money and so the orders were nullity. It was evident from the order dated 10.9.1990 that the Additional Sessions Judge was very much conscious of the fact that he was not the Designated Court under the provisions of Section 9 of the above Act.

The Sessions Judge (Designated Court) during absence from the station, at the relevant time, made provision by an order under Section 10 (3) of the Code of Criminal Procedure on the Additional Sessions Judge for disposal of any urgent application. The counsel Mr. "J" submits that the Designated Court having all powers of court of Session, to try offence under the Act in accordance with the provisions of the Code and therefore, the order passed by the Sessions Judge-cum-designated court under the provisions of Section 10 (3) of the Code would by way of procedure conferred power/jurisdiction on the Additional Sessions Judge for disposal of urgent application even for the cases under the TADA Act. The application disposed of under impugned orders was one under Section 451 of Cr.P.C. Whereas the public prosecutor submits that Section 14 (3) of the Act simply provides the procedure to try a case under the Act as a Sessions Case by a Designated Court in accordance with procedure prescribed in the Code for trial of Sessions Case...An order under section 10 (3) of the Cr. P.C. by a Sessions Judge-cum-Designated Court upon the Additional Sessions Judge, not being a Designated Court, would not consider jurisdiction on the Additional Sessions Judge to dispose of any application of a case under the Act, but that would only confer to cases other than cases under the Act. The provision under section 14 (3) is not unambiguous. It has plainly prescribed that a designated court shall have all powers of a Sessions Judge and shall try the Offence under the Act complying procedures under chapter XVIII of the Code Criminal Procedure. Therefore, the submissions of Mr. "J" carries no force; whereas submissions of Mr. "K" have substance and acceptable. An order under the provision of Section 10 (3) of the code of Criminal Procedure by a sessions Judge-cum-designated court during his absence simply confers powers to dispose of any urgent application concerning cases excluding cases under the Act, but if the court upon whom such power is conferred is a designated court under the provision of sub-session (8) of Section 9 of the Act. The Additional Sessions Judge in question was not Designated Court under sub section (8) of section 9 of the Act and therefore, he had no jurisdiction by virtue of that order under Section 10 (3) of the code to dispose of an application under Section 451 of Cr P.C. concerning a case under the TADA (P) Act Section 20 of the Act has clearly prescribed as to the applicability or non-applicability of the provisions of the code with regard to the cases/offences under the provision of the Act. It was not there that a Sessions Judge-cum-designated court, during its absence, can confer power to another court, not being designated, under the provision of Section 10 (3) of the Code for disposal of petitions of the cases under the above Act.[1]

The Additional Sessions Judge was conscious as appeared from the impugned order that it was not a designated court but acted upon for the observations made by the designated court in the bail order and after going through the case diary. The Additional Sessions Judge had no authority to go through the case diary of the case under the Act and to be led by the observations made by Designated Court in the bail order dated 17.8.1990 or the act on the basis that no incriminating material could be found in case diary by self-inspection. Observation of a Designated Court or examination of case diary by self would not confer jurisdiction on the Additional Sessions Judge to dispose of an application of case under the Act. It transpired that the Additional Sessions Judge lacks judicial conception, which was not expected from such a senior officer. Being conscious of the fact that he had no jurisdiction being not designated court, how could he pass an order releasing huge amount involved in the case under TADA (P) Act. Some motives other than discharge of judicial function on good faith cannot be rule out from suspicion.[2]

Even a reasonable order by a wrong forum is not order under the law and becomes a nullity. But the orders impugned cannot even be attributed as reasonable because the Additional Sessions Judge was conscious that he had no jurisdiction being the wrong forum. The impugned orders were without jurisdiction and so those were illegal nullity. It will be a chaos in the field of law and courts if such acts are allowed as done by the Additional Sessions Judge not being Designated Court. Special Act carries specified characteristics and the court must act within the provisions of the Act, the TADA (P) Act is one of such nature.[3]

The observation of the Designated Court in the bail order would not amount that the case had come out of the purview of the TADA (P) Act and stood only with the offence under Sec. 412 I.P.C. allowing other courts to deal with the case. The special nature and characteristics of the case under TADA (P) continuous unless the Investigation Agency submits final report in respect of the offences of that Act and the same is accepted by the Designated Court or unless the offences under investigation with the Act are quashed by any competent court.[4]

Functioning of Designated Court Administrative Problems as to their location- It has been stated on behalf of the prosecution that though earlier all the Sessions Judges were empowered as Designated Court within their respective jurisdiction, but now the Designated Court are at Guwahati and these courts exercise powers for the entire State. According to the counsel for the prosecution if he First Information Reports, in respect of all cases under the Act have to be sent forthwith to the Designated Court at Guwahati, it may create administrative problems for the State. This, in Court opinion cannot be a ground to fulfill the provisions of the Act and the Criminal Procedure Code, more particularly, when the country is committed to bring justice nearer to the people. The Court do not want to express any further opinion on this point, more particularly regarding inconvenience caused to the accused persons as the court understand that the notification of the Government constituting the Court at Guwahati under the Act for the entire State of Assam is under challenge before this Court.[5]

High Court, Under Section 482 Criminal Procedure Code has no jurisdiction to entertain an application for quashing the F.I.R. in which accusation of Commission of an offence under TADA Act is involved. Clearly reveals that the High Court has no jurisdiction in a case invoking arrest of any person on the accusation of having committed an offence punishable under the Tada Act or Rules made thereunder. The present is a case involving arrest of the petitioner on the accusation of having committed an offence punishable under the TADA Act. For decision whether or not the F.I.R. in question is liable to be quashed, the Court has to examine whether the accusation made in the report discloses the essential requirement of an offence under the Tada Act. But the Supreme Court[6] debars the High Court from examining the report as to whether it prima facie disclose Commission of an offence under the TADA Act. Therefore, under Sec. 482, Criminal Procedure Code the High Court has no jurisdiction to entertain an application for quashing the F.I.R. in which accusation of Commission of an offence under the TADA Act is involved.[7]

Jurisdiction: In Court V. State of Punjab,[8] it was observed as follows:

"It is futile to go into the question whether this court has inherent jurisdiction under Section 482 of Criminal Procedure Code 1973, to advise on a matter like this and correct the suggested error of domain jurisdiction. The fact remains that the Act has conferred the power to determine all questions arising as the jurisdiction of any Designated Court on the Central Government whose decision thereon shall be final. The jurisdiction of High Court automatically in the given situation is ousted, for it cannot determine any question arising as to the jurisdiction of any Designated Court. And additionally, the question is not of inherent jurisdiction of a Designated Court to try the case but is rather by which of the two Designated Courts should the case be tried. The jurisdiction to try the case is with one or the other and neither of them has jurisdiction to try the matter."

Preventive Detention- Legality- In habeas corpus therefore, the legality or otherwise of the detention shall also be considered on the date of final disposal of the petition.

Therefore, the detention became lawful when the two were arrested and produced by the civil police before the Magistrate for remand order as under-trial prisoners. In that view of the matter, the prayer

For writ of habeas corpus has become infructuous.[9]

Whether the High Court can grant appropriate relief under Article 226 of the Constitution in a case arising out of arrest of a person on the accusation of having committed an offence under TADA Act- In Kerala Education Bill, 1957. In re,[10] a Constitutional Bench of the Supreme Court has, while considering the jurisdiction of the High Court Under Article 226 held : "No enactment of a Legislature can as long as that Article stands, take away or a bridge the jurisdiction and power confer on the High Court by that Article."

The position, which emerges from the above decision is that where a statutory provision bars the jurisdiction of the High Court under Article 226 of the Constitution of India. Therefore, the TADA Act does not take away the remedies available under Article 226 of the Constitution. The observations made by the Supreme Court in para 12 of the judgment in Usmanbhai's[11] case. Therefore, the High Court in exercise of its jurisdiction under Article 226 may grant appropriate relief.[12]

Applicability of the Act to the State of Haryana- It is not in dispute that the provisions of the TADA Act, 1987 had been extended to cover the whole of the State of Haryana by a notification dated 18th November.[13]

Jurisdiction of Court- If the case is exclusively tribal by the Designated Court, the application for bail lies to the Designated Court in view of the law laid down by the Supreme Court in Usmanbhai Dawoodbhai Memon v. State of Gujarat,[14] accordingly, the petition is dismissed. The petitioner, if so advised, may approach the Designated Court for the relief prayed for by him.[15]

In Bimal Kaur Khalsa v. Union of India[16] in that case, one of the Civil Writ Petitions challenging the vires of the Terrorist and Disruptive Activities Act relating to a case under the Act of the same title of 1985. D.S. Tewatia. Chief Justice speaking for the Full Bench Judgment Section 6 of the Act 1985 and the analogus Section (also Section 6) of 1987 Act and concluded in para 127 As under:

"In view of the above, the offence qua this petitioner under Section 25 of the Arms Act would no longer attract the provision of Section 6 of the Act of 1985, because of the provisions of section 6 and Section 25 of the Act of 1987 nor would it attract in the present case the provision of section 6 of the Act of 1987, because the offence under Section 25 of the Arms Act herein was not committed with intent to the terrorist or disruptions, and there is no such allegation against the petitioner."

In Jaloba v. State of Haryana,[17] was contended that in the absence of any charge under Section 3 of the Terrorist and Disruptive Activities

Act, 1985 the offence was triable by the ordinary courts and not by the Designated Court. The contention was rejected as untenable. It was held as under :

"Section 6 lays down that if in any area notified by the State Government under the Act a person contravenes any provision or rule made under the Arms Act, the Explosive Substances Act and the Inflammable Substances Act then he is liable to enhanced punishment as provided for in the Section 9. Lays down that notwithstanding anything contained in the Code, every offence punishable under the Act or any rule made there under shall be triable only by the Designated Court within whose local jurisdiction it was committed. It therefore, follows that though the offence committed by the appellant was for contravention of section 25 of the Arms Act, it became exclusively triable by the Designated Court because of notification made by the State Government and the operation of section 6 of the act." Possession of unauthorized arms- In Baba Satyam Bhaiyya v. State of Gujarat,[18] it was observed as follows:

"Learned Advocate Shri Mehta has rightly submitted that while dealing with the matter under the Indian Penal Code and as well as the Arms Act and if the Court dealing with the matter holds against the accused of that case, while awarding the sentence it can certainly look to this provision of enhanced punishment as that would be the law applicable in the area because the State happens to be notified area under the Terrorist Act. However, by that fact alone it will not be necessary that the matter is required to be dealt with by the Designated Court under the Terrorist Act. To my mind, even resort to section 5 may no longer be necessary because so far as the enhanced punishment is concerned, by amending the provisions of the Arms Act, minimum sentence of six months, further enhanced to one year has been provided.

Though the discretion is left with Court to impose a lesser sentence for which special reasons are required to be recorded in the judgment. The result of the said discussion therefore, is that the conclusion of the Designated Judge in his order that possession of firearms in a notified area is an office punishable under the Terrorist Act is not correct. It is punishable being an offence under the Arms Act and not as per the provisions of the Terrorist Act. By this I mean that it is an offence under the former Act and not under the latter Act. So far as the quantum of Punishment is concerned, it being notified area as long as there is a difference between the quantum of punishment under the Arms Act on the one hand under the Terrorist Act on the other, no doubt, Section 5 of the Terrorist Act is not only required to be invoked but, there being non obstinate clause, it is Section 5 of the Terrorist Act that will prevail.

There is, therefore, no warrant to suggest that the possession of firearm unauthorized in a notified area is an offence punishable under the Terrorist Act.

To put it differently, I hold that the Terrorist Act would apply Provided the offence is corrected there under and then only the matter will be required to be dealt with by the Designated Court.

Propriety of trial by the Designated Court.-In Paras Ram v. State of Haryana,[19] it was observed as follows :

"Upon the authority of the judgment in Jaloba's[20] it must be held that the appellant before us was rightly tried by the Designated Court under the TADA Act, 1987."

Recovery of unauthorized Arms- It is only when the basic ingredients of Section 5 of the TADA Act are satisfied, namely, possession of an unauthorized fire-arm in a notified area, and in addition it must be prima facie established by the prosecution that such possession by the accused has direct nexus with terrorist and disruptive activities, that the provisions of TADA Act are applicable to a particular case. The Designated Court has jurisdiction to deal with this aspect of the matter by applying its mind to the facts of each case and decide whether the provisions of TADA Act are applicable or whether the matter would be forwarded to the regular court for trial.[21]

Direction for investigation by the Police.- The Magistrate can direct investigation of the case by the Police under Section 156 (3) of the Code of Criminal procedure, without taking cognizance, if, however he can order investigation by the police only under Section 202 of the Cr. P.C. and not under Section 156 (3) of the Cr. P.C.[22]

Investigation into an offence by the Police– Inference by the High Court.- The investigation into an offence is a statutory function of the Police and the Superintendence thereof is vested in the State Government and the Court is not justified without any compelling and justifiable reason to interfere with the investigation.[23]

The violation of the provision of Section 167 (5) Cr. P.C. could not result in vitiating the entire trial. –The legislature in its wisdom has barred the continuation of the investigation after the expiry of period of six month from the date of arrest of the accused. There is no indication, direct or indirect there from that the investigation already conducted within the period of six months would also stand vitiated or that the continuation of the investigation beyond the period of six months in summons cases vitiate the entire trial or result in acquittal of the accused...In other words, it can be well said that the evidence collected during the investigation beyond the period of six months would be rendered inadmissible by these provisions and not the evidence, which was collected earlier by the investigation. Consequently by no stretch of imagination, it can be held that the violation of the provisions of Section 167 (5) of Cr. P.C. 1973 could result in vitiating the entire trial.[26]

Use of statement made by the witness during investigation under Section 162 Cr. P.C. Section 162 of Cr. P.C. governs the statement made by the witness during the course of investigation and only the limited use of such a statement is to contradict the maker of the statement, when he is examined as a prosecution. For no other purpose, that statement can be used. One witness cannot be contradicted with reference to the Police Statement of another witness.[27]

"Absconding" –Meaning have. If a Police Officer goes to the house and does not find the occupant there, it cannot necessarily be said that man was absconding. "Absconding" does not mean absence on one day, but it means remaining out for some days.[28]

Reason to believe "–Meaning of– The expression reason to believe" occurring in Section 82 of Cr. P.C. contemplates subjective satisfaction on the basis of materials before the Magistrate making the order of proclamation.[29]

Attachment of property of person absconding:- The Court issuing a proclamation under Section 82 may, for reasons to be recorded in writing, at any time after the issue of the proclamation, order the attachment of any property, movable or immovable, or both, belonging to the proclaimed person :

Provided that where at the time of the issue of the proclamation the court is satisfied by affidavit or otherwise, that the person in relation to whom the proclamation is to be issued,-

(a) is about to dispose of the whole or any part of his property, or (b) is about to remove the whole or any party of his property from the local jurisdiction of the Court.

It may order the attachment simultaneously with the issue of the prosecution.

Such order shall authorize the attachment of any property belonging to such person within the district in which it is made; and it shall authorize the attachment of any property belonging to such person without such district when endorsed by the District Magistrate within whose district such property is situate.

If the property ordered to be attached us a debt or other movable property, the attachment under this section shall be made,

(a) by seizure ; or

(b) by the appointment of a receiver or

(c) by an order in writing prohibiting the delivery of such property to the proclaimed person or to any on his behalf; or

(d) by all or any two of such methods, as the Court thinks fit.

If the property ordered to be attachment is immovable, the attachment under this section shall, in the case of land paying revenue to the State Government, be made through the Collector of the district in which the land is situate; and in all other case,

(a) by taking possession; or

(b) by the appointment of a receiver, or

(c) by an order in writing prohibiting the payment of rent on delivery of property to the proclaimed person or to any one on his behalf; or

(d) by all or any two or of such methods, as the Court thinks fit.

If the property ordered to be attached consists of livestock or is of a perishable nature, the Court may if it think if expedient, order immediate sale there of, and in such case the proceeds of the sale shall abide the order of the Court.

The powers, duties and liabilities of a receiver appointed under this section shall be the same as those of a receiver appointed under the Code of Civil procedure, 1908.[30]

Claims and objections to attachment.- If any claim is preferred to, or objection made to the attachment of, any property attached under Section 83, within six months from the date of attachment, by person other than the proclaimed person, on the ground that the claimant or objector has an interest in such property, and that such interest is not liable to attachment under Section 83, the claim or objection shall be inquired into, and may be allowed or disallowed in whole or in part :

Provided that any claim preferred or objection made within the period allowed by this sub-section may, in the event of the death of the claimant or objector, be continued by his legal representative.

Claims or objections under sub-section may be preferred or made in the Court by which, the order of attachment is issued, or, if the claim or objection is in respect of property attached under an order, endorsed under sub-section 83, in the court of the Chief Judicial Magistrate of the district in which the attachment is made.

Every such claim or objection shall be inquired into by the court in which it is preferred or made :

Provided that, if it is preferred or made in the Court of a Chief Judicial Magistrate, he may make it over for disposal to any Magistrate subordinate to him.

Any person who claim or objection has been disallowed in whole or in part by an order under Subsection (1) may, within a period of one year from the date of such order, institute a suit to establish the right which he claims in respect of the property in dispute, but subject to the result of such suit, if any, the order shall be conclusive.[31]

Proclamation for person absconding.- In Section 8; any Court has reason to believe (whether after taking evidence or not) that any person against whom a warrant has been issued by it has absconded or is concealing himself so that such warrant cannot be executed, such Court may publish a written proclamation requiring him to appear at a specified place and at a specified time not less than thirty days from the date of publishing such proclamation.

The proclamation shall be published as follows:

(a) it shall be publicly read in some conspicuous place of the town or village in which person ordinarily resides,

(b) it shall be affixed to some conspicuous part of the house or homestead in which such person ordinarily resides or to some conspicuous place of such town or village, a copy thereof shall be affixed to some conspicuous part of the Court-House, the Court may also, if it thinks fit, direct a copy of the proclamation too be published in daily newspaper circulating in the place in which such person ordinarily resides.

A statement in writing by the Court issuing the proclamation to the effect that the proclamation was duly published on a specified in clause (i) of sub-section (2) shall be conclusive evidence that the requirements of this section have been complied with, and that the proclamation was published on such day.[33]

Release, sale and restoration of attached property:- If the proclaimed person appears within the time specified in the proclamation, the Court shall make an order releasing the property from the attachment. If the proclaimed person does not appear within the time specified in the proclamation, the property under the attachment, shall be at the disposal of the State Government but it shall not be sold until the expiration of six months from the date of the attachment and until any claim preferred or objection made under Section 84 has been disposed of under that section, unless it is subject to speedy and natural decay, or the Court considers that the sale would be for the benefit of the owner, in either of which cases the Court may cause it to be sold whenever it thinks fit.

If within two years from the date of the attachment, any person whose property is or has been at the disposal of the State Government. Under sub-section (2), appears voluntary or is apprehend and brought before the Court by whose order the property was attached, or the Court to which such Court to which such Court is subordinate, and prove to the satisfaction or such court that he did not abscond or conceal himself for the purpose of avoiding execution or the warrant, and that he had not such notice of the proclamation as to enable him to attend within the time specified therein, such property, or if the same has been sold, the proceeds of the sale, or, part only thereof has been sold, the net proceeds of the sale and the residue of the property, shall, after satisfying there from all costs incurred in consequence of the attachment, be delivered to him.[34]

Scope of – Section 9 empowers the Central Government as well as the State Governments to constitute by notification one or more Designated Courts for such area or arrears, or for such case or class or group of cases as may be specified in the notification.[35]

Conferment of powers of the designated Court:- The Sessions Judge, Kamrup, Gauhati was the designated Court under the provision of Section 9 of the Terrorist and Disruptive Activities (Prevention) Act, 1987. The designated Court was out of station on the relevant dates on which the Additional Sessions Judge passed the orders.

Admittedly, the Additional Sessions Judge was not a designated court under Section 9 of the above Act when the impugned orders were passed. An amount of Rs. 2 lakhs cash was seized from the accused person of the case. The Additional Sessions Judge vide impugned orders particularly dated 10.9.1990 released the seized money to the accused on executing a bond before the Investigating Officer of the case. Perused all the 3 impugned orders particularly dated 10.9.1990.

The Public Prosecutor submits that the Additional Sessions Judge, not being a designated court, had no jurisdiction to pass the impugned orders releasing the money and so the orders were nullity. It was evident from the order dated, 10.9.1990 that the Additional Sessions Judge was very much conscious of the fact that he was not the designated court under the provisions of Section 9 of the above Act.

The Sessions Judge (designated court) during absence from the station, at the relevant time, made provision by an order under Section 10 (3) of the code of Criminal Procedure on the Additional Sessions Judge for disposal of any urgent application. The counsel submits that the designated court having all powers of court of session to try offences under the Act in accordance with the provisions of the Code and therefore, the order pass by the Sessions Judge-cum-designated court under the provision of Section 10 (3) of the Code would by way of procedure conferred power jurisdiction on the Additional Sessions Judge for disposal of urgent application even for the case under the TADA Act. The application disposed of under impugned order was one under Section 451 of the Cr. P.C. Whereas the public prosecutor submits that Section 14

(3) of the Act simply provides the procedure to try a case under the Act as a sessions case by a designated court in accordance with the procedure prescribed in the Code for trial of Sessions case. An order under Section 10 (3) of the Cr. P.C. by a Sessions Judge-cum-Designated court upon the Additional Sessions Judge, not being a designated court, would not confer jurisdiction on the Additional Sessions Judge to dispose of any application of a case under the Act, but that would only confer to cases other than cases under the Act. The provision under Section 14 (3) is not unambiguous. It has plainly prescribed that a designated court shall all powers of a Sessions Judge and shall try the offence under the Act complying procedures under Chapter Vide Cr. P.C. 1973, Section XVIII of the Code of Criminal Procedure. Therefore, the submissions of the Counsel carries no force, whereas submissions of the public prosecutor have substance and acceptable. An order under the provision of Section 10 (3) of the Code of Criminal Procedure by a Sessions Judge-cum-designated court his absence simply confers powers to dispose of any urgent application concerning cases excluding cases under the Act. But if the court upon whom such power is conferred is a designated court under the provision of sub-section (8) of Section 9 of the Act. The Additional Sessions Judge in question was not a designated court under sub-section (8) of Section 9 of the Act. And therefore, he had no jurisdiction by virtue of that order under Section 10 (3) of the Code to dispose of an application under Section 20 of the Act has clearly prescribed as to the applicability or non applicability of the provisions of the code with regard to the cases/offences under the provision of the Act. It was not there that a Sessions Judge-cum-designated court, during its absence, could confer powers to another court, not being designated, under the provision of Section 10 (3) of the code for disposal of petitions of the case under the above Act.[36]

The Additional Sessions Judge was conscious as appeared from the impugned order that it was not a designated court but acted upon for the observations made by the designated court in the bail order and after going through case diary. The Additional Sessions Judge had no authority to go through the case diary of the case under the Act and to be led by the observations made by the designated court in the bail order dated 17.8.1990 or to act on the basis that no incriminating material could be found in case diary by self inspection. Observations of a Designated Court or examination of case diary by self would not confer jurisdiction on the Additional Sessions Judge to dispose of an application of a case under the Act. It transpired that the Additional Sessions Judge lacks judicial conception, which was not expected from such a senior officer. Being conscious of the fact that he had no jurisdiction being not designated court, how could he pass an order releasing huge amount involved in the case under TADA (P) Act. Some motives other than discharge of judicial function on good faith cannot be ruled out from suspicion.[37]

Even a reasonable order by a wrong form is no order under the law and becomes a nullity. But the orders impugned cannot even be attributed as reasonable because the Additional Sessions Judge was conscious that he had no jurisdiction being the wrong forum. The impugned orders were without jurisdiction and so those were illegal and nullity. It will be a chaos in the field of law and courts if such acts are allowed as done by the Additional Sessions Judge not being designated court Special Act carries specified characteristics and the courts must act within the provisions of the Acts, the TADA (P) Act is one of such nature.[38]

The observations of the designated court in the bail order would not amount that the case had come out of the purview of the TADA (P) Act and stood only with the offence under Section 412 IPC allowing other courts to deal with the case. The special nature and characteristics of the case under TADA (P) continues unless the Investigation Agency submits final report in respect of the offences of that Act and the same is accepted by the Designated Court or unless the offences under investigation with the Act are quashed by any competent Court.[39]

Cognizance of offence under Act by Magistrate- The offence under TADA shall be tried only by a designated Court established under Section 9 the Act and the designated court has to take cognizance of such offence upon a complaint of facts or upon a police report, and follow the procedure applicable to a trial of a sessions case.

When such a report is filed, he should return it to the concerned complaint or police officer to file it in the Designated Court. If on the other hand the Magistrate takes cognizance, his jurisdiction only extends to the extent of trying the other offences. But taking cognizance on the basis of such police reports or complaints involving punishable under TADA should be avoided by the First Class Magistrates. Otherwise, the very object for which TADA is enacted will be defeated. However, in the instant cases though the Magistrate has taken cognizance; such cognizance is not in accordance with the due process of law. Therefore, to that extent the proceedings involving the offences punishable under TADA are vitiated and the Criminal Courts like that of the First Class Magistrates or the Sessions Courts not being Designated Courts, cannot either enquire or proceed with the trial of those offences.[40]

Jurisdiction.— In Court v. State of Punjab,[41] it was observed as follows :

It is futile to go into the question whether this Court has inherent jurisdiction under Section 482 of Cr. P.C. 1973, to advice on a matter like this and correct the suggested error of domain jurisdiction. The fact remains that the Act has conferred the power to determine all questions arising as to the jurisdiction of any Designated Court on the Central Government whose decision thereon shall be final. The Jurisdiction of High Court atomically in the given situation is ousted, for it cannot determine any question arising as to the jurisdiction of a Designated Court to try the case but is rather by which of the two Designated Court should the case be tried. The jurisdiction to try the case is with one or the other and not that neither of them has jurisdiction to try the matter."

"Upon the authority of the judgment in Jaloba's[42] case it must be held that the appellant before us was rightly tried by the Designated Court under the provisions of the TADA Act 1987."

Allowing the addition of any provisions of the TADA Act during investigations- Although the jurisdiction of the High Court in respect of the judgment and other etc. passed by a Designated Court has been taken away, but the constitutional powers of this Court under Articles 226 and 227 of the Constitution are always available as has laid down by the apex Court and Gujarat High Court, as well as this Court. Accordingly, this Court is duty bound to direct all the Courts and Tribunals within the jurisdiction of this Court to implement the law laid down by the apex Court. Therefore, the Court holds that on receiving the First Information Report. The first duty of the designated Court is to apply its mind to the said report and other materials made available and shall take a decision keeping in view, the above ratio laid down by the apex Court and other court whether prosecution should be allowed to rope in a person under the act and in so doing, the designated Court is duty bound to record its satisfaction or otherwise as to whether the offence disclosed in the first information report could be dealt with under the normal law of the land and whether "the Government's law enforcing machinery has failed'. It is needless to that before passing the order, Designated Court may hear the public Prosecutor and the persons accused of the offence. If the Designated Court is of opinion that no prima facie case has been made out under the Act, the Designated Court may transfer the case to any other Court having jurisdiction under Criminal procedure code this has to be done promptly as the sword of Damocles need not be kept having unnecessarily without any point or purpose.

As a corollary of the above proposition a questing may arise, in fact it has arisen in the cases in hand whether subsequently provisions of the Act can be allowed to be added during investigation and if so by which

Court, admittedly when normal investigation by police in proceeding the competent Court is kept informed and subsequent addition of any section of the Act by the investigating agency cannot be allowed to be done by ordinary Criminal Court as the power of such Court under the Act is confirmed only to remand of a accused person. Such an order allowing the investigating agency can be passed only by the Designated Court and not by any other Criminal Court. In allowing the investigating agency to add any provisions of the Act it is duty of the Designated Court to examine very carefully all the materials produced before the Court and a speaking order has to be passed keeping in view ratio of the apex Court, as stated above regarding the application of the provisions of the Act. Such order shall not be passed mechanically and it shall be a speaking order with reasons. In the cases in hand, along with the prayer for adding the provisions of the Act, no material were disclosed and that, the orders were passed by a Magistrate in a most mechanical way without any reason. Not only these orders are without jurisdiction, these orders are also liable to be struck down for want of reasoned order, which is the basic judicial order.[43]

Scope of Section 12 of the Act empowers the Designated Court to convict a person of any offence any offence under any other law if he is found to have been guilty of the same during the course of a trial under that Act and to punish appropriately.[44]

In Umanbhai v. State of Gujarat,[45] observed as follows: "Where an enactment provides for a special procedure for the trial of certain offences, it is that procedure that must be followed and not the prescribed by the Code."

Duty of Court,–Section 12 (1) of the Act no doubt empowers the Designated court to try any offence punishable under any other stature along with the offence punishable under the Act if the former is connected with the latter. That, however, does not mean that even when the Designated Court comes to the conclusion that there exists no sufficient ground for framing a charge against the accused under Section 3 (1) of the Act it must proceed to try the accused for the commission of offences under other statutes. That would tentamout to usurping jurisdiction.[46] Change under TADA and IPC against several accused–question of jurisdiction of the Designated Court to try any other offence in respect of the accused in its Court. If Section 12 of the Act is analyzed, carefully, it is clear to us that when the Designated Court is trying any offence it may also try any other offence with which accused is charged under the Code at the same trial, if offence is connected with such other offence. It is, therefore, clear that the Designated Court may have a jurisdiction to try other offence in respect of the accused in its court provided that other offences are connected with such other offence under TADA. In the present case, since accused Nos. 4 and 5 have been discharged under TADA the offences alleged to have been committed by Accused Nos. 4 and 5 under sections 412 and 414 of the IPC cannot be tried along with other accused Nos. 1 to 3 whose offences were being being tried by the Designated Court. On the basis of the charge-sheet, Mr. Bahal submitted that here offenders as well as offences of Accused Nos. 4 and 5 are distinct qua the other accused and, therefore, Accused Nos. 4 and 5 cannot be tried along with other and therefore, Accused Nos. 4 and 5 cannot be tried along with other accused whose offences fall TADA and being trial by the Designated Court. Mr. Bahal in support of his submission drew our attention to a decision of the Supreme Court in Niranjan Singh Karma Singh Punjabi v. Jintendra Bhimraj Bijja,[47] in this reported decision the question that fell for consideration before the Supreme Court was whether provisions of TADA were applicable to the facts of the case. While holding that provisions of TADA did not apply to the facts and circumstances of the case, the Supreme Court in para 12 held as under:

"Once the designated court came to the conclusion that the evidence was not sufficient to frame a charge under Section 3 (1) of the Act, the Designated Court had no alternative but to resort to Section 18 and transfer the cases to the competent Court under the Code. We therefore, do not see any merit in the contention of the learned counsel for the State of Maharashtra that even the Designated Court came to the conclusion that no ground was made out under Section 3 (2) of the Act, it was duty bound by virtue of Section 12 (1) of the Act to proceed with the trial for the other offences under the Penal Code and the Bombay Police Act we think that the course adopted by the Designated Court in transferring the case to the Sessions Court is clearly in keeping with Section 18 of the Act."

It is true the Supreme Court in this case transferred the criminal case to regular Criminal Court under Section 18 of the TADA. That was because the Supreme Court came to the conclusion that provisions of Section 3 (1) of TADA have to application to the facts of that case. This decision, raised on behalf of the petitioner. Mr. Bahal then drew our attention to another decision of this Court in Rafiq Abid Patel v. Inspector of Police, Kashmira Police Station Thane,[48] in this reported decision also crime was registered against the petitioners along with one Asif Patel. Asif Patel alone had a revolver in his hand whereas petitioners were armed with stone, soda water bottles and other weapons. It was the case registered under Sections 307, 341, 147, 148, 324, 336 and 427 of the Indian Penal Code and Sections 25 (1) and 27 of the Arms Act.

The Circle Police Inspector Kashmira Camp, informed the TADA Court that provisions of Section 3 and 5 of the TADA have been applied to all the accused in the said case. While construing the scope and ambit of Sections 5 of the TADA, the court held that having regard to the phraseology used in Section 5 of the TADA, the said provisions couldn't be made applicable to the petitioners. The Division Bench of the Bombay High Court accordingly quashed the application of provisions of Sections 3, 5, and 6 of the TADA. The Police Officers were restrained from carrying out any investigation against the Petitioners under Sections 3, 5 and 6 of the TADA. It is true that in this case provisions of Section 12 of the TADA were not considered because question of transferring case it appears, did not arise. From paragraph 16 of the said judgment it appears, to us, that investigation was progress at that stage and, therefore, question of considering Section 12 did not arise.

'L' Learned Assistant Public Prosecutor however, urged that all offences connected with C.R. No.113/91 can be tried together in a Designated Court under the TADA with the aid of Section 12 of the Act. The Designated Court has been empowered to try any other offences of which offender accused was charged if such offences are connected with such other offence for which Accused Nos. 1 to 3 are being tried under TADA 'L' also urged role of Accused Nos. 4 and 5 for which they have been charges, is so intimately connected that separate trial is regards their offence by another Court would be inappropriate and contrary to Section 12 of the TADA.

The Designated Court which is trying any offence under TADA may try any other offence with which accused whose offence is being tried by the Designated Court, if charged with the offences connected with offence under TADA, may club together and try such offences. The position in the present case altogether different because order of discharge has been passed by the trial judge. Moment Accused Nos. 4 and 5 were discharged under TADA, then their trial by the Designated Court would be without jurisdiction. Section 12 would not be attracted to try accused Nos. 4 and 5 along with other accused is a Designated court.

In Court opinion, viewed from any angle, trial of accused No. 4 and 5 who have been discharged by the Designated court under TADA will be without jurisdiction and, therefore, under Section 18 of the TADA, the case of Accused No. 4 and will have to be transferred to the Competent Court for trial.[49]

Reliability of evidence of Police Officials. In Paras Ram v. State of Haryana,[50] it was observed as follows :

"It was submitted that the evidence against the appellant did not establish that he was guilty of an offence under Section 25 (1-B) (a) of the Arms Act, namely, of having in his possession an unlicensed firearm. We have examined the evidence and found no reason to question the conclusion of the Designated Court that the appellant was so guilty. That the evidence relied upon was of two police officials do not ipso facto give rise to doubt about its credibility. There is nothing on record to show that these police officials were hostile to the appellant and their evidence was not shaken in cross-examination. That the private party who was called as a witness by the prosecution did not support it, does not, in the circumstances, lead to the conclusion that the appellant was innocent.

The appellant being guilty of an offence under Section 25 (1-B) of the Arms Act is punishable with imprisonment for a term, which shall not be less than one year but which may extend to three years, and he is also liable to fine. In the circumstances of the case, we think that the appellant must undergo rigorous imprisonment for a term of one year and pay a fine of Rs. 200."

Whether provisions of the TADA Act can be subsequently allowed to be added during investigation and if so by which Court?- Although the jurisdiction of the High Court in rest act of the judgment and order etc. passed by a Designated Court has been taken away, but the constitutional powers of this Court under Article 226 and 227 of the constitution are always available as has been laid down by the apex court and the Gujarat High Court, as well as this court. Accordingly, this court is duty bound to direct all the courts and Tribunals within the Jurisdiction of the Court to implement the law laid down by the apex court. Therefore, the court hold that on receiving the First Information Report, the first duty of the Designated Court is to apply its mind to the said report and other materials made available and shall take a decision keeping in view, the above ratio laid down by the apex court and other court whether prosecution should be allowed to rope in a person under the Act and in so doing, the Designated Court is duty bound to record its Satisfaction or otherwise as to whether the offence disclosed in the First Information Report could be dealt with under the normal law of the land and whether the Government's law enforcing machinery has failed'. It is needless to say that before passing the order Designated Court may hear the Public Prosecutor and the persons accused of the offence. If the Designated Court is of opinion that no prima facie case has been made out under the Act, the Designated Court may transfer the case to any other court having jurisdiction under Cr. P.C. This has to be done promptly as the sword of pamocles need not be kept hanging unnecessarily without any point or purpose.

As a corollary of the above proposition, a question may arise in fact it has arisen in the case in hand whether subsequently provisions of the Act can be allowed to be added during investigation and if so by which court. Admittedly, when normal investigation by police in proceeding the competent court is kept informed subsequent addition of any Section of the Act by the investigating agency cannot be allowed to be done by ordinary criminal court as the power of such court under the Act is confirmed only to remand of an accused person. Such an order allowing the investing agency can be passed only by the Designated Court and not by any other criminal court. In allowing the investigating to add any provisions of the Act it is duty of the Designated Court to examine very carefully all the materials produced before the court and a speaking order has to be passed keeping in view ratio of the apex court, as stated above regarding the application of the provisions of the Act. Such order shall not be passed mechanically; it shall be a speaking order with reasons. In the cases in hand, along with the prayer for adding the provisions of the Act, no material were disclosed and that apart, the orders are passed by a magistrate in a most mechanical way without any reason. Not only these order are also liable to be struck down for want of reasoned order, which is the basic judicial order.[51]

Statement of accused- Court can act on such admission if it satisfied all the requirements of admission. (General A.S.Vaidya's Murder Case):

Section 313 of the Code of Criminal Procedure intended to afford a person accused of a crime and opportunity to explain the circumstances appearing in evidence against him, Sub-Section (1) of the section is in to parts: the first part empowers the Court to put such Question to the accused as it considers necessary at any stage of the inquiry or trial where as the second part imposes a duty and makes it imperative on the court to question him generally on the prosecution having completed the examination of its witnesses and before the accused is called on to enter upon his defense. Counsel for accused No. 5 submitted that since no circumstance had surfaced in evidence tendered by the prosecution against the said accused, there was nothing for him to explain and hence the learned trial judge committed a grave error in examining the said accused under Section 313 of the Code. He submitted that since the examination has to be made under the said provision after the prosecution has examined all its witnesses and rested, it is obligatory on the learned judge to decide which circumstance he considers established to seek the explanation of the accused. He submitted that the obligation to question the accused is a serious matter and not a were idle formality to be gone through by the trial court without applying its mind as to the evidence and circumstances necessitating an explanation by the accuse. Therefore, counsel submitted, if there is no evidence or circumstance appearing in the prosecution evidence implicating the accused with the commission of the crime with which he is charged there is nothing for the accused to explain and hence his examination under Section 313 of the Code would be wholly unnecessary and improper. In such a situation the accused cannot be questioned and his answers cannot be used to supply the gaps left by witnesses in their evidence. In such a situation counsel for accused No. 5 Jinda strongly submitted that his examination under section 313 should be totally discarded and his admissions, if any, wholly ignored for otherwise it may appear as if he trapped by the court. According to him the rules of fairness demand that such examination should be left out of consideration and the admissions made in the course of such examination cannot form the basis of conviction. Counsel for the accused No.1 also contended that the evidence adduced by the prosecution against the accused was so thin and weak that even if it was taken as proved that court would not have been in a position to convict him and therefore, it was unnecessary to examine him under Section 313 of the Code. Strong reliance was placed on Jit Bahadur Chetri v. State of Arunachal Pradesh,[52] and Asokan v. State of Kerala.[53]

Section 313 of the Code is a statutory provision and embodies the fundamental principle of fairness bases on the maxim Audi alter am parted. It is trite law that the attention of the accused must be specifically invited to inculcator pieces of evidence or circumstances laid on record with a view to give him an opportunity to offer an explanation if he chooses to do so. The Section imposes a heavy duty on the court to take great care to ensure that the incriminating circumstances are put to the accused and his response solicited. The words 'shall question him' clearly bring out the mandatory character of the clause and cast an imperative duty on the court and confer a corresponding right on the Accused to an opportunity to offer his explanation for such incriminating material against him. It is, therefore, true that the purpose of the examination of the accused under Section 313 is to give the accused an opportunity to explain the incriminating material, which has surface on record. The stage of examination of the accused under clause (b) of sub-section (1) of Section 313 reaches only after the witnesses for the prosecution have been examined and before the accused is called on to enter upon his defense. At the stage of closure of the prosecution evidence and before recording the statement under Section 313, the learned judge is not expected to evaluate the evidence for the purpose of deciding whether or not he should question the accused. After the Section 313 stage is over he has to hear the oral submission counsel on the evidence adduced before pronouncing on the evidence. The trial judge is not expected before he examine the accused under Section 313 of the Code, to sift the evidence and pronounce on whether or not he would accept the evidence regarding any incriminating material to determine whether or not to examine the accused on that material. To do so would be to prejudice the evidence without hearing the prosecution under section 314 of the Code. Therefore, no matter how a weak or scanty the prosecution evidence is in regard to a certain incriminating material. It is the duty of the court to examine the accused and seek his explanation thereon. It is only after that stage is over that the oral arguments have to the heard before the judgment is rendered. It is only where the court finds that no incriminating material has surfaced that the accused may not be examined under Section 313 of the Code. If there is material against the accused he must be examined. In the instant case it is not correct to say that no incriminating material has surfaced against the accused, particularly Accused No. 5 and hence the trial judge was not justified in examining the accused under Section 313 of the Code.

That brings us to the questions whether such a statement recorded under section 313 of the Code can constitute the sole basis for conviction. Since no oath is administered to the accused, the statements made by the accused will not be evidence strict to sense. That is why sub-section (3) says that the accused shall not render himself liable to punishment if he give false answers. Then comes sub-section (4) which reads :

"The answers given by the accused may be taken into consideration in such inquiry or trial, and put in the evidence for or against him in any other inquiry into, or trial for, any other offence which such answers may tend to show he has committed."

Thus the answers given by the accused in response to his examination under Section 313 can be taken into consideration in such inquiry or trial. This much is clear on a plain reading of the above sub-section. Therefore, though not strictly evidence, sub-section (4) permits that it may be taken into consideration in the said inquiry or trial[54] the Supreme Court in the case of Hate Singh v. State of Madhya Bharat,[55] held that an answer given by an accused under Section 313 examination can be used for proving his guilt as much as the evidence given by a prosecution witness. In Narain Singh v. State of Punjab,[56] this Court held that if the accused confesses to the commission of the offence with which he is charged the Court may, relying upon that confession, proceed to convict him to state the exact language in which the three Judge Bench answered the question it would be advantageous to reproduce the relevant observations at pages 684-685: "Under Section 342 of the code of Criminal Procedure by the first sub-section in so far as it is material, the court may at any stage of the enquiry or trial and after the witnesses for the prosecution have been examined and before the accused is called upon for his defense shall put questions to the accused person for the purpose of enabling him to explain any circumstances appearing in the evidence against him Examination under Section 342 is primarily to be directed to those maters on which evidence has been led for the prosecution to ascertain from the accused his version or explanation if any, of the incident which forms the subject matter of the charge and his defense. By sub-section (3), the answers given by the accused may 'be taken into consideration' at the enquiry or the trial. If the accused person in his examination under section 342 confesses to the commission of the offence charged against him the court may relying upon that confession, proceed to convict him, but if he does not confess and in explaining circumstances appearing in the evidence against him sets up his own version and seeks to explain his conduct pleading that he has committed no offence, the statement of the accused can only be taken into consideration in its entirety."

Sub-Section (1) of Section 313 corresponds to sub-section (1) of Section 342 of old Code except that it now stand bifurcated in two parts with the proviso added thereto clarifying that in summons cases where the presence of the accused is dispensed with his examination under clause (b) may also be dispensed with. Sub-section (2) of Section 313 reproduces the old subsection (2) except for the change necessitated on account of the abolition of the jury system. The present sub-section (4) with which we are concerned is a verbatim reproduction of the old sub-section (3). Therefore, the above stated observations apply with equal force.

Even on first principle no reason why the Court could not act on the admission or confession made by the accused in the course of the trial or in his statement recorded under section 313 of the Code, under Section 12 (4) of the TADA Act a Designated Court shall, for the purpose of trial of any offence, have all the powers of a Court of Session and shall try such offence as if it were a Court of Session so far as may be in accordance with the procedure prescribed in the Code for the trial before a Court of Session, albeit subject to the other provisions of the Act. The procedure for the trial of Session cases is outlined in Chapter XVIII of the Code. According to the procedure provided in that chapter after the case is opened as required by Section 226, if upon consideration of the record of the case and the documents submitted therewith, the Judge considers that there is no sufficient ground for proceeding against the accused, he shall discharge the accused for reasons to be recorded. If, however, the

Judge does not see reason to discharge he is required to frame in writing a charge against the accused as required by Section 228 of the Code. Where the Judge frames the charge, the charge so framed has to be read over and explained to the accused and the accused is required to be asked whether he pleads guilty of the offence charged or claims to be tried. Section 229 of Cr. P.C. next provides that if the accused pleads guilty, the Judge shall record the plea and may, in his discretion, convict him there on. The plain language of this provision shows that if the accused pleads guilty the Judge has to record the plea and thereafter decide whether or not the accused to convict the accused. The plea of guilt tantamount to an admission of all the facts constituting the offence. It is, therefore, essential that before accepting and acting on the plea the Judge must feel satisfied that the accused admits facts or ingredients constituting the offence. The plea of the accused must, therefore, be clear, unambiguous and unqualified and the court must be satisfied that he has understood the nature of the allegations made against him and admits them. The Court must act with caution and circumstances before accepting and acting on the plea of guilt. Once these requirements are satisfied the law permits the judge trying the case to record a conviction based on the plea of guilt. If, however, the accused does not plead guilty or the learned Judge does not act on his plea he must fix a date for the examination of the witness i.e. the trial of the case. There is nothing in this Chapter which prevents the accused from pleading guilty at any subsequent stage of the trial. But before the trial the Judge accepts and acts on that plea he must administer the same caution unto himself this plea of guilt may also be put forward by the accused in his statement recorded under Section 313 of the Code.

In the case of Jit Bahaduer Chetri, only one witness was examined and immediately thereafter the statement of the accused was recorded under Section 313 of the Code. The deposition of the sole witness did not reveal that he had seen accused causing injury in question. The question that was framed was not consistent with this evidence and hence the High Court found that the trial court had acted illegally. It was held that such an answer can not be construed as pleading guilty within the meaning of the provisions of the Code and hence the learned Magistrate had acted contrary to law in convicting and sentencing the accused on the basis of that plea. It will thus be seen that the Court came to the conclusion that the accused could not be stated to have pleaded guilty and hence the conviction was set aside. In the other case of Asokan the High Court of Kerala pointed out that in a criminal case the burden of establishing the guilt beyond doubt lies on the prosecution and that burden is neither takeaway, nor discharged, nor shifted merely because the accused sets up a plea of private defense. It was pointed out that if the prosecution has not placed any incriminating evidence such an admission made by the accused will be of no avail unless the admission constitutes an admission of guilt of any offence. In that case also the admission made by the accused read as a whole did not constitute an admission of guilt of the offence charged. On the contrary it was in the nature of a plea of private defense. In such circumstances, the High Court came to the conclusion that the absence of unequivocal, unmistakable and unqualified plea of guilt, the Court could not have convicted the accused on the statement made by him under Section 313 of the Code. This decision also does not, therefore, help the defense.

The accused were inter alias charged under Section 3 (2) (i) or (ii) and 3 (3) of TADA Act read with subrule (4) of Rule 23 of the rules framed there under. Section 3 provides the punishment for Terrorist Act. Section 10 lays down that when trying any offence a Designated Court may also try any other offence with which the accused may, under the code, be charged at the same trial if the offence is connected with such other offence. It is obvious that where an accused is up for trial for the commission of any offence under the Act or the rules made there under he can also be tried by the same Designated Court for the other offences with which he may, under the Code, be charged at the same trial provided the offence is connected with such other offence. In the instant case, the accused were tried under the aforesaid provisions of TADA Act and rules made there under along with the offences under Sections 120-B, 302, 307, 419, 468, 471, and 645 of I.P.C. They were also charged for the commission of the aforesaid offences with the aid of Section 34, I.P.C. As pointed out earlier under sections 12 (4) the procedure, that the Designated Court must follow is the procedure presided in the Code for the trial before a Court of Session. Accordingly, the Designated Court tried the two accused persons since they were charged for the commission of offences under the TADA Act. The Designated Court, however, come to the conclusion that the charge framed under Section 3 of the TADA Act read with the relevant rules had not been established and therefore, acquitted the accused persons on that court. It is not necessary for us to examine the correctness of this finding as we also come to the conclusion that capital punishment is warranted. It also acquitted all the accused persons of the other charges framed under the Penal Code save and except accused Nos. 1 and 5 as stated earlier. The accused were also convicted under Section 307 and 307/34 respectively for the injury caused to PW.106 Bhanumati Vaidya. Thus accused conviction of accused Nos. 1 and 5 is outside the provisions of TADA Act and, therefore, it was open to the Designated Court to award such sentence as was provided by the Penal Code. Section 17 (3) of the TADA Act makes Sections 366 to 371 and Section 392 of the Code applicable in relation to a case involving an offence trial by a Designated Court. The Designated Court having come to the conclusion that this was a case falling within the description of 'the rarest of a rare' awarded the extreme Penalty of death to both the accused Nos. 1 and 5 for the murder of Vaidya. In doing so, the Trial Court placed strong reliance on the decision of this court in Kehar Singh and others v. State (Delhi Administration).[58] The learned Trial Judge took the view that since the murder of General Vaidya was also on account of the same footing a and hence fell within the 'rarest of a rare' category. The accused persons had no remorse or repentance; in fact they felt proud of having killed General Vaidya in execution of their plan and hence we find no extenuating circumstance to make a departure from the ratio of Kehar Singh's case.

In Allauddin Mian v. State of Bihar,[59] the defense counsel submitted that in the present case also since the conviction and sentence were pronounced on the same day, the capital sentence awarded to the accused should not be confirmed. In the decision relied on, which one of us (Ahmadi, J.) was a party and who spoke for the Court, it was emphasized that Section 235 (2) of the Code being mandatory in character, the accused must be given an adequate opportunity of placing material bearing on the question of sentence before the Court. It was pointed out that the choice of sentence had to be made after giving the accused an effective and real opportunity to place his antecedents, social and economic background, mitigating and extenuating circumstances etc., before the Court for otherwise the Court's decision may be vulnerable. It was then said Paragraph 10 at Page 21:

"We think as a general rule the trial courts should after recording the conviction adjourn the matter to a future date and call upon both the prosecution as well as the defense to place the relevant material bearing on the question of sentence before it and thereafter pronounce the sentence to be imposed on the offender."

The above decision was rendered on 13th April 1989 whereas the present decision was pronounced on 21st October 1989. Yet contended learned counsel for the accused the Court did not appreciate the spirit of Section 235 (2) of the Code. The ratio of Allauddin Mian's case was affirmed in Milkiat Singh v. State of Punjab.[60] On the other hand the learned Additional Solicitor General invited our attention to a subsequent decision of this Court in Jumman Khan v. State of U.P.[61] That decision turned on the facts of that case. In the case the Court refused to entertain the plea on the ground that it was not raised in the courts below and sought to be raised for the first time in the apex court. That decision, therefore, does not assist the prosecution. Reliance was then placed on the third proviso to Section 309 of the Code, which reads as under :

"Provided also that no adjournment shall be granted for the purpose only of enabling the accused persons to show cause against the sentence proposed to be imposed on him."

This proviso must be read in the context of the general policy of expeditious injury and trial manifested by the main part of the section. That section emphasizes that an inquiry or trial once it has begun should proceed from day to day till the evidence of all the witnesses in attendance has been recorded so that they may not be unnecessarily vexed. The under lying object is to discourage frequent adjournment. But that does not mean that the proviso precludes the Court from adjourning the matter even where the interest of justice so demands. The proviso may not entitle an accused to an adjournment but it does not prohibit or preclude the court from granting one in such serious cases of life and death to satisfy the requirement of justice as enshrined in Section 235 (2) of the Code. Expeditious disposal of criminal case is indeed the requirement of Article 21 of the Constitution, so also a fair opportunity to place all relevant material before the court equally the requirement of the said article. Therefore, if the Court feel that the interest of justice demands that the matter should be adjourned to enable both sides to place the relevant material touching on the question of sentence before the Court, the above extracted proviso cannot preclude the court from doing so. But in the instant case court found that both accused decided to plead guilty. Accused No.1 had done so at the earlier stage of the trial when he filed the statement Exh. 60-A. Accused No. 5 had also made up his mind when he filed the statement Exh. 922 even before his examination under Section 313 of the Code. Accused No.1 had reiterated has determination when he filed the statement Exh. 919. Thus both accused had mentally decided to own their involvement in the murder of General Vaidya before their statement were recorded under Section 313 of the Code. Not only that their attitude reveals that they had resolved to kill him an enemy of the Sikh community since he had desecrated the Akal Takht. They also told the trial court that they were proud of their act and were not afraid of death and were prepared to sacrifice their lives for the article of their faith, namely, the realization of their dream of a separate State of Khalistan. It is thus apparent that before they made their statement admitting their involvement had mentally prepared themselves for the extreme penalty and therefore, if they desired to place any material for a lesser sentence they had ample opportunity to do so. But after the decision of this Court in Kehar Singh's case having regard to the well planned manner in which they executed their revolve to Kill General Vaidya, they were aware that there was every likelihood of the Court imposing the extreme penalty and they would have, if they so desired, place material in their written statement or would have requested the Court for time when the statements under Section 313 of the Code were recorded, if they desired to pray for a lesser sentence. They resolve not to do so is reflected in the fact that they have not chosen to file any appeal against their convictions by the Designated Court. Held that in them presents case the requirements of section 235 (2) of the Code have been satisfied in letter and no prejudice is shown to have occurred to the accused.[62] "Public Prosecutor" means any person appointed under Section 24 of Cr. P.C. 1973, and includes any person acting under the directions of a Public Prosecutor.[63]

Scope of—From a bare reading of sub-section (5) of Section 14 of the Act, it is clear that it pertains to the stage when evidence is to be recorded. In the present case the evidence stage has not reached as yet. The accused have not even charge-sheeted. The case is yet at the stage when the Court has to see whether any prima facie case is made out against the accused persons or not. If the prima facie case is not made out against any or all of the accused persons, such person or persons are entitled to be discharged.

Moreover, the Court has a right even to examine any or all of the accused persons before framing of charge sheets, and may put question to them, as it may deem fit.

For the said purpose the presence of all the accused persons is necessary even before the evidence stage and the respondents are legally bound to produce all the accused persons before the designated Court on all such hearing as fixed by it.

This is now well-established law that speedy trial in a criminal case has assumed the status of a fundamental right under Article 21 of the Constitution of India and any impediment there to is voilative of the constitutional guarantees.

In these circumstances of the case, the Designated Court is duty bound to take all necessary immediate steps for the speedy trial of the case. It is sufficient to write only letters to the Government for production of the accused person. The court has all the powers under law to procure their presence. It can issue warrants to the concerned authorities where they are detained for procuring their presence. It can proceed against them for contempt of the Court, if its orders are not complied with. It can even exempt them from their personal appearance in the court and proceed with the case, at least against the persons who are brought before it. After all, under law an accused is presumed to be innocent till guilt is proved against him. This is a glaring violation of the constitutional guarantee to keep a person in custody without any trial for years together. The court has the power to admit such persons to bail, if for the default of the respondents, the trial of the case has been thwarted.64

Cognizance of offence under Act by Magistrate.- The offence under TADA Act shall be tried only by a Designated Court established under Section 9 of the Act and the Designated Court has to take cognizance of such offence upon a complaint of facts or, upon a police report, and follow the procedure applicable to a trial of a sessions case.

When such a report is filed, he should return it to the concerned complaint or police office to file it in the Designated Court. If on the other hand the Magistrate takes cognizance, his jurisdiction only extends to the extent of trying the other offences. But the First Class Magistrates should avoid taking cognizance on the basis of such police reports or complaint involving offence punishable under TADA.

Otherwise, the very object for which TADA is enacted will be defeated. However, in the instant cases though the Magistrate has taken cognizance, such cognizance is not in accordance with the due process of law.

Therefore, to that extent the proceedings involving the offences punishable under TADA are vitiated and the Criminal Court like that of First Class Magistrates or the Sessions Courts not being Designated Courts, cannot either enquire or proceed with the trial of those Offences.65

Summary trial.- Relevant Provisions of Cr. P.C. 1973 are given below:-

Record in summary trials- In every case tried summarily, the Magistrate shall enter, in such form as the State Government may direct, the following particulars, namely

(a) the serial number of the case;

(b) the date of the commission of the offence;

(c) the date of the report or the complaint;

(d) the name of the complaint (if any);

(e) the name percentage and residence of the accused.

(f) the offence complained of and the offence (if any) proved, and in cases coming under clause (ii), clause (iii), or clause (iv) of sub-section (i) of Section 260 the value of the property in respect of which the offence has been commited;

(g) the plea of the accused and his examination (if any);
(h) the finding;
(i) the sentence or other final order;
(j) the date on which proceedings terminated.

Judgment in case tried summarily- In every case tried summarily in which the accused does not plead guilty, the Magistrate shall record the substance of the evidence and a judgment containing a brief statement of the reasons for the finding.

Language of record and judgment- Every such record and judgment shall be written in the language of the Court.

The High Court may authorize any Magistrate empowered to try offences summarily to prepare the aforesaid record or judgment or both by means of an officer appointed in this behalf by the Chief Judicial Magistrate, and such Magistrate shall sign the record or judgment so prepared.

Power of Supreme Court to transfer cases and appeals. Whenever it is made to appear to the Supreme Court that an order under this section is expedient for the ends of justice, it may direct that nay particular case or appeal be transferred from one High Court to subordinate to one High court to another Criminal Court equal or superior jurisdiction subordinate to another High Court.

The Supreme Court may act under this section only on the application of the Attorney- General of India or of a party interested, and every such application shall be made by motion, which shall, accept when the applicant is the Attorney General of India or the Advocate-General of the State, be supported by affidavit or affirmation.

Where any application for the exercise of the power conferred by this section is dismissed, the Supreme Court may, if it is of opinion that the application was frivolous or vexatious, order the applicant to pay by way of compensation to any person who has opposed the application such sum not exceeding one thousand rupees as it may consider appropriate in the circumstances of the case.[66]

Confession made by an accused in custody of Police Admissibility under Section 26 of the evidence Act no part of the confession made by the accused to a police Officer is held admissible under section 26 of the Evidence Act, the confession made in the presence of a police Officer becomes admissible although it is made by an accused who is in custody of the police, provided it is made in the presence of the Magistrate.

Be that as it may there is nothing in the Evidence Act that precluded an accused from relying upon his confession for his own purpose. This advantage, no doubt, the prosecution does not have because of the total ban enacted under Section 25 in making use of the confession is made of it under Section 26 provided the confession is made in the presence of a Magistrate. The accused is not untrammeled by either of these sections in case he desires to rely on the confession.[67]

Confession of co-accused- Whether can be relied upon for conviction? – The Deputy Government Advocate submitted that besides evidence of discovery there is other evidence of confession by the accused 'M', while making the confession under section 164 Criminal Procedure Code, implicated co-accused 'R', as one of the anticipants the crime, who committed dacoit and was involved in the offences, that confession cannot be relied upon for convicting accused 'R' for two reasons : (i) there is no independent evidence to connect the accused 'R' with the crime and (ii) the confession so made was exculpatory, it does not implicate the maker to the same extent as the other accused person against whom confession is sough to be used as 'M' has confessed that he was standing outside. Such type of confession by the co-accused can not be used against another co-accused as it cannot give rise to a conclusion of guilt beyond reasonable doubt, and can not be trusted.[68]

References

1. See State of Assam V. Prasenjeet Narzary. (1991) 1 crimes 709 (Gau) S. Hque J.
2. Vide State of Assam V. Prasenjeet Narzery, (1991) 1 Crimes 709 at 710, 711 (Gau).
3. VIDE Pandurang v. State of Maharashtra, AIR 1987 SC 535; Usmanbhai Dawoodbhai Menon v. State of Gujarat, AIR 1988 SC 922 : 1998 Cr. L.J. 938.
4. State of Assam v. Pransenji Narzary, (1991) 1 Crimes 709 at 711 (Gau).
5. Shri Sampatmall Jain v. State of Assam, 1992 Cr.L.J. 919 at 927, 928 (Gau) (S.N. Phukan, J.) See also Usmanbhai Dawoodbhai Memon v. State of Gujarat, AIR 1988 SC 922 : 1988 Cr.L.J. 938; Niranjan Singh Karam Singh Punjabi v. Jitendra Bhimaji Bijja, AIR 1990 SC 1962 : 1990 Cr. L.J. 1869, Ayubkhan Kalandarkhan Pathan v.State of Gujarat, 1991 Cr.L.J. 1085; (1990) 1 Crimes 183.
6. Vide Usmanbhai v. State of Gujarat, AIR 1988 SC 922 : 1988 Cr.LJ. 938.
7. Girish Chandra Kakati v. Union of India, 1992 Cr.L.J. 460 at 461 (Gau) (Manisena and Smt. M. Sarma, JJ.).

8. 1990 Cr. L.J. 76 P & H paragraph 7.
9. Shri Bacha Bora v. State of Assam, 1991 Cr. L.J. 2782 at 2784 (Gau).
10. AIR 1957 SC 956.
11. AIR 1988 SC 922.
12. Girish Chandra Kakati v. Union of India, 1992 Cr. L.J. 460 at 461, 462 (Gau) (Manisana and Smt. M. Sarma, JJ.).
13. Paras Ram v. State of Haryana, 1993 Cr. L.J. 416 at 617 (SC).
14. AIR 1988 SC 922 : 1988 Cr. L.J. 938.
15. Rattan Singh v. State of Háryana, 1991 Cr. L.J. 7724 at 725 (P.H.) (A.P. Chowdhari, J.).
16. AIR 1988 P & H 95 ; 1988 Cr. L.J. 869.
17. 1990 SCC (Cri.) 46.
18. (1992) 2 Crimes 80 at 85 (Guj).
19. 1993 Cr. L.J. 416 at 417 (SC).
20. 1989 SCC Supp. (2) 197.
21. Bhalchandra v. Sr. Inspector of police, (1992) 2 Crimes 336 (337) (Bom) (S.W. Puranik and D.J. Moharir, JJ.).
22. Rajaram Venkatesh v. State of A.P., 1993 Cr.L.J. 707 at 719 (A.P.).
23. Jayant Vitamins Ltd. v. Chaitanyakumar, 1992 Cr. L.J. 3450 at 3451 (SC).
24. Rajaram Venkatesh v. State of A.P., 1993 Cr. L.J. 707 at 719 (A.P.).
25. Jayant Vitamins Ltd. v. Chaitanyakumar, 1992 Cr. L.J. 3450 at 3451 (SC).
26. State of Punjab v. Amar Singh, 1992 Cr. L.J. 1000 (P & H). Relying on State v. Jai Bhagwan Singh. 1985 Cr. L.J. 932 (Del); Ravinder Pal Singh v. U.T. Chandigarh, (1987) 1 PLR 391 : 1986 Cr. L.J. 1371: Gange Ram v. Union Territory, Chandigarh, (1986) RCR 139.
27. Jodha Khoda Rabari v. State of Gujarat, 1992 Cr. L.J. 3298 at 3354 (Guj).
28. Gaurishankar v. State of Bihar, 1973 Cr. L.J. 137 (Pat).
29. Abdul Kader v. Union of India, AIR 1977 Mad. 386 : 1977 Cr. L.J. 1708.
30. Vide Cr. P.C. 1973, Section 83.
31. Vide Cr. P.C. 1983, Section 84.
32. Vide Cr. P.C. 1973, Section 82.
33. Vide Cr. P.C. 1973, Section 82.
34. Vide Cr. P.C. 1973, Section 85.

35. Niranjan Singh v. Jitendra Bhimraj Bijja, 1990 Cr. L.J. 1889 at 1873 (S.C.).
36. See State of Assam v. Prasenjit Narzary, (1991) 1 Crimes 709 (Gau) (S. Haque, J.).
37. Vide State of Assam v. Prasenjit Narzary, (1991) 1 Crimes 709 at 710, 711 (Gau).
38. Vide Pandurang v. State of Maharashtra, AIR 1987 S.C. 535 : Usmanbhai Dawoodbhai Memon v. State of Gujarat, AIR 1988 S.C. 922 : 1988 CR L.J. 938.
39. State of Assam v. Prasenjit Narzary, (1991) 1 Crimes 709 at (Gu).
40. Karna Siva Kanchi Reddy v. State of A.P., 1990 CR LJ 2734 at 2746, 2749 (A.P.).
41. 1990 CR LJ. 76 (P&H), Paragraph 7.
42. 1989 SCC Supp (2) 197.
43. Sampatmall Jain v. State of Assam, 1992 Cr LJ 919 at 928 (Gau) S.N. Phukan, J.) See also
    (i) Usmanbhai Dawoodbhai Memon v. State of Gujarat, AIR 1988 SC 922 : 1988 Cr LJ 938.
    (ii) Niranjan Singh Karam Singh Punjabi v. Jitendra Bhimraj • Bijja, AIR 1992 SC : 1990 Cr LJ 1869.
    (iii) Ayubkhan Kalandarkhan Pathan v. State of Gujarat 1991 Cr LJ 1085 : (1990) Crimes 183.
44. Para's Ram v. State of Haryana, 1993 Cr LJ 416 at 418 (SC) : State of Maharashtra v. Sukhdeo Singh, (1993) 1 Bom CR 233.
45. AIR 1988 SC 922 : 1988 CR LJ 938 quoted in 1990 Cr LJ 2743 at 2747 (AP), (Para 17 of SC).
46. Nairanjan Singh v. Jitendra Bhimraj Bijja, 1990 Cr LJ 1869 at 1877 (SC).
47. AIR 1990 SC 1992 : 1990 Cr LJ 1869.
48. 1992 Cr LJ 394 (Bom).
49. Santosh Dattarm More v. State of Maharashtra, 1992 Cr LJ 3409 at 3413, 3414 (Bom) (S.P. Kurdukar and W.M. Sambre, JJ.).
50. 1993 Cr LJ 416 at 416 at 418 (SC).
51. Sampatmall Jain V. State of Assam, 1992 Cr LJ 919 at 928 (Gau) (S.N. Phukan, J.). See also
    (i) Usamanbhai Dawoodbhai Memon V. State of Gujrat, AIR 1988 SC 922 : 1988 Cr LJ 938.
    (ii) Niranjan Singh Karan Singh Punjabi v. Jitendra Bhimraj Bijja, AIR 1990 Cr LJ 1962 : 1990 Cr LJ 1869.
    (iii) Ayubkhan Kalandarkhan Pathan v. State of Gujarat, 1991 Cr LJ 1085 : (1990) 1 Crimes 183.

52. 1977 Cr. L.J. 1833 (Gauhati).
53. 1982 Cr. L.J. 173 (Kerala).
54. See State of Maharashtra v. R.B. Chaudhari, (1967) 3 SCR 708.
55. 1953 Cr. L.J. 1933 (S C) : AIR 18953 S C 468.
56. (1963) 3 SCR 678.
57. 1977 Cr. L.J. 1833.
58. (1988) 3 SCC 609 : AIR 1988 SC 1883.
59. (1988) 3 S CC 5 : (1989) 3 S C J 163.
60. JT (1991) 2 S C 190 (Paragraph 18).
61. (1990) Suppl. 3 S C R 398 : AIR 1991 S C 345. F.-8.
62. State of Maharashtra v. Sukhdeo Singh, (1992) 3S C J 330 : (1993) 1 Bom CR 233 (S C).
63. Vide Cr. P.C. 1973, Section 2 (u). Also see Cr. P.C. Section 24 and 25.
64. Ali Mohamad Mir v. State, (1992) 2 Crimes 185 at 186 (J & K) (S.M. Rizvi, J.).
65. Karna Siva Kanchi Reddy v. State of A.P. 1990 Cr L.J. 2743 at 2746, 2749 (A.P.).
66. Vide Cr. P.C. 1973, Section 406.
67. Madaiah v. State, 1992 Cr. L.J. 502 at 506 (Karn). See also Lal Khan's case, 1949 Cr. 977 Mottai Thevar's case, 1952 Cr. L.J. 1210.
68. Chandan v. State of Rajasthan, 1988 Cr. L.J. 842 (S C) : 1988 CAR 89 ; Babu v. State of M. P., 1972 JLJN 69. See also Khalak Singh v. State of M. P.' 1992 Cr L.J. 1150 at 1155, 1156 (P).

2

EVIDENTIAL VALUE AND COURTS DUTY IN TERRORIST CASES

Evidentiary value of extra-judicial confession- The extra judicial confession is not a weak piece of 'Evidence'. On the contrary, if it is credible and the Court finds that the confession was made voluntarily, it can form the basis of conviction. One thing has to be kept in mind while considering the extra judicial confession. It has to be seen whether the person making confession knows the person before whom such a confession was made, that is, the confession is not made before a stranger. Normally a person would not make an implicate statement before a stranger. If the person before whom the confession is made is a close relative of the person making confession, or has possibility of being in his confidence, the same can be a plea of evidence to be utilized against the accused. Hence, when the three independent witnesses have spoken about the confession, they were co-villagers and not strangers. Therefore, in Court's considered opinion, the Sessions Judge has rightly believed it and has acted upon.[1]

Voluntary and trustworthy confession- Recording of.- Before recording the confession, the Magistrate gave all due caution to the accused and cautioned him that if he made a confessional statement that may be used against him. The confession was recorded in chamber at that time no police personnel was present. The accused understood that he was making the statement before a Magistrate and not police officer and on query of the Magistrate the accused specifically stated that police had not influenced him in any manner by way of threat or promise. After recording confession he explained the same to the accused who accepted it to be correctly recorded. He gave a certificate to that effect.

The confessional statement is marked Exh. 6. The accused has made the confession voluntarily and at the same time the court from the facts and circumstances of the case that there is a general corroboration to the confessional statement. As such the confession is not only voluntary but it is trustworthy. The council for the Appellant has assailed the confession as according to him the same suffers from some serious infirmities; for example, the Magistrate did not put any question the accused as to why he was going to make a confession.[2]

When extra judicial confession can formulate the basis for conviction. Generally extra judicial confession by itself is known to be a weak piece of evidence, hence scrutiny of it with caution is necessary. When fact of extra judicial of an accused comes through witnesses having no interest to falsely implicate the accused and it is found free from any suspicion as to its voluntary character and bears a ring of truth in it then its evidentiary value becomes more stronger carrying high probative value and deserves to be acted upon the instant extra judicial confession came through 6 witnesses having no reason to falsely implicate the accused and further more it was corroborated by circumstantial evidence indicated above. Hence extra judicial confession of accused was of voluntary character and came through non-interested witnesses corroborated by circumstantial evidence and the same had been proved. Hence extra judicial confession formulates the basis for conviction.[3]

Evidence of defense witnesses- Contents of inquest report can be looked into to test the veracity. When examined under section 313, Cr. P.C. 1973 the accused stated that a worthy quarrel ensued between him and his wife and at that time he was having a licensed gun with him. He was carrying the gun because of enemies in the village. He was in a drunken condition and during the grappling the gun went off accidentally as a result of which the deceased received a gunshot injury and died. He appears to have filed an application before the D.S.P. stating these facts. He also examined D.Ws. 1 to 3 in support of his plea. The trial Judge accepted the evidence of the eyewitness P.W. 3, the mother of the deceased and also the medical evidence and held that the accused went and brought the gun and shot at the deceased. He rejected the plea of the accused and the evidence of D.Ws. 1 to 3. Therefore, the question that arises for consideration is whether it was an accident as pleaded as per the prosecution version. D.Ws. 1 and 2 were examined to depose that P.W. 3 was later brought from her village and that she was not at the scene of occurrence. D.W. 2 was a panch witness in the inquest report which he attested. And in which the presence of P.W. 3 is given as witness of the occurrence. D.W. 2 has no explanation except stating that he did not read the contents. Admittedly he knows Punjabi language in which the inquest report was written. Therefore his explanation is not acceptable. The evidence of D.W. 2 therefore is not of much consequence. D.W. 3 deposed that he is brother-in-law of the accused and that his wife had taken the son and daughter of the accused from the village. His evidence is not of much consequence. D.W.I also deposed that he heard an alarm from the house of the accused and went to the house of accused and saw the accused and his wife grappling and he tried to intervene but before he could do so, the gun of the accused fired accidentally. Therefore he took the accused to D.W. 2 Village Sarpanch and thereafter they went to the Police Station and gave a report. But as stated above D.W. 2 was a panch witnesses in the inquest report wherein the version was that the accused shot at the deceased. No doubt, the contents of the inquest report cannot be treated as evidence but they can be looked into to test the veracity of D.W. 2. Thus the evidence of D.Ws. 1 to 3 is not of any help to the accused.[4]

Application of evidence of injured persons,- In Swaran Singh v. State of Himachal Pradesh,[5] wherein it has been held that :

"There is no rule either of law or prudence which requires that evidence of injured persons with respect to the cause of their injuries should not be believed and acted upon simply because it has not been corroborated by some independent witnesses of the occurrence. As in the instant case, independent witnesses may not be present at all at the time of the occurrence, that would not mean that the prosecution case, however, true, should be thrown out simply for the reason that the prosecution has not procured independent eyewitnesses. Again, it is pertinent to remember that though the injured person examined at the trial is hostile to the assailants and interested in the prosecution, it is most unlikely that he would deliberately spare the true assailants and substitute in their place the names of the other enemies out of malice or enmity. This is all the more unlikely in case where the victim had full opportunity to identify his assailants. The desire to punish assailants is so powerful in human being that he would unhesitant name the real culprits without thinking of substituting them by others who may be inimical to him. After all victim can have no better sympathy with his real assailants then his other enemies and this applies all the more in case of an offence involving the very life of the victim. A person may falsely implicate his enemy in place of the real culprit but this is likely only when he is not sure about the identity of his assailant, for example, where the offence is committed under the cover of darkness and the culprit manages to escape. It is also not improbable that while naming the assailants, the victims may add some innocent persons out of malice and enmity, which factor the Courts must bear in mind while appreciating the evidence of such interested persons."[6]

Evidentiary value of interested witnesses. In state of Punjab v. Wassan Singh,[7] in para 27 that report this is what the Supreme Court has said :

"It is true that both these witnesses are related to the deceased and, as such, are interested witnesses. Their antecedents also are of a questionable nature. But their antecedents or mere interestedness was not a valid ground to reject their evidence. Persons with such antecedents are not necessarily untruthful witnesses. Nor mere relationship with the deceased was a good ground for discarding their testimony, when, as we have already held, their presence at the scene of occurrence was probable. All that was necessary was to scrutinize their evidence with more than ordinary care ad circumspection, with reference to the part or role assigned to each of the accused. An effort should have been made to shift the rain from the chaff : to accept what appeared to be true and to reject the rest. The High Court did not adopt this methodology in appreciating their evidence. Instead, it took a short cut to disposal and rejected their plea already discussed, are manifestly untenable"[8].

Eyewitnesses- Evidence cannot be discarded on being related to or interested in the deceased or even on grounds of enmity with the accused. The evidence of a witness who has enmity with the accused is required to be examined with care and caution. However, his evidence cannot be thrown as away merely because he has enmity with the accused. On the contrary, a person who has received an injury in an accident for a person whose relative has been murdered in as incident will not like to allow the real assailant to go scot-free and implicate his enemies merely on account of his enmity.

Suffice it to say that the court fully agree with the view taken by the Sessions Judge that the evidence of the eye witnesses in the present case can not be discarded merely because they are either relatives of the deceased or they are interested in the deceased or even on the ground of enmity.

If the presence of the witness at the scene of the incident could not be disputed, and if he himself has been injured in the incident, it would be most unlikely that he would like the real culprit to go scot-free, and falsely implicate his other enemy. Here in this case, the presence of Purshotam Mulji at the scene of the incident could not be and has not been disputed. He had sustained as many as eight fire arm injuries as revealed by the medical evidence, which is not challenged. When he was taking treatment at the Civil Hospital, Ahmedabad, by surgical intervention, from his body, one Order 32 deformed lead bullet weighing about 6.17 gms. was removed. Of course that bullet, according to the Forensic Science Laboratory expert, though was a fired lead bullet, such a bullet is not ordinarily used in short gun cartridge. The fact remains that he received as many as eight firearm injuries. Such a person who has received such extensive injuries would hardly think of allowing the real culprit to escape and implicate his other enemies.[9]

First Information Report- appreciation and purpose.- A first information report is not supported to be a detailed document. The F.I.R. is a document which sets the criminal law into motion and it has to be appreciated keeping in the facts and circumstances of each individual case.[10]

Non-examination of the prosecution witness won over by the accused not to affect the probative value of the evidence of other prosecution witness.

In Allauddin Mian v. State of Bihar,[11] it has been observed as under :

"It was next submitted by learned Counsel for the accused that sum of the prosecution witnesses, namely, Jallaluddin, Bhikhari Mian and Ramchandra Prasad who were admittedly preset at the scene of the occurrence according to the prosecution and had witnessed the entire incident were deliberately dropped with a view to suppressing the truth. The Supreme Court can not accept this contention for the simple reason that apart from both P.W. 5 and P.W. 6 having deposed that they were pressurized by the defense, the High Court has found in paragraph 36 of its judgment that efforts were made by the defense to scare away the witnesses from giving evidence. There is ample material on record to conclude that considerable pressure was exerted on the prosecution witnesses to stay away from the witness box. Some succumbed to the threats and pressure while some others did not displayed courage to give evidence and state the truth. In this backdrop, if the prosecution did not examine Jallaluddin, Ram Chandra Prasad and Bhikari Mian on learning that they were won over, it cannot be said that the prosecution was unfair to the accused persons. Mr. Garg submitted that there was nothing to show that the Accused persons were in any way guilty of pressurizing or threatening the witnesses. That is beside the point. What is relevant is the fact it so happened. Therefore, the non-examination of the aforesaid witnesses cannot affect the probative value of the evidence of other prosecution witnesses."

If there is some material going to show that the prosecution witness has been won over by the accused then the non-examination of that witness by the prosecution can certainly not be a matter of criticism.

Omission in F I R-Can not render evidence of one witness in any manner infirm- In Jodha Khoda Rabari v. State of Gujarat,[12] it was observed as follows:

"Here, the Court has to bear in mind that there was all of a sudden assault by a large number of persons armed with firearms on a party of about 25 person traveling in a trailer about 13 who were females. The Court has also to remember that there is consistent evidence to show that the first shoot was fired by Jasubha accused no.11 on the tire of the tractor took a result of which the tire was deflated and the tractor took a turn and came to a stop. There is again consistent evidence to show that the second shot was also fired by Jasubha accused No. 11 and that shot almost decapitated or be headed Bai Diwali who was in the trailer. It was thereafter that other shots were fired and one of those other shots hit Pragji on his elbow. One has to visualize the mental condition of Pragji Mavji, under those circumstances. He had with his own eyes seen Jasubha having fired a shot on the tyre of the tractor. He has seen Bai Diwali being decapitated by another shot fired by Jasubha, and it was thereafter that he was hit. He must have been to an extent dumb founded, but life being dearest to every one, so it was to Pragji and therefore Pragji jumped out of the trailer and ran for his life towards village Timba, that is, towards north. But, then even while running away towards north out of human curiosity, he looked back, when he had already run about two or three rope lengths equivalent to about 50 to 60 paces as stated by para 9 of his deposition and then he saw four other persons besides the seven named assailants. As stated by him, in para 9 of his deposition he had identified by their faces, two out of the four other persons but he had not been able to see the faces of the remaining two. According to him, one of those two was of Chomal and the other of Sandh Khakhara. Thus, it is clear that at the time he made the statement Mark 'A' he must have been under some shock, he having witnessed a ghastly incident and he himself having been injured. Therefore, the omission on his part to state in the FIR about Jasubha having fired a shot on the tire of the tractor and about Diwaliben having been killed on the spot is in Court's opinion not of any significance. That omission could certainly be explained on the argument that at the time Pragji made this statement Mark "A" he must have been under some shock. But even when making that statement he had given sufficient details about the incident. The facts about Jasubha having fired the shot at the tire of the tractor and the second shot fired by Jasubha having decapitated Bai Diwali have been clearly deposed by the witness and there is clear evidence that Pragji came to be hit after these first two shots were fired by Jasubha. He must have, therefore, witnessed these two facts. Mere omission on his part to mention these two facts in the FIR cannot render his evidence in any manner infirm.

Other witnesses cannot disbelieve witness merely on the ground of discrepancy in number of accused persons seen. In Jodha Khoda Rabari v. State of Gujarat,[13] it was observe as follows:

"Then, it was submitted on, behalf of the defense that though Pragji and some other witnesses implicated only seven accused in the case, Ganesh implicates eleven accused and therefore, as regards the four accused (11 minus 7), the deposition if Ganesh should not be accepted. Firstly, factually, the argument is not wholly correct. Pragji as the High Court has indicated here in above has implicated not only seven persons but he has implicated (7+4=11) persons. It is a different matter that he has not been able to identify two out of those eleven for he had not seen their faces but he positively proves the presence of eleven persons at the scene of offence. Parashottam Mulji speaks of the presence of seven persons named by him and two other. Of course, Madhu Naran speaks of the presence of only seven persons. But from these facts Ganesh cannot be disbelieved when he speaks about the presence of eleven persons. It is required to be noticed that whereas Pragji Mavji, Madhu Naran and Parashottam Mulji as also Dhanji Bhagwan were injured, this witness Ganesh had fortunately escaped unscathed. On account of having been hit, the power of perception of witness Madhu Naran, Pragji Mavji and Dhanji Bhagwan might have been, to some extent impaired while for Ganesh there were no such reasons for impairment of his power of perception. Therefore, when Ganesh speaks about the presence of eleven persons, he can not be discarded on the argument that Parashottam Mulji and Madhu Naran speak about the presence of only seven persons. In this connection, reference may be made to the decision in the case of Shiv Charan v. State of Haryana,[14] that was a case of a running train dacoit by six dacoits. Three of the witnesses produced at the trial were not able to identify the appellant Shiva Charan, of that case and each one of the other dacoits, while the fourth witness Allabu had recognized all the accused. Of course Allabux after the incident had participated at the T.I. Parade where he had identified all the five accused to be the dacoits but merely on the ground that some other witness had not identified Shiv Charan, Allabux not disbelieved when he identified Shiv Charan as one of the dacoits. Of course, there was an additional feature that Allabux had participated at the T.I. Parade where he had identified Shiv Charan. The Supreme Court confirmed the conviction of Shiv Charan. Applying the same logic here, merely because some other witnesses spoke about only seven accused and Ganesh speaks about eleven, Ganesh cannot be disbelieved. In this case, it was not at all necessary for Ganesh to participate at T.I. Parade for all the accused named by him were very much known to him since much prior to the incident. What we emphasize is that merely because Parashottam Mulji and Madhu Naran have spoken about the presence of seven accused. Ganesh can not be disbelieved when he speaks about the presence of eleven accused."

Witness cannot be faulted, merely because he left leaving behind his wife and relations to their luck at the place of incident. In Jodha Khoda Rabari v. State of Gujarat,[15] it was observed as follows :

The evidence of Pragji was criticized on the ground that he ran away immediately from the scene, leaving his wife and brother to their luck. According to the Advocate for the accused such a conduct of Pragji is unnatural. This argument leveled by the Advocate for the accused cuts at the very root of the earlier argument that Pragji must left the place soon on having received the injury and he would then have no opportunity to witness the other parts of the incident. What Pragji has done in running away from the place of incident, he has done? Merely because he left the place, leaving his wife, brother and other relative to their luck for that he can not be faulted. It is to be noted here that the instant of self-preservation is paramount in the mind of every human being, under ordinary circumstances, one would like to take care of his wife and other relatives if there is a cloud of danger, on their head. But if the person himself is under danger as when there is likelihood of losing his life, he could not be faulted if he takes to his heels and does not care for his wife, brother and other relatives who might also be in similar danger."

References

1. Arjun Pradhan v. State, 1992 Cr. L.J. 3614, 3616 (ORI) (A. Pasayat and D.M. Patanaik, JJ.).
2. Sarkar Mardi v. State of West Bengal, 1992 Cr. L.J. 367 at 369, 370 (Cal).
3. Jarina Khatun v. State of Assam, 1992 Cr. L.J. 733 at 735 (Gau). See also Piara Singh v. State of Punjab, AIR 1977 S C 2274 : 1977 Cr. L.J. 1941.
4. Kuldip Singh v. State of Punjab, 1992 Cr. L.J. 3592 at 3593 (S C).
5. (1984) 3 Crimes 12, paragraph 21 : 1984 Cr L.J. NOC 147.
6. Vide Jodhan Khoda Rabari v. State of Gujarat, 1992 Cr. L.J. 3298 at 3333 (Guj).

7. AIR 1981 S C 697 : 1981 Cr. L.J. 410.
8. See Jodha Khoda Rabari v. State of Gujarat, 1992 Cr. L.J. 3298 at 3333 (Guj).
9. Jodha Khoda Rabari v. State of Gujarat , 1992 Cr. L.J. 3228 Para 54, 57, 77 (Guj).
10. Jodha Khoda Rabari v. State of Gujarat, 1992 Cr. L.J. 3298 at 3329 (Guj).
11. AIR 1989 S C 1456, para 7 : 1989 Cr. L.J. 1466.
12. Jodha Khoda Rabari v. State of Gujarat, 1992 Cr L.J. 3298 at 3360 (Guj).
13. 1992 Cr. L.J. 3298, para 64 (Guj).
14. AIR 1987 S C 1 : 1987 Cr. L.J. 695.
15. 1992 Cr. L.J. 3298 at 3334 (Guj.).

3

PROCEDURE AND TRIAL OF TERRORIST AND RULES AND SOME RELATED ACTS

Scope of- The language of Section 18 of the Act does not require any obligation for the party connected to make application under Section 18. The Designated Court can also sue motu act under Section 18 of the TADA act.[1]

Charges under TADA Act and IPC against several accused- When the Designated Court may have a jurisdiction to try any other offences in respect of the accused in this Court- 1 If section 12 of the Act analyzed, carefully, it is clear to us that when the Designated Court is trying any offence it may also try any other offence with which accused is charged under the code at the same trial, if offence is connected with such other offence. It is therefore, clear that the Designated Court may have a jurisdiction to try any other offence in respect of the accused in its court provided that other offences are connected with such offence under TADA. In the present case, since accused a Nos. 4 and 5 have been discharged under TADA the offence alleged to have been committed by Accused Nos. 4 and 5 under Section 412 and 414 of the Indian Penal Code can not be tried along with other accused Nos. 1 to 3 whose offences were being tried along with other accused Nos. 1 to 3 whose offences were being tried by the Designated Court. On the basis of the chargesheet Mr. 'B' submitted that here offenders as well as offences of Accused Nos. 4 and 5 are distinct qua the other accused and therefore accused Nos. 4 and 5 can not burried along with other accused where offences fall under TADA and being trial by the Designated Court. Mr. 'B' in support of his submission drew Court's attention to a decision of the Supreme Court in Niranjan Singh Karam Singh Punjabi v. Jitendra Bhimraj Bijja,[2] in this reported decision the question that fell for consideration before the Supreme Court was whether provisions of TADA were applicable to the facts of the case. While holding that provisions of TADA did not apply to the facts and circumstances of the case, the Supreme Court in para 12 held as under:

"Once the Designated Court came to the conclusion that the evidence was not sufficient to frame a charge under Section 3 (1) of the Act, the Designated Court had no alternative but to resort to Section 18 and transfer the case to the competent Court under the Code. We therefore do not see any merit in the contention of the counsel for the State of Maharashtra that even after the Designated Court came to the conclusion that no ground was made out under Section 3 (2) of the Act, it was duty bound by virtue of Section 12 (1) of the Act to proceed with the trial for the other offences under the Penal Code and the Bombay Police Act. We think that the Course adopted by the Designated Court in transferring the case to the Sessions Court is clearly in keeping with Section 18 of the Act".

It is true that the Supreme Court in this case transferred the criminal case to regular Criminal Court under Section 18 of the TADA. That was because; the Supreme Court came to the conclusion that the provisions of Section 3 (1) of TADA have no application to the facts of that case. This decision, supports the contention raised on behalf of the petitioner. 'B' then drew our attention to another decision of this Court in Rafiq Abid Patel v. Inspector of Police, Kashmira Police Station, and Thane,[3] in this reported case with one Asif Patel. Asif Patel alone had a revolver in his hand whereas petitioners were armed with stone, Soda water bottle and other weapons. It was the case registered under sections 147, 148, 149, 307, 324, 336, 341 and 427 of the Indian Penal Code and Sections 25 (1) and 27 of the Arms Act. The Circle Police Inspector, Kashmira Camp, informed the TADA Court that provisions of Section 3 and 5 of the TADA have been applied to all the accused in the said case. While construing the scope and ambit of Section 5 of the TADA, the Court held that having regard to the phraseology used in section 5 of the TADA, the said provisions can not be made applicable to the petitioners. The Division Bench of the Bombay High Court accordingly quashed the application of provisions of Sections 3, 5 and 6 of the TADA. The Police Officer was restrained from carrying out any investigation against the Petitioners under sections 3, 5 and 6 of the TADA. It is true that in this case provisions of Section 12 of the TADA were not considered because question of transferring case it appears, did not arise from paragraph 16 of the said judgment it appears, that investigation was under progress at that stage and therefore, question of considering Section 12 did not arise.

Mr. 'L' the Assistant Public Prosecutor, however, urged that all offences connected with C.R. No. 113/91 can be tried together in a Designated Court under the TADA with the aid of Section 12 of the Act. The Designated Court has been empowered to try any other offences of which offender accused was charged if such offences are connected with such other offence for which accused Nos. 1 to 3 are being tried under TADA. Mr. 'L' also urged that role of accused Nos. 4 and connected 5 for which they have been charged, is so intimately that separate trial as regards their offences by another Court would be inappropriate and contrary to Section 12 of the TADA.

The Designated Court which is trying any offence under TADA may try any other offence with which accused whose offence is being tried by the Designated Court, if charged with the offences connected with offence under TADA, may club together and try such offences. The position in the present case in altogether different because order of discharge has been passed by the trial Judge. Moment accused Nos. 4 and 5 were discharged under TADA, then trial by the Designated Court would be without jurisdiction. Section 12 would not be attracted to try accused Nos. 4 and 5 along with other accused in a Designated Court.

In Court's opinion, viewed from any angle, trial of accused nos. 4 and 5 who have been discharged by the Designated Court under TADA will be without Jurisdiction and therefore, under section 18 of the TADA the case of accused Nos. 4 and 5 will have to be transferred to the competent court for trial.[4]

Cognizance of an offences. Whether provisions of Cr. P.C. equally applicable to the Designated courts under TADA Act.- The Court, under the scheme of the Code of Criminal Procedure, can take the cognizance of any offence after investigation is complete.

In fact taking cognizance means judicial application of mind to the facts as disclosed, inter alia, in the police report for taking further action. These provisions of the Code of the code of Criminal Procedure are equally applicable to the Designated Court under the TADA Act. Save and except to the extent to which they are over ridden or modified by the TADA Act. Section 18 of the TADA Act would be attracted only at the Stage where the Designated Court takes cognizance of an offence i.e. after the investigation is complete and police report, generally known as a charge sheet, is filed. The contention of 'L' that the Designated Court can exercise its powers under Section 18 even during the pendency of investigation has no merit.[5]

Duty of Court:- Section 18 of the Act provides that where after taking cognizance of any offence the Designated Court is of the opinion that the offence is not triable by it, it shall, not withstanding that it has no jurisdiction to try such offence, transfer the case for the trial of such offence to any Court came to the conclusion that there was no prima facie evidence to frame a charger under Section 3 (1) of the Act, it was justified in transferring the case to the court of Session, Ahmadnagar, which alone had jurisdiction under the Code.[6]

Duty of the Court to interfere in non-disclosure of an offence- In the case of State of West Bengal v. Swapan Kumar Guha,[7] the Supreme Court has observed as follows (at p. 842 of Cr. L.J.).

"Whether an offence into which an investigation is made or to be made is disclosed or not must necessarily depend on the facts and circumstances of each particular case and in considering that question the Court has mainly to take into consideration the complaint or F I R. On a consideration of the complaint or F I R, and all the relevant materials, the Court has to come to the conclusion whether an offence is disclosed or not. If on such consideration, the court is satisfied that offence disclosed, the court will normally allow the investigation into the offence and will generally allow the investigation into the offence to be completed for collection material for proving the offence. If, on the other hand, the court is satisfied that no offence is disclosed, it will be the duty of the Court to interfere with any investigation and to stop the same to prevent any kind of uncalled for unnecessary harassment to an individual.[8]

Mala-fide exercise of power by investigation:- Restrain on the police officer by issuing writ of mandamus by the High Court- In S.N. Sharma v. Bipen Kumar Tiwari,[9] the Supreme Court said that tough the code of Criminal Procedure gives to the police unfettered power to investigate all cases where they suspected that a cognizable offence has been committed, in appropriate cases an aggrieved person can. Always seek a remedy by invoking the powers of the High Court under Article 226 of the Constitution under which, if the High Court could be convinced that the power of investigation has been exercised by a police officer mala-fide, the High Court can always issue a writ of mandamus restraining the police officer from misusing his legal powers.[10]

Non-disclosure of any offence under TADA Act- Exercise of powers of the High Court under Article 226 of the Constitution. If the investigation which is being conducted is challenged by a affected person on the ground that no offence is disclosed under TADA Act, as in the present case, or on any other adequate ground, the Court do not see any reason why the High Court can not, in a suitable case, examine this contention in exercise of its powers under Article 226 of the Constitution of India.

It is only at the stage of taking cognizance of the offence after filling of the charge sheet that the Designated Court can exercise its powers under Section 18 of the TADA Act and till then, if the investigation has taken a considerable period of time, as in the present case, and if no prime-facie case is disclosed for applying the provision of the TADA Act, the Court can exercise its powers under Article 226 of the Constitution of India to entertain a petition. In the present case, does the material which is before us and the F I R relating to C.R. No. I-43/ of 1991, disclose any offence by the petitioners which would attract the application of the provision of Sections 5 and 6 of the TADA Act.[11]

Scope of Section 19 provides for an appeal to the Supreme Court both on facts and on law from any judgment, sentence or order, other than interlocutory order, of a Designated Court.[12]

Resort to the TADA Act even in ordinary cases- Direction issued to the Designated Court by invoking the provisions of Article 227 of the Constitution to observe law laid down in this regard by the apex Court. The Public Prosecutor has rightly urged that in view of the provisions of Law laid down in Section 19 of the Terrorist and Disruptive Activities (Prevention) Act, 1987, this Court has no jurisdiction to interfere with the orders of Designated Court.

This Act came up before the apex Court in two cases viz. Usmanbhai D. Memon v. State of Gujarat,[13] and Niranjan Singh Karam Singh Punjabi v. Jitendra Bhimraj Bijja,[14] in Usmanbhai (supra) in para. 15, the apex Court observed that the act is extreme measure to be resorted to when the Police cannot take the situation under the ordinary penal law. The intendment is to provide special machinery to combat the growing menace of terrorism in different parts of the country. The Court further held that the Act being a drastic measure, it should not ordinarily be resorted to unless the Government's law enforcing machinery fails. This was reiterated in Niranjan Singh (supra) and in para 8 of the judgment the ratio laid down is as follows:

"To put it differently the ratio of the decision is that the proviso of the act need not be resorted to it if the nature of the activities of the accused can be checked and controlled under the ordinary law of the land. It is only in those cases where the law enforcing machinery finds the ordinary law to be inadequate or not sufficient effective for tackling the menace of terrorist and disruptive activities that resort should be had to the drastic provision of the Act. While invoking a criminal statute such as Act the prosecution is duty bound to show from the record of the case and the documents collected in course of investigation that facts emerging there from prima facie constitute an offence within the letter of the law..."

This law laid down by the apex Court is binding on all Courts within the territory of India as laid down in Article 141 of the Constitution of India, and as such this Court is duty bound to enforce the above law laid down. It has come to the notice of this Court that even in the ordinary cases, Sections 3 and 4 of the above Act are added by the prosecution which is absolutely illegal. Though this court cannot interfere with the impugned order. This court can definitely direct the Designated Court, by invoking the provisions of Article 227 of the Constitution to observe the law lay down by the Supreme Court.[15]

Superintendence of Subordinate Court and Tribunal. It is a settled law that by exercising power of Superintendence under Article 227 of the Constitution, High Court can keep the subordinate Courts and Tribunal within the bound of its authority.[16] The designated court or Magistrate by exercising powers under Criminal Procedure Code is not acting in accordance with law, suitable direction can be given by this Court.[17]

Writ- If it is a matter conducted by a Court of Sessions under code of Criminal Procedure, the accused before the said Court of Sessions can approach this Court either by way of Revision or Appeal as matter of Course and as a matter of right under the Code; while that may not be the position if that matter is dealt with the Designated Court.

Apart from these practical implications, the aforesaid question raised in the petition, namely that the Designated Court could not have exercised its power in the instant case because the Terrorist act itself is not attracted would certainly be a subject matter of enquiry under Articles 226 and 227 of the Constitution of India.[18]

THE TERRORIST AND DISRUPTIVE ACTIVITIES (PREVENTION) RULES 1987

Notification No. G.S.R. 84 3 (E), dated October 7, 1987, published in the gazattee of India, (Extra), Part II, Section 3 (I), dated 7th October, 1987,- In exercise of the powers conferred by Section 28 of the Terrorist and Disruptive Activities (Prevention) Act, 1987 (28 of 1987), the Central Government hereby makes the following rules, namely:-

Short title and commencement:- (1) These rules may be called the Terrorist and Disruptive (Prevention) Rules, 1987.

They shall come into force on the date of there publication in the

Official Gazettee.

Definitions:- In these rules, unless the context otherwise requires:-

(a) "Act" means the Terrorist and Disruptive Activities (Prevention) Act, 1987 (28 of 1987);

(b) "empowered authority" means any authority being the

Central Government or a State Government or the Administrator of a Union territory under Article 239 of the Constitution or an Officer of the Central Government not lower or an Officer of a State Government or a Union territory Administration not lower in rank than that of a District Magistrate or an Officer competent to exercise under any law the powers of a District Magistrate;

(c) "Prohibited place" means a prohibited place as defined in clause (8) of Section 2 of the Official Secrets Act, 1923 (19 of 1923).

THE NATIONAL SECURITY GUARD ACT, 1986

An act to provide for the constitution and regulation of an armed force of the Union for combating terrorist activities with a view to protecting State against internal disturbances and for matter connected there with. Be it enacted by Parliament in the Thirty- Seventh year of the Republic of India as follows:-

Statement of Object and Reasons:- For quite sometime past, terrorist has been steadily assuming menacing proportions in the country. These elements have been indulging in wanton killings, arson, looting and other heinous crimes such as hijacking, mass murders, etc. with the object to over awe the Government to terrorist, create fear and panic in the minds of citizens and to disrupt communal peace and harmony. With a view effectively combating such terrorist activities in different States and to project the State against internal disturbances, the Central Government decided to raise a special armed force. Consequently, the National Security Guard was raised in the middle of 1984 when the Directorate-General of National Security Guard was set up under the command of a senior Police Officer Designated as the Director-General of the National Security Guard.

The National Security Guard shall serve as a contingency Deployment force to deal with terrorist activities in various states. However, considering the nature and purpose of the force and the experience gained during the last two years 'It has been felt that the force should be regulated by a self contained statute, which will provide or its special needs more particularly in matters of discipline.

While taking care, that the National Security Guard does not lose its character as an armed force of the Union charged with combating terrorist aetivities within the Country, the Bill seeks to ensure that highest standards of efficiency and discipline are maintained in this force.

Accordingly, the drafting of the present Bill, the provision of the Army Act, 1950 and Border Security Force Act, 1958 have been borne in mind. The Bill provides for the constitution of the National Security Guard and for deeming the existing National Security Guard.

References

1. Bhalchandra v. Senior Inspector of Police, (1992) 2 Crimes 336 at 337 (Bom) (S.W.) Puranik & D.J. Moharir, JJ.).
2. AIR 1990 S C 1962 : 1990 Cr. L.J. 1869.
3. 1992 Cr. L.J. 394 (Bom).
4. Santosh Dattaram More v. State of Maharashtra, 1992 Cr. L.J. 3409 at 3413, 3414 (Bom) (S.P. Kurdukar and W.M. Sambre, JJ.)
5. Rafiq Abid Patel v. Inspector of Police, 1992 Cr. L.J. 394 : (Bom) (Mrs. Sujata Manohar and B.N. Srikrishna JJ.).
6. Niranjan Singh v. Jitendra Bhimraj Baija, 1990 Cr. L.J 1869 at 1877 (S C).
7. 1982 Cr. L.J. 819 : 1982 1 SCC 561.
8. See also Rafiq Abid Patel v. Inspector of Police 1992 Cr. L.J. 394 at 396 (Bom.).
9. AIR 1970 S C 786 (1970) 1 Cr. L.J. 764.
10. Vide Rafiq Abid Patel v. Inspector of Police, 1992 Cr. L.J. 394 at 396, 397 (Bom.).
11. Rafiq Abid Patel v. Inspector of Police, 1992 Cr. L.J. 394 at 396, 397 (Bom.).
12. Niranjan Singh v. Jitendra Bhimraj Bijja, 1990 Cr. L.J. 1869 at 1872 (S C) See also, P.K. Bhausar v. Sadiq (1993) 2 JT (S C) 435.
13. A I R 1988 S C 922 : 1988 Cr. L.J. 938.
14. A I R 1990 S C 962 : 1990 Cr. L.J. 1869.
15. Harem Brahma v. State of Assam. 1992 Cr. L.J. 1351 at 1352 (Gau) (S.N. Shanker, J.) See also P.K. Bhausar v. saiq, (1993) 1 J T (S C) 435.
16. Sampatmal Jain v. State of Assam, 1992 Cr. L.J. 919 at 929 (Gau). See also Nvaryam Singh v. Amarnath, A I R 1954 SE 215.
17. Sampatmal Jain v. State of Assam, 1992 Cr. L.J. 919 at 929 (Gau) : (1991) 3 crimes 319.

18. Babu Satyam Bhaiyya v. State of Gujarat, (1992) 2 Crimes 80 at 91 (Gau) (N.J. Pandya, J.).
19. Enforced on 16.10.1986, vide S.O. 735 (E), at 16th October 1986. F- 18.

THE ARMS ACT, 1959 (Act 54 of 1959)[1]
(23rd December 1959)

CONTENTS

17. Variation, suspension and revocation of licenses.
18. Appeals.

CHAPTER IV

Power and Procedure

19. Powers to demand production of license, etc.
20. Arrest of persons conveying arms, etc.

Under suspicious circumstances.

21. Deposit of arms etc., on posses.

1. Reg has extended this Act to Goa, Daman and Diu. 12 of 1962, Section 3 and Sch., to Dadra and Nagar Haveli (w.e.f. 1.7.1965) by Reg. 6 of 1963, Section 2 and Sch. I, to Pondicherry (w.e.f. 1.10.1963) by Reg. 7 of 1963, Section and Sch. I, to the State of Sikkim (w.e.f. 1.8.1976) vide notification No. GSR 461 (E) dated 21.7.1976.

THE ARMS RULES 1962[1]

CONTENTS

25. Sale of keeping for sale certain arms and ammunition.
26. Identification marks on fired arms.
27. Record of transactions in arms and ammunition.
28. Inspection of premises, stock and record,
29. Restrictions upon import or export for re-import of arms or ammunition.
30. Import by sea or air.
31. Vessels entering the territorial water of India.
32. Import by land or river of arms and ammunition.

References

1. Vide G.S.R. 987, Dated the 13th July, 1962.

THE EXPLOSIVE ACT, 1884
(Act No. IV of 1884)
(26th February 1884)

CONTENTS

Sections

6-C Refusal of licenses.

6-D Licensing authority competent to impose conditions in addition to prescribed conditions.

6-E Variation, suspension and revocation of licenses. An Act to regulate the manufacture, import and export of explosive.

6-F Appeals.

7. Power to make rules conferring powers of inspection, search, seizure, detention and removal.

8. Notice of accidents.

9. Inquiry into accidents.

9-A Inquiry into more serious accidents.

9-B Punishments of certain offences.

9-C Offences by companies.

10. Forfeiture of explosives.

11. Distress of aircraft for vessel.

12. Abetment and attempts.

13. Power to arrest without warrant persons committing dangerous offences.

14. Saving and power to exempt.

15. Saving of Indian Arms Act, 1878.

16. Saving as to liability under other law.

17. Extension of definition of "explosive" to other explosive substances.

17-A Power to delegate.

18. Procedure for making publication and confirmation of rules. An Act to regulate the manufacture, possession, use, sale[1] (transport, import and export) of explosives.

References

1. Subs. by Act 32 of 1978.
   F-51.

4

IMPORTANT JUDGMENTS ON TERRORIST AND DISRUPTIVE ACTIVITIES (PREVENTION) ACT, 1987

(SUPREME COURT)

A.M. Ahmadi and N.M. Kasliwal, JJ.

Niranjan Singh Karam Singh Punjabi, Advocate
Versus
Jitendra Bhimraj Bijja and others
With
State of Maharashtra
Versus
Jitendra Bhimraj Bijja and Others
With
Jitendra Bhimraj Bijja and Others
Versus
State of Maharashtra

(Criminal Appeal Nos. 703 with 712 of 1989 and 13 of 1990, with Special Leave Petition (Cri.) No. 2459 of 1989, Decided on 7th August, 1990).

(a) Terrorist and Disruptive Activities (Prevention) Act, 1987, Section 3(1)- Whether offence under Section 3(1)-

Whether offence creates terror under Act- In gang rivalry offence or murder committed- Statement of accused that by elminating rival persons accused would cause terror and fear- Held, it does not constitute terrorists act.

The Designated Court was right to coming to the conclusion that the intention of the accused persons was to eliminate R and K for gaining supremacy in the underworld. A mere statement to the effect that the show of such violence would create terror or fear in the minds of the people and none would dare to oppose them can not constitute an offence under Sections 3(1) of the Act. That may indeed be the fall out of the violent act but that cannot be said to be the intention of the perpetrators of the crime. It is clear from the statement extracted earlier that the intention and gain supremacy in the underworld so that they may be known as the bullies of the locality and would be dreaded as such. But it cannot be said that their intention was to strike in the people or a section of the people and thereby commit a terrorist act. (Para 11)

(b) Terrorist and Disruptive Activities (Prevention) Act, 1987, Sections 12(1) and 18— Accused persons triable under Act-Duty of Court-Designated Court, Coming to conclusion that charge for offence under Act, cannot be framed — Held, under such case Designated Court cannot try accused for commission of offences under other statutes.

Sections 12(1) no doubt empowers the Designated Court to try any offence punishable under any other statute along with the offence punishable under the act if the former is connected with the letter that, however, does not mean that even when the Designated Court comes to the conclusion that there is exists no sufficient ground for framing a charge against the accused under Section 3(1) of the Act it must proceed to try the accused for the commission of offence under other statutes. That would tantamount to usurping, jurisdiction. Sections 18, therefore, in terms provides that whether after taking cognizance of any offence the Designated Court is of the opinion that the offence is not triable by it, it shall, notwithstanding that it has no jurisdiction to try such offence, transfer the case for the trial of such offence to any Court having jurisdiction under the Act.

(Para 12)

JUDGMENT

Ahmadi, J- These three appeals arise out of the Charge leveled by the police against the five petitioners of the above special Leave Petition under Section 3 of the Terrorist and Disruptive Activities (Prevention) Act, 1987, (hereinafter called "the Act"). Sections 302, 397 read with Section 147, 148 and 149 IPC and Section 37 of the Bombay Police Act, 1951, for the murder of one Raju alies Avtar Singh, son of the Appellant of Criminal Appeal no. 703/89, and for injuries caused to his companion Keshav Vithal, the first informant. The facts giving rise to these proceedings are as under :

On the afternoon of the 12th July, 1989 when Raju and his companion Keshav were proceeding on a Motor Cycle at about 3.00 p.m they were intercepted by the accused Jitendra and one another known as a wrestler. Following some altercation and heated exchange of words between them, the order three accused persons arrived at the spot. Two of them were armed with knives and the third possessed an iron-rod. On seeing them Keshav who was on the pillion seat took to his heels whereupon Raju who was in the driver's seat abandoned the motor-cycle and ran in another direction two of the accused persons ran after Raju while the others including the wrestler chased Keshav. On being over taken accused Vijay gave a knife blow on the vhest of Keshav and his campanion Santosh dealt blows with the iron-rod. Thereafter all the three fled from the scene of occurrence. The other two who had chased Raju are alleged to have killed him as he was found laying in an unconscious conditions on the road. Both the injured were removed to the hospital. Keshav, however, responded to medical treatment and has survived to give evidence.

On the same day at about 5.30 p.m. the First Information Report was lodged by the injured Keshav. On the basis there of an entry was made in CR No. 138/89 and a case under Sections 302 and 307 read with Sections 147, 148 and 149 IPC and Section 37 of the Bombay Police Act was registered. The accused were arrested on 15th July, 1989 and were taken on remand for 9 days which period was extended upto 29th July, 1989 on which date the Investigating Officer invoked Section 3 of the Act. On 3rd August, 1989 the accused moved an application in the Designated Court, Jalgaon, for bail, inter alia, contending that the provisions of the Act had been wrongly and maliciously invoked. The said application was heard and decided by the Designated Court on 2nd September, 1989 which took the view that Section 3 of the Act was wrongly applied. Against that order the State of Maharashtra has preferred Criminal Appeal No. 712/89.

LATEST AMENDMENT PREVENTION OF TERRORISM (AMENDMENT) ACT, 2003[1] (4 of 2004) (2nd January, 2004)

An act to amend the Prevention of Terrorism Act, 2002. Be it enacted by Parliament in the Fifty-Fourth Year of the Republic of India as follows:

Received the assent of the President on 2-1-2004 and Published in the Gazette of India, Extra, Part II, Section 1 dated 5-1-2004.

COMMENT

Statement of Objects and Reasons: 1. The Prevention of Terrorism Act, 2002 has been enacted to make provisions of and for prevention of, and for dealing with, terrorist activities and for matters connected therewith. Sub-section (1) of Section 60 of the said Act provides that the Central Government and each State Government shall, when necessary, constitute one or more Review Committees for the purpose of the said Act. Sections 19, 40 and 46 of the said Act assign the specific functions to the Review Committee. At present, the recommendations or directions of the Review Committee except those explicitly provided in the said Act are not binding on the Central Government and the State Governments and are only advisory in nature. In order to have an effective safeguard against the likely misuse of the powers conferred by the said Act, it was considers necessary that the mechanism of the Review Committee needs to be strengthened.

2 Keeping in view the above, Section 60 of the Prevention of Terrorism Act, 2002 was amended by the Prevention of Terrorism (Amendment) Ordinance, 2003 (Ord. 4 of 2003) and was promulgated on 27th October, 2003 by which new subsections (4), (5) and (6) in Section 60 of the said Act were inserted. The new subsections empower the Review Committee to review, on an application by any aggrieved person, whether there is a prim facie case for proceeding against the accused under the said Act and issue directions accordingly. The directions of the Review Committee shall be binding on the Central Government, the State Government and the police officer investigating the offence. Where the directions relating to the same offence under the said Act, have been made by a Review Committee constituted by the Central Government and the Review Committee constituted by the State Government, the directions of the Central Review Committee shall prevail over those of the State Review Committees.

3. The Bill seeks to replace the said Ordinance.

Part I: POTA, 2002, Section 1- Constitutional validity of POTA- Supreme Court cannot go into and examine the 'need' of POTA. It is a matter of policy. Once legislation is passed the Government has an obligation to exercise all available options to prevent terrorism within the bounds of the Constitution. Moreover, Court would like to point out that Supreme Court has repeatedly held that mere possibility of abuse cannot be counted as a ground for denying the vesting of powers or for declaring a statute unconstitutional.[1]

Part I: POTA, 2002, Section 3(1)-I.P.C. 1860, Section 121- What constitutes a terrorist act — Comparison between POTA and TADA-Comparison of POTA and TADA shows that the two statues define terrorist act, with substantial similarity, the difference being that in TADA 'acts intended to overawe the Government as by law established and acts intended to alienate any section of the people or to adversely affect the harmony amongst different sections of the people' were terrorist acts. These categories of acts, are found missing in POTA but 'acts done with intention to threaten the unity, integrity, security or sovereignty of India, are terrorist acts under both statues. The 'acts' have to be by use of arms, ammunition, noxious substances or chemicals referred to in both provisions. Court find that the purport and intent is substantially common.

It was held that a criminal activity becomes a terrorist act, where it is committed with the requisite intention as contemplated by Section 3 (1) of TADA by use of such weapons as have been enumerated in Section 3(1) and which cause or are likely to result in the offence mentioned in said Section. The court, in the context of the Constitution Bench Judgment in Kartar Singh's case[2], which upheld the constitutional validity of TADA observed: 'it is, thus, seen that most of the criminal activities constituting a terrorist Act, and offences under the penal law, do overlap.'

All Counsels agreed that indeed what happened on 13-12-2001 at Parliament House in the forenoon was a terrorist act, as defined in POTA. Notwithstanding that none disputed that it was a terrorist act, Court shall none the less deal with it in relation to the evidence on record since it is a case involving capital sentence and should not return Court's finding on Counsels concessions[3].

PART I: POTA, 2002, Sections 3(2), 4(b)- Explosive Substances Act 1988, Sections 3 and 4 — I.P.C. 1860, Sections 120-B, 121, 307-Criminal conspiracy- Attempt to murder—Terrorist attack on Parliament House— Where five slain terrorists had made an entry into Parliament House complex in a white Ambassador car which had a red light on its roof. Those five terrorists were intercepted by the security personnel near Vice President's gate. There was firing between security personnel and the five terrorists. As a result, all five terrorists were shot down by the security personnel. The said terrorists were armed with automatic assault rifles, pistols, grenades, rifle grenades and had ammunition with them. There was recovery of 11 electric detonators, 14 hand grenades and 16 rifle grenades from the site. Apart from the aforesaid explosives, many electronic devices were found at the site. 58 used cartridges of AK-47 rifle and 118 live cartridges were seized at the spot. Mobile phones sized revealed the information about many associates in the act. Accused persons were arrested and recoveries were made. Disclosure statement was recorded and confessions were also recorded. The accused Afzal was held to be a part to conspiracy to attack Parliament when it was in Session. He had procured hide outs from terrorists and was instrumental in smuggling of arms and ammunition used by terrorists. Shaukat's role in conspiracy was that of an active participant. Accused Gilani was on close and intimate terms with accused Afzal and Shaukat but there was no evidence on record to establish that he remained in touch over the telephone with terrorists. Held that charge of conspiracy against the accused Afzal and Shaukat to attack Parliament of India stood established. Conviction under Section 3(2), POTA was recorded and death sentence was awarded for the accused Afzal and Shaukat but the accused Gilani and Afzal Guru were acquitted of the charges.[4]

Part 1: POTA, 2002, Section 14- Constitution of India, Articles 14, 19, 20 (3), 21— Any person could be compelled to give information about terrorist Act to Police- Section 14 giving power to police not violative of Articles 14, 19, 20, 20, 21 of Constitution.— Section 39 of the code of criminal Procedure, 1973 casts duty upon every person of furnish information regarding offences. Criminal justice system cannot function without the co-operation of people. Rather it is the duty of everybody to assist the State in detection of the crime and bringing criminal to justice. Withholding such information cannot be traced to right to privacy, which itself is not an absolute right. Section 14 confers power to the investigating officer to ask for furnishing information that will be useful for or relevant to the purpose of the Act. Furthermore, such information could be asked only after obtaining a written approval from an officer not below the rank of a Superintendent of Police. Such power to the investigating officer is quite necessary in the detection of terrorist activities or terrorist.

It is settled position of law that a journalist of lawyer does not have a sacrosanct right to withhold information regarding crime under the guise of professional ethics. A lawyer cannot claim a right over professional communication beyond what is permitted under Section 126 of the Evidence Act. There is also no law that permits a newspaper or journalist to withhold relevant information from Courts though they have been given such power by virtue of Section 15 (2) of the Press Council Act, 1978 as against Press Council.[5]

Part 1: POTA, 2002, Sections 14, 19 — Review Committee— Mere presence of non-judicial members no ground to declare Section 19 invalid.— It is urged that Section 18 or 19 is invalid based on the inadequacy of judicial members, in the Review Committee. As per

Section 60, Chairperson of the Review Committee will be a person who is or has been a judge of High Court. The mere presence of non-judicial members by itself cannot be treated as a ground to invalidate Section 19.[6]

Part 1: POTA, 2002, Sections 18, 19-Constitution of India, Articles 14, 19 (1) (a), (1) (c)- Validity of notification/de-notification of terrorist organization—Sections 18, 19 constitutionally valid—The right of citizens to form association or union that is guaranteed by Article 19 (1) (c) of the Constitution is subject to the restriction provided under Article 19 (4) of the Constitution. Under Article 19(4) of the Constitution the state can impose reasonable restriction, inter alia, in the interest of sovereignty and integrity of the country. POTA is enacted to protect sovereignty and integrity of India from the menace of terrorism, imposing restriction under Article 19(4) of the Constitution also includes declaring an organization as a terrorist organization as provided under POTA. Hence Section 18 is not unconstitutional. It is contended that before making the notification whereby an organization is declared as a terrorist organization there is no provision for pre-decisional hearing. But this cannot be considered as a violation of audi alteram partem principle, which itself is not absolute. Because in the peculiar background of terrorism it may be necessary for the Central Government to declare an organization as terrorist organization even without hearing that organization. At the same time under Section 19 of POTA the aggrieved persons can approach the Central Government itself for reviewing its decision. If they are not satisfied by the decision of the Central Government they can subsequently approach Review Committee and they are also free to exercise their Constitutional remedies. The post-decisional remedy provided under POTA satisfies the audi alteram partem requirement in the matter of declaring an organization as a terrorist organization.

As regards the reasonableness of the restriction provided under Section 18, it has to be noted that the factum of declaration of an organization as a terrorist organization depends upon the 'belief' of Central Government. The reasonableness of the Central Government's action has to be justified based on material facts upon which it formed the opinion. Moreover the Central Government is bound by the order of the Review Committee. Considering the nature of legislation and magnitude of presence of terrorism, it cannot be said that Section 18 of POTA imposes unreasonable restrictions of fundamental right guaranteed under Article 19(1) (c) of the Constitution. Supreme Court upheld the validity of Sections 18 and 19.[7]

Part 1: POTA, 2002, Section 22 (3)- Meaning of word "terrorism":-

The word terrorism cannot be construed as per scheme of Section 22 and, therefore, will have to be given a requisite meaning, i.e. terrorism created by such terrorist organizations, which are enlisted in Schedule of Section 18 of the Prevention of Terrorism Act.

On the backdrop of these provisions, prosecution must have evidence to show that a person has provided money or property or knows or has reasonable cause to suspect that such money or property will or may be used for the purposes of terrorism by such organization. The sum and substance of this provision is that prosecution must show in order to attract the provisions of subsection (3) of Section 22 of the Prevention of terrorism Act that the person has provided money or property to the Terrorist organization and/or at least he knows or had reasonable cause to suspect that it may be used for terrorism either by the organization or by individual, who is member of such terrorist organization. It is no doubt true that explanation to sub-section (1) of Section 3 provides that raising fund intended for the purpose of terrorism either by the terrorist organization or by individual is a terrorist act and is punishable under Section 3 of the Prevention of Terrorism Act. However, offence under Section 22 is in respect of fund raising for the terrorist organization and, therefore, it will have to be viewed and construed accordingly.[8]

Part 1: POTA, 2002, Section 31- Interview of accused shown by media did not amount to violation of fair trial.—After the terrorist attack on Parliament House interview of accused Mohd. Afzal was allowed to be taken by the reporters of various channels which was prominently telecasted. Trial had commenced after more than Six month, but media coverage continued for approximately five months. Held that it did not amount to violation of fair trial.[9]

Part 1: POTA, 2002, Section 32- Prosecution should not rely on confessional statement of co-accused.— Prosecuting agency to be aware of these legal aspects of provisions of Section 32(1) of the POTA and should conduct investigation keeping in view all this vital aspects in respect of admissibility of confession recorded under Section 32(1) of the POTA, and not to repeat such mistake of solely relying on the confessional statement of the accused, time and again, to prove the offence/offences against the co-accused and regard must be had to the provisions of Section 32 (1) of the POTA. Prosecuting agency is expected to collect independent evidence to conduct the offender with the crime under the provisions of POTA and should not rely solely on confessional statement of co-accused for this purpose in order to bring home the guilt of the accused under the provisions of the Special Act.[10]

Part 1: POTA, 2002, Section 32 — Section 32 not invalid on ground that it empowers police to record confession.— If the recording of confession by police is found to be necessary by Parliament and if it is in tune with the scheme of law, then an additional safeguard under Section 32(4) and (5) is a fortiori legal. The provision that requires producing such a person before the Magistrate is an additional safeguard. It gives that person an opportunity to rethink over his confession. Moreover, the Magistrate's responsibility to record the statement and the enquiry about the torture and provision for subsequent medical treatment makes the safer. It will deter the police officers from obtaining a confession from an accused by subjecting him to torture. It is also worthwhile to not that an officer who is below the rank of a Superintendent of Police cannot record the confession statement. It is a settled position that if a confession was forcibly extracted, it is a nullity in law. Non-inclusion of this obvious and settled principle does not make the section invalid. Ultimately it is for the concerned Court to decide the admissibility of the confession statement. Judicial wisdom will surely prevail over irregularity, if any in the process of recording confessional statement. Therefore Court was satisfied that the safeguards provided by the Act and under the law is adequate in the given circumstances and Supreme Court do not think it is necessary to look more into this matter. Consequently Supreme Court upheld the validity of Section 32.[11]

Part I: POTA, 2002, Section 34 — Without an order of Special Court, no appeal lies to High Court.— The provisions of POTA are in clear contradiction with that of Code of Criminal procedure where no appeal is provided against an order of Special court and unless there is an order of the Special Court refusing bail, the accused will have no right to file an appeal before the High Court praying for grant of bail to them. Existence of an order of the Special Court is, therefore, sine qua non for approaching the High Court.

In the present case, the respondents did not chose to apply for bail before the Special Court for offences under POTA and consequently there was no order of refusal of bail for offences under the said act. The learned Single Judge exercising powers under Section 439 read with Section 482 Cr.P.C. granted them bail. The order of the High Court is clearly without jurisdiction as under the scheme of the Act the accused can only file an appeal against an order of refusal of bail passed by the Special Court before a Division Bench of the High Court and, therefore, the order under challenge cannot be sustained and has to be set aside.[12]

Part 1: POTA, 2002, Section 49 — Effect of charge sheet not filed within 90 days — Where charge — Sheet had not been filed within 90 days and period of detention beyond 90 days was not extended by the Special Court. Even assuming that there was specific reasons for detention of the petitioner beyond the period of 90 days, the period of detention could be extended up to one hundred and eighty days only, and since the petitioner had been in judicial custody and even the period of 180 days as contemplated by Section 49 (2) of the Act had already elapsed. Therefore, the petitioner was entitled to be released on bail as a matter of right.[13]

Part 1: POTA, 202, Section 50- Appropriate Government should complete procedural mandatory formalities regarding sanction for prosecution without wasting time.— Court expect the appropriate Government to complete procedural mandatory formality of granting sanction, if necessary, without wasting any time and fulfill the mandatory requirement of Section 50 of POTA. The appropriate Government is expected to keep in mind the far-reaching consequences in case the procedural requirement mandated by provisions of Section 50 is not fulfilled. Inaction or delay on the part of the appropriate Government in this regard shall, undoubtedly, not only frustrate the object of the Act but also result in giving benefit to the unscrupulous elements.[14]

Part V: TADA Act, 1987, Section15—Voluntary confession admissible in evidence and could be relied upon for conviction without any further corroboration.—Whenever an accused challenges that his confessional statement is not voluntarily, the initial burden is on the prosecution for it has to prove that all requirement under Section 15 of TADA Act and Rule 15 of the TADA Rules have been complied with. Once this is done the prosecution discharges its burden and then it is for the accused to show and satisfy the Court that the confessional statement of the accused can be relied upon for the purpose of conviction, and no further corroboration is necessary if it relates to the accused himself.[15]

Part V: TADA Act, 1987, Section 15 — Tada (Prevention) Rules, 1987, Rule 15 — Police Officer need not himself record the statement in his own handwriting.—When a confessional statement is dictated to a steno and typed on a typewriter, the same amounts to a confessional statement being in writing. This view is supported by an authority of this Court in the case of State of Tamil Nadu v. Sivarasan.[16] In this case it has been held that the words "recorded in writing" in Section 15 includes a typewritten confessional statement.

SCHEDULE (See Section 18)
TERRORIST ORGANISATIONS

1. Babbar Khalsa International.

2. Khalistan Commando Force.
3. Kalistan Zindabad Force.
4. International Sikh Youth Federation.
5. Lashkar-E-Taiba/Pasban-E-Ahle Hadis.
6. Jaish-E-Mohammed/Tahrik-E-Furqan.
7. Harkat-Ul-Mujahideen/Harkat-Ul-Ar/Harkat-Ul-Jehad-E Islami.
8. Hizb-Ul-Mujahideen/Hizb-Ulmujahideen Pir Panjal Regiment.
9. Al-Umar-Mujahideen.
10. Jammu and Kashmir Islamic Front.
11. United Liberation Front of Assam (ULFA).
12. National Democratic Front of Bodoland (NDFB).
13. People's Liberation Army (PLA).
14. United National Liberation Front (UNLF)
15. People's Revolutionary Party of Kangleipak (PREPAK)
16. Kangleipak Communist Party (KCP)
17. Kangle Yaol Kanba Lup (KYKL)
18. Manipur People's Libration Front (MPLF).
19. All Tripura Tiger Force.
20. National Liberation Front of Tripura.
21. Liberation Tigers of Tamil Eelam (LTTE).
22. Students Islamic Movement of India.
23. Deendar Anjuman.
24. Communist Pary of India (Marxist-Leninist)- People's War, All Its Formations And Front Organisations.
25. Maoist Communist Centre (MCC). All Its Formations and Front Organisations.

Explanation — For the purpose of this Schedule, serial numbers 24 and 25 shall be deemed to have been included with effect from the date of publication of S.O. No. 1194(E), dated the 5th December 2001.

General- To deal with the situation arising in certain provinces on account of the partition of the country in 1947, the Governor General issued four Ordinances, namely: (1) The Bengal Disturbed Areas (Special Powers of Armed Forces) Ordinance, 1947 (11 of 1947); (2) The Assam Disturbed Areas (Special Powers of Armed Forces) Ordinance, 1947, (14 of 1947); (3) The East Punjab and Delhi Disturbed Areas (Special Powers of Armed Forces) Ordinance, 1947 (17 of 1947); and (4) The United Provinces Disturbed Areas (Special Powers of Armed Forces) Ordinance, 1947 (22 of 1947). These Ordinances were replaced by the Armed Forces (Special Powers) Act, 1948 (Act No. 3 of 1948).[17]

The Armed Forces (Special Powers) Act as enacted in 1958 to enable certain special powers to be conferred upon the members of the

Armed Forces in the disturbed areas in the State of Assam and the Union Territory of Manipur. By Act 7 of 1972 and Ac 69 of 1986, the Central Act was amended and it extends to the whole of the State of Arunachal Pradesh, Assam, Manipur, Meghalaya, Mizoram, Nagaland and Tripura; Chandigarh Disturbed Areas Act, 1983, it extends to the whole of Union Territory of Chandigarh; The Terrorist Affected Areas (Special Courts) Act, 1984, it extends to the whole of India except the State of Jammu and Kashmir, Punjab Disturbed Areas Act, 1983, it extends to the whole of State of Punjab; Disturbed Areas (Special Courts) Act, 1976, it extends to the whole of India, except the State of Jammu and Kashmir.

The expression "Disturbed Areas" has been defined in Section 2(b) of the Chandigarh Disturbed Areas Act, 1983, means the area which is for the time being declared by notification under Section 3 of the said Act, as may be specified in the notification, is a disturbed area, also the disturbed area has been defined in Section 2(b) of the Disturbed areas (Special Courts) Act, 1976, means an area declared as a disturbed area under Section 3 of the said Act.

The State Act was enacted with a view to make better provision for the suppression of disorder and for restoration and maintenance of public order in the disturbed areas in Assam. Section 2 of the State Act, also defined disturbed area to mean an area which is for the time being declared by notification under Section 3 to be a disturbed area. Section 3 lays down that the State Government may, by notification in the official Gazette of Assam, declare the whole or any part of any district of Assam, as may be specified in the notification, to be a disturbed area. Sections 4 and 5 confer on a Magistrate or Police Officer not below the rank of Sub-Inspector or Havaldar in case of Armed Branch of the Police or any officer of the Assam Rifles not below the rank of Havaldar/Jamadar powers similar to those conferred under clauses (a) and (b) of Section 6 of the Central Act. Section 6 confers protection similar to that conferred by Section 5 of the Central Act.[18]

The Police Act of 1861, in Sub-Section (1) of Section 15, empowers the State Government to issue a proclamation declaring that any area subject to its authority has been found in a disturbed or in a dangerous state and thereupon in exercise of the power-conferred under sub-section (2), the Inspector-General of Police or other officer authorized by the State Government in that behalf car employ any police force in addition to the addition to the ordinary fixed complement, to be quartered in the area specified in such proclamation. Sub-section (6) of Section 15 prescribes that every such proclamation issued under sub-section (1) shall indicate the period for which it is to remain in force, but it may be withdrawn at any time or continued from time to time for a further period or period as the State Government may in each case think fit to direct. The Police Act makes no provision for deployment of Armed Forces.[19]

Under Section 3 of the Armed Forces (Special Powers) Act, 1958 as amended by Act 7 of 1972, the Central Government has been empowered to declare an area to be a disturbed area. There is no requirement that it shall consult the State Government before making the declaration. As a consequence of such a declaration the power under Section 4 of the Armed Forces (Special Powers) Act, 1958 can be exercised by the Armed Forces and such a declaration can only be revoked by the Central Government. The conferment of the said power on the Central Government regarding declaration of areas to be disturbed areas does not, however, result in taking over of the State Administration by the Army or by other Armed Forces of the Union, because after such declaration by the Central Government, the powers under Section 4 of the said Act, can be exercised by the personnel of the Armed Forces, only with the co-operation of the authorities of the State Government concerned. It is, therefore, desirable that the State Government should be consulted and its co-operation sought while, making a declaration.[20]

It would be useful to refer to the report of the Sarkaria Commission, Part I, pp. 198, 199, on Central States Relations which has also dealt with this aspect. The commission has observed:-

"7.5.01........Clearly, the purpose of deployment which is to restore public order and ensure that effective follow up action is taken in order to prevent recurrence of disturbances, cannot be achieved without the active assistance and co-operation of the entire law enforing machinery of the State Government. If the Union Government chooses to take unilateral steps to quell an internal disturbance without the assistance of the State Government, these can at best provide temporary relief to the affected area and none at all where such disturbances are chronic."

"7.5.02........ Thus, practical consideration, as indicated above, make it imperative that the Union Government should invariably consult and seek the co-operation of the State Government, if it propose either to deploy suo motu its Armed Forces in that State or to declare an area as 'disturbed', the constitutional position notwithstanding. It need hardly be emphasized that without the State Government's co-operation, the mere assertion of the Union Government's right to deploy its Armed Forces cannot solve public order problems."

"7.5.03........ We recommend that, before deploying Union Armed and other Forces in a State, in aid of the Civil Power otherwise than on a request from the State Government, or before declaring an area within a State as 'disturbed area', it is desirable that the State Government should be consulted, wherever feasible, and its co-operation sought by the Union Government. However, prior consultation with the State Government is not obligatory."

There the words "in the course of any trial under this Act of any offence pertain to the trial in respect of an offence for which sanction has been accorded by the authority as contemplated under Section 20-A(2) of the TADA. Similarly the words "any other offence under this Act or any rule made there under or under any other law" denote all offences other than those falling in the first category. The intention of the Parliament in conferring such a power on the Designated Court is to prevent unmerited escape of offenders from the clutches of penal consequences even in cases where the Designated Court is satisfied during a valid trial that some other offences has been established beyond reasonable doubt. Once cognizance of any offence under TADA has been taken valid by the Designated Court with a proper sanction the Court is not disabled from convicting an accused for any other offence proved during the trial, whether or not sanction has been accorded in respect of such other offence. The reason d'etre is that it is the Court of Law which after a judicial scrutiny is satisfied on the materials placed before it that another offence has been made out and such satisfaction is of a higher caliber that the satisfaction of a sanctioning authority. The sanction envisaged in Section 20-A of TADA is, of course, a curb imposed on the prosecution agency to approach the Designated Court with a case. But once such approach is validly made with the proper sanction then the Court gets a wider jurisdiction to deal with the offenders in respect of all offences made out in the trial.[21]

"Aid"- Meaning of. — The word "Aid" postulates the continued existence of the authority to be aided. This would mean that even after deployment of the Armed Forces, the civil power will continue to function.[22]

"Harbours"- Meaning of. — The word "harbours" used in TADA must be understood in its ordinary, meaning as for penal provisions. In Black's Law Dictionary, its meaning is show as "to afford lodging to, to shelter or to give a refuge to".

It is, therefore reasonable to attribute a mental element (such as knowledge that the harboured person was involved in a terrorist act) as indispensable to make it a penal act. That apart, there is nothing in the Act, Either expressly or even by implication, to indicate that mens rea has been excluded from the offence under Section 3(4) of TADA.[23]

Section 52-A of the Indian Penal Court defines the word "harbour" as including:-

"Supplying a person with shelter, food, drink, money, clothes, arms, ammunition or means of conveyance, or the assisting a person by any means, whether of the same kind as those enumerated in this section or not to evade apprehension.[24]

"In Aid of the Civil Power" — Meaning of.— The expression "in aid of the civil power" in Entry 2-A of List 1 and in Entry I of List II, implies that deployment of the Armed Forces of the Union shall be for the purpose of enabling the Civil Power in the State to deal with the situation affecting maintenance of public order which has necessitated the deployment of the Armed Forces in the State.[25]

Applicability of provisions of Cr PC. — The provisions of Cr Pc governing search and seizure have to be followed during the course and seizure conducted in exercise of the powers conferred under Section 4(d) of the Armed Forces (Special Powers) Act, 1958. [26]

"Disturbed Area"— What is?— The expression "disturbed area" has been defined in Section 2(b) of the Armed Forces (Special Powers) Act, 1958 to mean an area which is for the time being declared by notification under section 3 of the said Act to be disturbed area. It has assailed the validity of the said provision on the ground that it is vague inasmuch as it does not lay down any guidelines for declaring an area to be a "disturbed area". Section 2 (b) of the said act has to read with section 3 of the said Act which contains the power to declare an area to be a "disturbed area". In the said section a declaration about disturbed area can be made where the Governor of the State of the administrator of the Union Territory of the Central Government is of the opinion that the whole or any part of such State or Union Territory, as the case may be, is in such a disturbed or dangerous conditions that the use of Armed Forced in Aid of the civil power is necessary. Since the use of Armed Forces of the Union in aid of the civil power in a State would be in discharge of the obligation imposed on the Union, under Article 355 of the Constitution to protect the State against internal disturbance, the disturbance in the area to be declared as "disturbed area" has to be of such a nature that the Union would be obliged to protect the State against such disturbance. In this context, reference can also be made to Article 257-A of the Constitution which was inserted by the Forty-Second Amendment along with Entry 2-A of the Union List. Although, Article 257-A has been deleted by the Forty-second Amendment, it can be looked into since it gives an indication regarding the disturbance which would be required for deployment of Armed Forces of the Union for use of the Civil power. The said article provided that the Government of India may deploy any Armed Forces of the Union for dealing with any grave situation of law and order in any

State. It can, therefore, be said that for an area to be declared as "disturbed area" there must exist a grave situation of law and order on the basis of which the Governor/Administrator of the state/Union Territory of the Central Government can form an opinion that area is in such a disturbed or dangerous conditions that the use of Armed Forces in aid of the civil power is necessary. It cannot, therefore, be said that an arbitrary and unguided power has been conferred in the matter of declaring an area as disturbed area under Section 2(b), read with Section 3 of the Armed Forces (Special Powers) Act, 1958.[27]

Avoidance of pernicious preventive laws.— What is needed in India is minimum education with a sense of social awareness so that each individual realizes his responsibility. The methods of training the police need redical changes and the police must be made responsible to the people. Similarly the bureaucrats and the politicians should have like servants of the society and be sufficient to punish those indulging in disruptive and terrorist activities. The pernicious preventive laws which always remind us of British colonial days should be abolished altogether. It is only in grave situations of external war or threat of war, or situation of civil war or insurgency that existing provisions of emergency can be used to maintain unity integrity of the country.[28]

Constitutional validity of TADA.— The uncivilized features of TADA especially Sections 5, 14(3) and 19 as Section 20(8) are unparallel in any democratic country. In fact TADA was packed with undemocratic and inhuman provisions. See Text of Terrorist and Disruptive Activities (Prevention) Act. And though the constitutional validity of the Act was upheld by the Supreme Court in Kartar Singh's Case,[29] yet the Court laid stress on checks and balance on its use.

The fact of its gross misuse is evident from the statement of arrest under TADA, given by the Union Home Ministry in April, 1995.[30] The total number of TADA arrest all over India were 77,571, out of which Gujarat alone accounted for 18,686; followed by Punjab, Assam and Jammu & Kashmir with 15, 314, 12, 715 and 616 arrest, respectively. A study conducted by PUDR in 1994 had shown 53,000 total persons detained under TADA out of which the cases of 30,000 had been pending for years. The number of TADA arrests in Punjab were 17,000, in Jammu & Kashmir 10,000 and in a peaceful State, like Gujarat and alarming 19,000.[31] And added to this, if the conviction rate is taken into account, which as per the National Human Rights Commission is said to be only one per cent[32] the magnitude of injustice perpetrated through the Act sends a chill down the spine. The real picture can be even more appealing if we also take into account to fact that TADA has been also used" as a weapon of threat by the Police to harass vulnerable sections of the minority communities and to extort money from hapless people." Interview of Chairman of National Commission of Minorities, the misuse of TADA came under attack from other human rights and civil liberties organization like PUCL, PUDR, AFDR and International bodies, like Amnesty International and Asia Watch. As far as the stand of the political parties is concerned, it ranged from outright opposition to total support for the Act. As deadlines of May 23, 1995 was approaching, for the lapse of the controversial Act, the Government found itself under mounting pressure not only from the opposition parties but also some sections of the Congress Party. Thus opposition to any further extension cut across even party affiliations. The ruling party also found itself divided into pro and anti TADA groups.[33]

"Terrorism"— Extreme forms of Violence.— The issue of terrorism has become an important aspect of all countries. Now-a-days terrorism is used as a weapon to fulfill their demands by the terrorists. Terrorism is one of the extreme forms of violence. No doubt all individuals have an instinct to violence but not all are equally inclined to resort to violent activities. In fact violence becomes a form of human behavior only in special conditions and not in the natural State of civilized human life. This show that certain internal forces drive a person towards violent behavior, whatever may be the object of the terrorist activities, creation of panic, or fear in the minds of the people is the widely accepted means or weapon of all terrorists. The fear might be physical or mental.[34]

Terrorism is found in many forms depending upon the object sought to be achieved by a terrorist or a group of terrorists. Thus the prevailing forms of terrorism are— individual terrorism, group terrorism, state terrorism, revolutionary terrorism and international terrorism. The leading factors, responsible for the growth of terrorism are political frustration, economic disparities, foreign support and financial assistance etc.[35]

Terrorism is not a new phenomenon for India. It has been used as an important means to achieve freedom from the colonial rule. The relevant sections of the Indian Penal Code, 1860, the Leading Criminal Law, dealing with terrorism are:-

(i) Concealing a design to commit an offence (Section 120).
(ii) Criminal Conspiracy (Section 120-B).
(iii) Offence against the State (Sections 121 to 131).
(iv) Promoting enmity between classes (Section 153-A).
(v) Assertions prejudicial to national integration (Section 153-B).
(vi) Harbouring robbers of dacoits (Section 216-A).
(vii) Maliciously insulting the religion or the religious beliefs of any classes (Section 295-A).

(viii) Offences against the human body (viz., Sections 302, 304-A and 304-B, etc.).

(ix) Extortion (Section 384).

Besides the Indian Penal Code, there are some other specific Laws which have been enacted to prevent terrorist and anti-national activities. They include the Explosives Act, 1884. The Explosives Substances Act, 1908, the Arms Act, 1959, the unlawful Activities (Prevention) Act, 1967, the Anti-Hijacking Act, 1982; and the Prevention of Damage to Public Property Act, 1984. Reference may also be made here of the SAARC convention (Suppression of Terrorism) Act, 1993. This Act was enacted with a view to give effect to the SAARC Convention against Terrorism. It came into force on April 26, 1993 dealing with hostage-taking, hijacking, offences against diplomatic agents, murder, etc. The Act also makes provisions for extradition of Criminals.[36]

Absence of delegation of power to State by Central Government.—The conferment of power to issue a declaration under Section 3 of the Armed Forces (Special Powers) Act, 1958 on the Governor of the State is invalid since it amounts to delegation under Section 3 of the said Act, since it amounts to delegation of power of the Central Government and that for the purpose of issuing a declaration the application of mind must be that of the central Government with respect to the circumstances in which such deployment of Armed Forces is to take place and that conferment of the power to make a declaration on the Governor of the State cannot be held to be valid. There is a basic infirmity in this contention. There is a distinction between delegation of power by a statutory authority and statutory conferment of power on particular authority/authorities by the Legislature. Under Section 3 of the said Act there is no delegation of power of the Central Government to the Governor of the State. What has been done is that the power to issue a declaration has been conferred by Parliament on three authorities, namely: (1) the Governor of the State; (2) the Administration of Union territory; and (3) the Central Government. In view of the information available at the local level, the Governor of the State or the Administrator of the Union Territory is in a position to assess the situation and form an opinion about the need for invoking the provisions of the Central Act for use of the Armed Forces of the Union in Aid of the Civil Power for the purpose of dealing with situation that has arisen in the concerned State or the Union Territory. Moreover, the issuance of a declaration by itself would not oblige the Central Government to deploy the Armed Forces of the Union. After such a declaration has been issued by the Governor/Administrator, the Central Government would have to take a decision regarding deployment of the Armed Forces of the Union in the Area that has been declared as a "disturbed area". The conferment of power on the Governor of the State to make the declaration under Section 3 of the Armed Forces (Special Powers) Act 1958 cannot, therefore, be regarded a delegation of power of the Central Government.[37]

Absence of evidence- Conviction illegal.— No evidence led by the prosecution to prove that the gun was in working condition and that the cartridges which were found from the person of the appellant were live cartridges. Neither ASI had stated so nor was any report from an export obtained to establish that the gun was in working condition and that five cartridges were live. What was found in the gun were two empties and not live cartridges and therefore, it was not proper to presume that it was in working condition. In absence of any evidence to that effect, the conviction of the Appellant in both Acts (Arms Act, 1959, Section 25 and TADA, Section 5) cannot be upheld.[38]

Absence of evidence regarding possession of arms — Conviction under Section 5 of TADA illegal.— Aggrieved by the order of acquittal, the State has filed this appeal. Court is of the opinion that the counsel is right in contending that the view taken by the Designated Court that in absence of sanction for prosecuting an accused under the Arms Act, he cannot be prosecuted even under Section 5 of TADA Act is wrong. But it is not necessary to allow this appeal and remand the case to the Designated Court as the respondent deserves to be acquitted even otherwise on merits. Though the evidence of PW 1 PW 3 establishes that the respondent was found in possession of one-12-bore DBBL gun and four live cartridges, there is no satisfactory evidence to show that the said gun and the cartridges were sent for examination by the Central Forensic Scientific Laboratory. There is no report from the forensic Scientific Laboratory or any other evidence to prove that the said gun was in a working condition or that the said cartridges were live cartridges. An entry made in the Malkhana register was relied upon by the prosecution. It does not mention that gun bearing No. 14119-88 was sent to the Central Forensic Scientific Laboratory nor does it contain any description of the cartridges.

Therefore, in absence of any evidence to show that the respondent was found in possession of one-12-bore DBBL gun in a working condition and four live cartridges, the respondent cannot be convicted under Section 5 of TADA Act.[39]

Armed Forces as substitute of Civil Power.— In view of the provision contained in Sections 4 and 5 of the Armed Forces (Special Powers) Act, 1958, the question must be answered in the negative. The power conferred under clause (a) of Section 4 of the said Act can be exercised only when any person is found acting in contravention of any law or order for the time being in force in the disturbed area prohibiting the assembly of five or more persons or the carrying of weapons or of things capable of being used as weapons or of fire arms, ammunition or explosive substances. In other word the said power is conditional upon the existence of a prohibitory order issued under a law, e.g., Cr PC or the Arms Act, 1959. Such prohibitory orders can be issued only by the civil authorities of the State. In the absence of such a prohibitory order the power conferred under clause (a) of Section 4 of the said Act cannot be exercised. Similarly, under Section 5 of the said Act, there is a requirement that any person who is arrested and taken into custody in exercise of the power conferred by clause (c) of Section 4 of the Act shall be made over to the officer-in-charge of the nearest Police Station with the least possible delay, together with a report of the circumstances occasioning the arrest. Maintenance of public order involves cognizance of offences, search, seizure and arrest followed by registration of reports of offences (FIRs), investigation, prosecution, trial and, in the event of conviction, execution of sentences. The powers conferred under the Central Act, only provide for cognizance of offences, search, seizure and arrest and destruction of arms dumps and shelters and structures used as training camps or as hide-outs for armed gangs. The other functions have to be attended by the State Criminal Justice machinery, viz., the Police, the Magistrates, the Prosecuting Agency, the Courts, the jails, etc. This would show that the powers that have been conferred under Section 4 of the said Act do not enable he Armed Forces of the Union to supplant or act as substitute for the civil power of the State and the Central Act, only enables the Armed Forces to assist the Civil power of the State in dealing with the disturbed conditions affecting the maintenance of public order in the disturbed area.[40]

Armed Forces Act confirms power to destroy any arms dump.—Section 4(b) of the Armed Forces (Special Powers) Act, 1958 confers the power to destroy any arms dump, prepare or fortified position of shelter from which armed attacks are made or are likely to be made or are attempted to be made or any structure used as training camp for armed volunteers or utilized as a hide-out by armed gangs or absconders wanted for any offence. It is urged that the said power is very wide in its scope and that apart from destruction of any arms dump, fortified positions, shelters and structures used by armed groups for attacks, it extends to destruction of a structure utilized as a hide-out by absconders wanted for any offence and that, to that extend, it is invalid. Absconders wanted for an offence are persons who are evading the legal process. In view of their past activities the possibility of their repeating such activities cannot be excluded and the conferment of the power to destroy the structure utilized as a hide-out by such absconders in order to control such activities cannot be held to be arbitrary or unreasonable.[41]

Armed Forces not a colourable legislation.- The Armed Forces (Special Powers) Act, 1958 cannot be regarded as a colourable legislation or a fraud on the Constitution. It is not a measure intended to achieve the same result as contemplated by a proclamation of emergency under Article 352 or a proclamation under Article 356 of the Constitution of India.[42]

Civil Force in dispersal.— Dispersal of assembly by use of civil force.—(1) Any Executive Magistrate or Officer-in-charge of a Police Station or, in the absence of Such officer-in-charge, any police officer, not below the rank of a Sub-Inspector, may command any unlawful assembly, or any assembly of five or more persons likely to cause a disturbance of the public peace to disperse; and it shall thereupon be the duty of the members of such assembly to disperse accordingly.

(2) If, upon being so commanded, any such assembly does not disperse, or if, without being so commanded, it conducts itself in such a manner as to show a determination not to disperse, any Executive Magistrate or Police Officer referred to in sub-section (1), may proceed to disperse such assembly by force, and may require the assistance of any male person, not being an officer or members of the Armed Forces and acting as such, for the purpose of dispersing such assembly and, if necessary, arresting and confining the persons who form part of it, in order to disperse such assembly or that they may be punished according to law.[43]

Civil Power and Armed Forces — Use of.— The provisions contained in Sections 130 and 131 of Cri PC, cannot be treated as comparable and adequate to deal with the situation requiring the use of armed forces in aid of civil power as envisaged by the Armed Forces (Special Powers) Act, 1958.

The Armed Forces (Special Powers) Act, 1958 does not displace the civil power of the Assam Disturbed Areas Act, 1955 (19 of 1955) by the armed forces of the Union and it only provides for deployment of armed forces of the Union in aid of the civil power.[44]

Compensation to victim.— In order that the people may feel assured that there is an effective check against misuse or abuse of powers by the members of the armed forces it is necessary that a complaint containing an allegation about misuse or abuse of the powers conferred under the

Armed Forces (Special Powers) Act, 1958 should be thoroughly inquired into and, if it is found that there is substance in the allegation, the victim should be suitably compensated by the State and the requisite sanction under Section 6 of the said Act should be granted for institution of prosecution and/or a civil suit or other proceeding against the person/persons responsible for such violation.

A complaint containing an allegation about misuse or abuse of the power conferred under the Central Act, shall be thoroughly inquired into and, if on enquiry it is found that the allegations are correct, the victim should be suitably compensated and the necessary sanction for institution of prosecution and/or a suit or other proceedings should be granted under Section 6 of the Armed Forces (Special Powers) Act, 1958.[45]

Conferment of power — Not delegation of power.— The conferment of the power to make a declaration under Section 3 of the Armed Forces (Special Powers) Act, 1958 on the Governor of the State cannot be regarded as delegation of the power of the Central Government.[46]

Conferment of power — Not Violative of Constitution — The conferment of the power to issue a declaration under Section 3 of the Armed Forces (Special Powers) Act, 1958 on the Central Government on the ground that the words "in aid of the civil power" postulate that the state alone should consider whether the public order requires Armed Forces of the Union to be called in aid of civil power and that the Conferment or such a power on the Central Government is destructive of the federal scheme which is a part of the basic structure of the Constitution. Whether a situation has arisen which requires the making of a declaration under Section 3 of the said Act, so as to enables the armed forces of the Union to be deployed in aid of the civil power is a matter which has to be considered by the governor of the State/Administrator of the Union Territory as well as Central Government because the co-operation of both is required for handling the situation. By virtue of Article 355 of the Constitution, the Union owes a duty to protect the States against internal disturbance and since the deployment of Armed Forces in aid of civil power in a State is to be made by the Central Government discharge of the said constitutional obligation, the conferment of the power to issue a declaration on the Central Government cannot be held to be violative of the federal scheme as envisaged by the Constitution.[47]

Conferment of power to make a declaration — Not violative of federal scheme.— The conferment of the power to make a declaration under Section 3 of the Armed Forces (Special Powers) Act, 1958 on the Central Government is not violative of the federal scheme as envisaged by the Constitution.[48]

Conviction by Designated Court as unreliable evidence liable to be set aside.— The Designated Court after having rejected the evidence of identification of parade on the ground that the suspects were possibly shown to the witnesses, relied upon the evidence of identification of the accused in the court by the two witnesses, and on that evidence recorded conviction against the appellants. No doubt, the evidence of identification parade is not substantive evidence, but its utility is for purposes of corroboration. In other words, it is utilized or corroboration of the sworn testimony of witnesses in Court as to the identity of the accused who are strangers to them. The real and substantive evidence of the indentity of the accused comes when witnesses given statement in the Court, identifying the accused. It is true that in the present case, prosecution witness identified the two accused who are the appellants before this Court. But, the question arises; what value could be attached to the evidence of identity of accused by the witnesses in the court when the accused were possibly shown to the witnesses before the identification parade in the police station. The Designated Court has already recorded a finding that there was wrong possibility that the suspects were shown to the witnesses. Under such circumstances, when the accused were already shown to the witnesses, their indentification in the Court by the witnesses was meaningless. The statement of witnesses in the court identifying the accused in the court lost all its value and could not be made basis for recording conviction against the accused. The reliance of evidence of identification of the accused in the Court by prosecution witness by the Designated Court was an erroneous way of dealing with the evidence of identification of the accused in the Court by the two eye-witnesses and had caused failure of justice. Since conviction of the appellants has been recorded by the Designated Court on wholly unreliable evidence, the same deserves to be set aside. Court accordingly set aside the judgment and order passed by the Additional Judge, Designated Court for Greater Bombay convicting the appellants. The appellants are acquitted of charges.[49]

Court empowered to close prosecution evidence after two years if offence punishable with 7 years imprisonment.— In case where the trial is for an offence punishable with imprisonment for a period not exceeding seven years, whether the accused is in jail or not, the Court shall close the prosecution evidence on completion of a period of two years from the date of recording the plea of the accused on the charges framed whether the prosecution has been examined all the witnesses or not, within the said period and the Court can proceed to the next step provided by law for the trial of the case. If the accused has been in jail for a period of not less than one half of the maximum period of punishment prescribed for the offence, the Trial Court shall release the accused on bail forthwith on such conditions as it deems fit.

If the offence under trial is punishable with imprisonment for a period exceeding 7 years, whether the accused is in jail or not, the court shall close the prosecution evidence on completion of three years from the date of recording the plea of the accused on the charged framed, whether the prosecution has examined all the witnesses or not within the said period and the Court can proceed to the next step provided by law for the trial of the case, unless for very exceptional reasons to be recorded and in the interest of justice, the Court considers it necessary to grant further time to the prosecution to adduce evidence beyond the aforesaid time-limit.

But if the inability for completing the prosecution within the aforesaid period is attributable to the conduct of the accused in protracting the trial, no Court is obliged to close the prosecution evidence within the aforesaid period in any of the cases covered by clauses (i) to (iii).

Where the trial has been stayed by orders of court or by operation of law such time during which the stay was in force shall be excluded from the aforesaid period for closing prosecution evidence.[50]

Declaration of disturbed area by Armed Forces not proper.— Section 3 of the Armed Forces (Special Powers) Act, 1958 does not confer an arbitrary or unguided power to declare an area as a "disturbed area". For declaring an area as a "disturbed area" under Section 3 of the said Act there must exist a grave situation of law and order on the basis of which the Governor/Administrator of the State/Union Territory or the Central Government can form an opinion that the area is in such a disturbed or dangerous condition that the use of the armed forces in aid of the civil power is necessary.[51]

Declaration of review not in law but obligation to review not illegal.— The provisions of Section 3 of the Armed Forces (Special Powers) Act, 1958 have been assailed by the counsel for the petitions on the ground that there is no requirement of a periodic review of a declaration issued under Section 3 of the said Act and that a declaration once issued can operate without any limit of time. The definition of "disturbed area" in Section 2(b) of the said Act talks of "an area which is for the time being declared by notification under Section 3 of the said Act to be a "disturbed area". The words "for the time being" imply that the declaration under Section 3 has to be for a limited duration and cannot be a declaration which will operate indefinitely. It is no doubt true that in Section 3 there is no requirement that the declaration should be reviewed periodically.

But since the declaration is intended to be for a limited duration and a declaration can be issued only when there is grave situation of law and order, the making of the declaration carries within it an obligation to review the gravity of the situation from time to time and the continuance of the declaration has to be decided on such a periodic assessment of the gravity of the situation.[52]

Declaration with consultation of State.—Although a declaration under Section 3 of the Armed Forces (Special Powers) Act, 1958 can be made by the Central Government suo motu without consulting the concerned State Government, but it is desirable that the State Government should be consulted by the Central Government while making the declaration.[53]

Different Case or crime does not effect admissibility of confessional statement under Section 15 of TADA Act.— Police charge sheeted the cases which were registered at two other police stations as against respondent and some others. The Designated Court began proceeding to try those cases. While the trial was in progress, the public prosecutor felt that the confessional statements recorded by the police during investigation of the case registered at police station under section 15 of the TADA have to be used as prosecution evidence as those statements related to events which are subject-matter of the cases registered in police stations. It was then that the Public Prosecutor filed application for permission to use such confessional statements. The application was opposed on the main ground that the confession made in another case cannot be used in the crime registered by police stations.

As these special leave petitions were pending an important development happened.— "fourth respondent died and the case against him got abated. Nevertheless, the question remains alive as the confessional statement attributed to the second respondent is also sought to be used in the cases registered by Police Station. For considering the said question Court looks at Section 15(1) of the TADA which reads thus;—

"15. Certain confessions made to police officers to be taken into consideration.- (1) Notwithstanding anything in the Code or in the Indian Evidence Act, 1872 (1 of 1872), but subject to the provision of this section, a confession made by a person before a police officer not lower in rank than a Superintendent of Police and recorded by such police officer either in writing or on any mechanical device like cassettes, tapes or sound tracks from out of which sounds or images can be produced, shall be admissible in the trial of such person (or co-accused, abettor or conspirator) for an offence under this Act or rules made there under."

It is clear from the above section that a confessional statement recorded in accordance with the requirements contained in the section becomes admissible in spite of the ban contained in Section 25 of the Evidence Act or Section 162 of the Code of Criminal Procedure. The requirements stipulated in Section 15(1) of the TADA for admissibility of a confession made to a police officer are — (1) the confession should have been made to a police officer not lower in rank than a Superintendent of Police; (2) it should have been recorded by the said police officer; (3) the trial should be against the maker of the confession; (4) such trial must be for an offence under TADA or the rules there under. If the above requirements are satisfied the confession becomes admissible in evidence and it is immaterial whether the confession was recorded in one particular case or in a different case.

When there is no statutory inhibition for using such confession, on the permission that it was not recorded during the investigation of the particular offence which is under trial there is no need or reason for the Court to introduce a further fetter against the admissibility of the confessional statement. It often happens that a confessor would disclose very many acts and events including different facets of his involvement in the preparation, attempt and commission if crimes including the acts of his co-participators therein. But to expel every other incriminating disclosure than those under investigation of a particular crime from the ambit of admissibility is not mandated by any provision of law.

The court has, therefore, absolutely no doubt that a confession, if usable under Section 15 of the TADA, would not become unusable merely because the case is different or the crime is different. If the confession covers that different crime it would be a relevant item of evidence in the case in which that crime is under trial and it would then become admissible in the case.[54]

Dispersion of assembly by Armed Force.— When the public security is manifestly endangered by any such assessable and no Executive Magistrate can be communicated with, any commissioned or gazette officer of the armed forces may disperse such assembly with the help of the armed forces under his command, and may arrest and confine any persons forming part of it, in order to disperse such assembly or that they may be punished, according to law, but if, while he is acting under this section, it becomes practicable for him to communicate with an Executive Magistrate, he shall do so, and shall thence forwarded obey the instructions of the Magistrate, as to whether he shall or shall not continue such action.[55]

Disturbed Area — Aid of Armed Force.— The primary task of the Armed Forces of the Union is to defend the country in the event of war or when it is faced with external aggression. Their training and orientation is to defeat the hostile forces. A situation of internal disturbance involving the local population requires a different approach. Involvement of Armed Forces in handling such a situation brings them in confrontation with their countrymen. Prolonged or too frequent deployment of Armed Forces for handling such situations is likely to generate a feeling of alienation among the people against - the Armed Forces who by their sacrifices in the defense of their country have earned a place in the hearts of the people. It also has an adverse effect on the moral and discipline of the personnel of the Armed Forces. It is, therefore, necessary that the authority exercising the power under Section 3 to make a declaration so exercises the said power that the extent of the disturbed area is confined to the area in which the situation is such that it cannot be handled without seeking the aid of the Armed Forces and by making a periodic assessment of the situation after the deployment of the Armed Forces the said authority should decide whether the declaration should be continued and, in case the declaration is required to be continued, whether the extent of the disturbed area should be reduced.[56]

Disturbed Area and applicability of Section 4 of Armed Forces (Special Powers) Act, 1958 — The power conferred under Section 4(a) of the Armed Forces (Special Powers) Act, 1958 must be so construed that it can be exercised only against armed persons and that the word "or" between the words "assembly of five or more persons" and the words "carrying of weapons" should be read as "and". The language of Section 4(a) does not support the said construction. Clause (a) of Section 4 of the said Act empowers the use of force against any person who is acting in contravention of any law or order for the time being in force in the disturbed area. It contemplates two types of such orders, viz. (a) an order prohibiting the assembly of five or more persons; and (b) an order prohibiting the carrying of weapons or of things capable of being used as weapons or of fire-arms, ammunition or explosive substances. The two order are different in nature in the sense that an order prohibiting the assembly of five or more persons can be issued under Section 144, Cr PC, while an order prohibiting the carrying of weapons or of things capable of being used as weapons or of fire-arms, ammunition or explosive substances has to be passed under the Arms Act, 1959 or other similar enactment. The word "or" links the two prohibitory orders and if it is read as "and", as suggested by 'D', the result would be that action only be taken under clause (a) where both the prohibitory orders were contravened by a person/persons. Such a construction would defeat the purpose of the provision and cannot be accepted.[57]

Effective action with minimum force.— While exercising the powers conferred under Section 5(a) of the Armed Forces (Special Powers) Act, 1958, the officer in the armed forces shall use minimum force required for effective action against the person/persons acting in contravention of the prohibitory order.[58]

Emergency power of Constitution.— It has to be borne in mind that Articles 352 and 356 of the Constitution contain emergency powers which can be invoked by the President exercising the executive power of the Union subject to such action being approved by both the Houses of Parliament within a specified period. The Central Act, on the other hand, has been enacted by Parliament in exercise of its legislative power under Article 246 and 248 of the Constitution.

Prior to the amendment of Article 352 of the Constitution by the Forty-fourth Amendment of the Constitution it was open for the President to issue a proclamation of emergency if he was satisfied that a grave emergency exists whereby security of India or of any part of the territory thereof is threatened whether by war or external aggression or "internal disturbance". By the Forty-Fourth Amendment, the words "internal disturbance" in Article 352 have been substituted by the words "armed rebellion". The expression "internal disturbance" has a wider connotation than "armed rebellion" in the sense that "armed rebellion" is likely to pose a threat to the security of the country or a part thereof, while "internal disturbance", though serious in nature, would not pose a threat to the security of the country or a part thereof. The intention underlying the substitution of the country or a part thereof. The intention underlying the substitution of the word "internal disturbance" by the word "armed rebellion" in Article 352 of the Constitution is to limit the invocation of the emergency powers under Article 352 only to more serious situations where there is a threat to the security of the country or a part thereof on account of war or external aggression or armed rebellion and to exclude the invocation of emergency powers in situation of internal disturbance which are of fusser gravity. This has been done because a proclamation of emergency under Article 352 has serious implications having effect on the executive as well as the legislative powers of the States as well as the Union. As a result of a proclamation under Article 352, the Parliament can make a law extending the duration of the House of the People (Article 83(2), Proviso); Parliament gets the power to legislate with respect to any matter in the State List (Article 250); the executive power of the Union is enlarged so as to extend to the giving of directions to any State as to the manner in which the executive power thereof is to be exercised (Article 353(a)); power of parliament to make laws with respect to any matter is enlarged to include power to make laws, conferring powers and imposing duties or authorizing the conferring of powers and the imposition of duties upon the Union or Officers and authorities of the Union as respects that matter, notwithstanding that it is one which is that enumerated in the Union List (Article 353 (b)); the President can pass an order directing that all or any of the provisions of Articles 268 to 279 of the Constitution relating to disturbance of revenue shall have effect subject to such exceptions or modification as he thinks fit (Article 354 of Constitution); the provisions of Article 19 are suspended (Article 358); and the enforcement of other rights conferred by Part III (except Article 20 and 21) can be suspended by the President (Article 359). The consequences of a proclamation of emergency under Article 352 are thus much more drastic and far reaching and, therefore, the Constitution takes care to provide for certain safeguards in Article 352 for invoking the said provision. There is no material on the record to show that the disturbed conditions in the States to which the Central Act has been Extended are due to an armed rebellion. Even if the disturbance is as a result of armed rebellion by a section of the people in those States the disturbance may not be of such a magnitude as to pose a threat to the security of the country or a part thereof so as to call for invocation of the emergency powers under Article 352. If the disturbance caused by armed rebellion does not pose a threat to the security of the country and the situation can be handled by deployment of Armed Forces of the Union in the disturbed area, there appears to be no reason why the drastic power under Article 352 should be invoked. It is, therefore, not possible to hold that the Central Act, which is primarily enacted to confer certain powers on Armed Forces when deployed in aid of civil power to deal with the situation of internal disturbance in a disturbed area, has been enacted to deal with a situation which can only be dealt with by issuing a proclamation of emergency under Article 352 of the Constitution.[59]

Enhancement of sentence legal under Article 142, if it is inadequate.—Powers of the Supreme Court in appeals filed under Article 136 of the Constitution are no restricted by the appellate provisions enumerated under the Code of Criminal Procedure or any other statute. When exercising appellate jurisdiction, the Supreme Court has power to pass any order. The aforesaid legal position has been recognized by a Constitution Bench of this Court in Durga Shankar Mehta's Case[60] and letter followed in a series of decisions.

The present appeals have not been filed under Article 136 of the Constitution, but under Section 19 of TADA. Hence it was contended that while dealing with a statutory appeal, plenary, powers of the

Supreme Court cannot be exercised. Accepting the said contention the Court pointed out that even otherwise this Court has wide and residual powers to deal with the situation like this, which are well enclosed in Article 142 of the Constitution.

It is now well-settled law that Supreme Court's powers under Article 142 of the Constitution are vastly broad based. That power in its exercise is circumscribed only by two conditions, first is that it can be exercised only when Supreme Court otherwise exercises its jurisdiction and the other is that the order which Supreme Court passes must be necessary for doing complete justice in the cause or matter pending before it. The first condition is satisfied here as the appellate jurisdiction of the Supreme Court is exercisable by virtue of Section 19 of TADA.

The Court is aware that powers under Article 142 are not to be exercised frequently but only sparingly. The occurrence described in this case is not the usual type of crimes reaching this Court. When all the four accused were caught red-handed while making nocturnal movements towards some targeted destination, in the densely crowded city with highly lethal and quickly explosive articles, it is a matter of reasonable imagination that, had they not been timely intercepted by the alert and vigilant police force, the consequences would have been disastrous and calamitous. Court has no manner of doubt that sentence of imprisonment of five years for the offence under Section 5 of the Tada in the circumstances of this case is too inadequate and it warrants enhancement.

The next question to be considered is, what should be the extent of the sentence. Section 5 of TADA prescribes punishment of "imprisonment for a term which shall not be less than five years, but which may extend to imprisonment for life" besides fine. When court found that the minimum sentence prescribed is too inadequate, the Court has to consider whether the maximum sentence prescribed is attracted.

Christopher, J. Emmins MA in his "A Practical to sentencing", has suggested that the maximum sentence should be reserved for the gravest instances of offence likely to occur as a principle of common sense (vide p. 110). The Court does not think that the maximum sentence prescribed in the section need be awarded in this case, since on a consideration of all aspects of the case, Court feels that the said upper limit is on the higher side. Nevertheless, after bestowing serious consideration in the matter, the court is of the definite opinion that imprisonment for a period of at least 10 years would necessary to meet the ends of justice looking at the manner in which the offence was perpetrated by the four accused persons.[61]

In Delhi case and also in Union Case,[62] this court made the petition clear that power under Article 142 of the Constitution is entirely of different level and is of a different quality which cannot be limited or restricted by provisions contained in statutory law. No enactment made by the Central or State Legislature can limit or restrict the power of this Court under Article 142 , though while exercising it the Court may have regard to statutory provisions. In Mohammed Anis's Case[63] Ahmadi, J., the Chief Justice by following the dictum in the above mentioned decisions has observed in paragraph 6, as followes:-

"This power has been conferred on the Apex Court, only and the exercise of that power is not dependent or conditioned by any statutory provision. The constitutional plenitude of the powers of the Apex Court is to ensure due and proper administration of justice and is intended to be co-extensive in each case with the needs of justice of a given case and to meeting any exigency. Very wide powers have been conferred on this Court, for due and proper administration of justice and whenever the Court sees that the demand of justice warrants exercise of such powers it will reach out to ensure that justice is done by resorting to this extraordinary power conferred to meet precisely such a situation".

In E.K. Chandrasenan's case[64] the Supreme Court has traced its power in Article 142, for the purpose of enhancing the sentence awarded to the accused who filed the appeal challenging the conviction passed by the High Court. The following observations in the said decisions are apposite:

"What is contained in Article 142 would any case provide sufficient power to this Court to pass an order like the one at hand, if this Court were to be of the view that the same in necessary for doing complete justice."

Exclusion of District in fear psychosis state.— What High Court could see is whether the material on the basis of which the opinion is formed is relevant but the Court could not go into the sufficiency of that material. The Apex Court has carefully perused the report sent by the Governor of Assam. On the basis of the said report it cannot be said that the districts which have been excluded from the notification by the High Court could not be declared as "disturbed area" inasmuch as in his report the Governor has referred to the entire State of Assam, and has said:-

"Apart from killings, according to reports received, many people were kidnapped and released after the ransom was paid. The extortion, to begin with, was on a limited scale. Magnitude of loot and plunder, however, become colossal in due course of time, presumably in view of the State Government's failure to Act."

The Governor has mentioned that the districts of Tinsukia, Dibrugar, Sibsagar, Jorhat and Nagoan on the South Bank of Brahmaputra and those cf Dhemaji, Lakhimpur, Sonitpur, Darrang, Nalbari and Barpeda on the North Bank of Brahmaputra are the worst sufferers. But that does not mean that other areas were not affected. In the concluding part of this report the Governor has said:-

"The cumulative consequences of all this is that the entire State is gripped by a fear psychosis. The holders of public offices have been rendered totally ineffective. The Statutory authorities are in a state of panic incapable of discharging their functions. The holders of constitutional offices stand totally emasculated so much so that the State Cabinet cannot even discuss the situation."

"The loss of faith in the efficiency and the credibility of the Government apparatus is so great that the thin distinction between ULFA, ASSU and AGP, which existed at some stage, stand totally obliterated. Glooms hang over the whole state. By the fall of the dusk, the people are huddled in their homes, nobody's life, limb, property or honor is safe. The basic attribute if a civilized and orderly society stand annihilated."

It cannot, therefore, be said that there was no material before the Central Government on the basis of which it could form the requisite opinion for the purpose of making a declaration under Section 3 of the Armed Forces (Special Powers) Act, 1958 covering the entire State of Assam. The impugned direction given by the High Court that the notification, dated November 27, 1990 issued under Section 3 of the Armed Forces (Special Powers) Act, 1958 shall not apply to the districts aforementioned cannot, therefore, be sustained and has to be set aside.[65]

Executive Magistrate empowered under Section 130, Cr. PC to seek help of Armed Forces to remove disturbance.— The adequate provisions are contained in Sections 130 and 131 of Cr. PC to deal with a situation requiring the use of Armed Forces in aid of civil power and that there is no justification for having a special law, as the Central Act, Armed Forces (Special Powers) Act. 1958, unless it can be shown that the said provisions in Sections 130- and 131, Cr. PC are not adequate to meet the situation. It has been submitted that Sections 130 and 131, Cr. PC contains several safeguards for the protection of the rights of the people and that the powers conferred under Section 4 of the Armed Forces (Special Powers) Act, 1958 are much more drastic in nature. If there are adequate provisions to deal with the situation in the general law (Cr. PC), the enactment of more drastic provisions in Section 4 of the said Act, to deal with the same situation is discriminatory and unjustified. Section 130 of Cr PC makes provisions for the Armed Forces being asked by the Executive Magistrate to disperse an unlawful assembly which cannot be otherwise dispersed and such dispersal is necessary for the public security. The said provision has a very limited application inasmuch as it enables the Executive Magistrate to deal with a particular incident involving breach of public security arising on account of an unlawful assembly and the use of the Armed Forces for dispersing such unlawful assembly. The Armed Forces (Special Powers) Act, 1958 makes provisions for dealing with a different type of situation where the whole or a part of a State is in a disturbed or dangerous condition and it has not been possible for the civil power of the State to deal with it and it has become necessary to seek the aid of the Armed Forces of the Union for dealing with the distance. Similarly, under Section 131, Cr PC a commissioned or gazette officer of the Armed Forces has been empowered to deal with an isolated incident where the public security is manifestly endangered by any unlawful assembly. The provisions of Section 130 and 131, Cr. PC cannot thus be treated as comparable and adequate to deal with the situation requiring the continuous use of Armed Forces in aid of the power for certain period in a particular area as envisaged by the Central Act, Armed Forces (Special Powers) Act, 1958 and it is not possible to hold that since adequate provisions to deal with the situation requiring the use of Armed Forces in aid of civil power are contained in Sections 130 and 131, Cr PC, the conferment of the power on officer of the Armed Forces under Section 4 of the Armed Forces (Special Powers) Act, 1958 to deal with a grave situation of law and order in a State is discriminatory in nature and is violative of Article 14 of the Constitution.[66]

Existence of means rea.— The legal proposition that unless the statute clearly excludes means rea in the commission of an offence the same must be treated as essential ingredient of the criminal act to become punishable.[67]

Finding or sentence when reversible by reason of error, omission or irregularity.--- (1) Subject to the provisions hereinbefore contained, on finding, sentence or order passed by a Court of competent jurisdiction shall be reversed or altered by a Court of Appeal, confirmation or revision on account of any error, omission or irregularity in the complaint, summons, warrant proclamation, order judgment or other proceedings before trial or in any inquiry or other proceedings under this Code, or any error, or irregularity in any sanction for the prosecution, unless in the opinion of that Court, a failure of justice has in fact been occasioned thereby.

(2) In determining whether any error, omission or irregularity in any proceeding under this Code, or any error or irregularity in any

proceeding under this code, or any error, or irregularity in any sanction for the prosecution has occasioned a failure of justice, the Court shall have regard to the fact whether the objection could and should have been raised at an earlier stage in the proceedings.[68]

Grant of compensation for illegal detention — legal and valid.— Since the appellant has been made a victim of prolonged illegal incarceration due to machination of prosecution witnesses and other police personnel of I.S.B.T. Police Post, the court directed the Delhi Government to pay him a sum of Rs. 50,000/- as compensation. The payment should be made within two months from the date of receipt of the order. The State Government will, however, be at liberty to recover the said amount from the erring police officers.[69]

Grant of refusal of sanction by Armed Forces to Central Government.— Section 6 of the Armed Forces (Special Power) Act, 1958, insofar as it confers a discretion on the Central Government to grant or refuse sanction for instituting prosecution or a suit or proceedings against any person in respect of anything done in exercise of the powers conferred by the Act does not suffer from the vice of arbitrariness. Since the order of the Central Government refusing or granting the sanction under Section 6 is subject to judicial review, the Central Government shall pass an order giving reasons.[70]

Guard on use of Preventive Detention.— the frames of the Constitution were of the view that in free India, when there will be democratic and representative Government, the need for framing such preventive detention laws will rarely arise and shall be sparingly and cautiously used. But it was right in 1950 that the Parliament passed the preventive Detention Act to curb the "violent and terrorist" activities of the communists in Hyderabad, West Bengal and Madras State. The Constitutional validity of the Act was upheld by the Supreme Court in terms of the Parliament's power to enact such a law but Chief Justice Kania and Justices Mahajan and Mukherjee, observed in A.K. Gopalan's case[71] that preventive detention laws were repugnant to democratic constitutions and did not "exist in democratic countries. In another Ram Krishna Bhardwaj's case[72] the Supreme Court (Patanjali Shastri, Chief Justice) stated: "Preventive detention is a serious invasion of personal liberty and such meager safeguards as the Constitution has provided against improper exercise of the power must be jealously watched and safeguarded by the Supreme Court."[73]

Illegal possession of arms — Sanction-Accordance of.— If it was felt that such a report can believed it is not necessary that the Director should have waited for the result of the analysis conducted by the laboratory upon those arms. That the sanctioning authority really intended to launch prosecution for the offence of illegal possession of arms is quite clear from the statements made in the order. True, the Section for the offence (Section 5 of TADA) has not been specifically mentioned therein but that is of no serious consequence as long as the authority has specified the fact and mentioned further that for the offence arising from such facts, sanction is accorded.[74]

Implementation and extension of TADA Act, after Punjab Scenario.— The early eighties witnessed, the phenomenal rise of militancy and terrorism in some parts of India, especially Punjab. The extraordinary, situations, created by the onslaught of terrorists and secessionist led the Parliament to enact the Terrorist Affected Areas (Special Court) Act, 1984 (See Act 61 of 1984), which was to be applicable to the whole of India, except Jammu and Kashmir. But soon it was found insufficient to deal with the situation arising out of continuous terrorist activities resulting in wanton killings, arson, looting of properties and other heinous crimes mostly in Punjab and Chandigarh. Hence, a more stringent and harsh law in the form of Terrorist and Disruptive Activities (Prevention) Act 1985. See, the Text of Terrorist and Disruptive Activities (Prevention) Act, 1985 was passed. In the prefatory note of the Act it was stated that "the new and overt phase of terrorism which requires to be taken serious note of and dealt with effectively and expeditiously". Thus, it is very clear that behind the much maligned TADA was the Punjab Scenario full of blood and gore. Initially passed for two years, the Act was given extensions after every two years. The first extention given through the Terrorist and Disruptive Activities (Prevention) Act, 1987, further strengthened its stringent provisions. Further extensions were given by Act 16 of 1989, Act 35 of 1991 and Act 43 of 1993, till 23rd May, 1995. When it could not be extended because of the wide spread criticism it attracted for the misuse of its obnoxious provisions.[75]

Inference of conscious possession cannot be drawn by mere knowledge about weapon and explosive.— it was alleged against the appellant that the said firearms were recovered from his Engar Khowa house. While replying to that allegation he clearly stated that it was recovered from the house of another person situated at a distance of 1½ to 2 kms. from his house. Though he stated that "one Shri "A", President, Achalik Parishad of ULFA, directed to keep that in that house" he did not say that 'A' had directed him to keep those firearms in that house. While admitting that he led the police to that house he denied extremist and that he was connected with the occurrence. If these statements made by the appellant were considered carefully by the Designated Court it would have realized that they did not constitute an admission of guilt. Only inference that can be drawn from the answer give by the appellant is that he knew that the said two guns and the cartridges were kept at that place but more knowledge that they were kept at that place cannot amount to conscious possession of those things. It is, therefore, obvious that on the basis of the said answer it was not proper to convict the appellant under Section 5 of the TADA Act.[76]

Internal disturbance- Invoking of Article 356 of the Constitution.— In view of the provision under Article 355 of the Constitution, the Union Government is under an obligation to take steps to deal with a situation of internal disturbance in a State. There can be a situation arising out of internal disturbance which under Article 356 of the Constitution, enabling the President to assume to himself all or any of the functions of the Government of the State. That would depend on the gravity of the situation arising on account of such internal disturbance and on the President being satisfied that a situation has arisen where the Government of the State cannot be carried on in accordance with provisions of the Constitution. A proclamation under Article 356 of the Constitution has serious consequences affecting the executive as well as the legislative powers of the State concerned. By issuing such a proclamation the President assumes to himself all or any of the functions of the Government of the State and all or any of the powers vested in or exercisable by the Governor or anybody or authority in the State other than the Legislature of the state and declares that the powers of the Legislature of the State shall be exercisable by or under the authority of Parliament. Having regard to the drastic nature of the consequences flowing from a proclamation under Article 356 of the Constitution, it is required to be approved by both Housed of Parliament within a prescribed period and it can be continued only with the approval of both Houses of Parliament and it cannot remain in force for more than three years. The provisions of the Central Government to discharge the obligation imposed on it under Article 355 of the Constitution and to prevent the situation arising due to internal disturbance assuming such seriousness as to require invoking the drastic provisions of Article 356 of the Constitution. The Central Act does not confer on the Union, the executive and legislative powers of the States in respect of which a declaration has been made under Section 3 of the Armed Forces (Special Powers) Act, 1958. It only enables the personnel of Armed Forces of the Union to exercise the power conferred under Section 4 of the said Act, in the event of a notification declaring an area to be a disturbed area being issued under Section 3 of the said Act. Having regard to the powers that are conferred under Section 4 of the said Act, the Apex Court are unable to appreciate, how the enactment of the Central Act can be equated with the exercise of the power under Article 356 of the Constitution.[77]

Law providing for deployment of Armed Forces:- The power to make a law providing for deployment of the Armed Forces of the Union in aid of the Civil Power of a State does not includes within its ambit the power to enact a Law which would enable the Armed Forces of the Union to supplant or act as a substitute for the civil power in the State. The armed forces of the Union would operate in the State concerned in co-operation with the civil administration so that the situation which has necessitated the deployment of Armed Forces is effectively dealt with and the normalcy is restored.[78]

Maintenance of public order:- The Assam Disturbed Areas Act, (19 of 1955) is in pith and substance a law in respect of maintenance of public order enacted in exercise of the legislative power conferred on the State Legislature under Entry 1 of List II.[79]

Periodic review of declaration.— A declaration under Section 3 of the Armed Forces (Special Powers) Act, 1958 has to be for a limited duration and there should be periodic review of the declaration before the expiry of six months.[80]

The period of one year is unduly long and has invited the court's attention to the provision contained in Article 352 and 356 of the Constitution which postulate periodic review of a proclamation issued under the said provisions after every six months. There is no reason why a longer period should be required for review of a declaration under Section 3 of the Armed Forces (Special Powers) Act, 1958. Keeping in view the fact that the declaration about an area being declared as a "disturbed area" can be issued only in a grave situation of law and order as well as the extent of the powers that can be exercised under Section 4 of the said Act in a disturbed area, the Apex Court are of the view that a periodic review of the declaration made under Section 3 of the said Act should be made by the Government/Administration that has issued such declaration before the expiry of a period of six months.[81]

Personal restraint and Prevention Detention.— The Prayer is divided into three parts. The first part briefly deals with the historical aspect of liberty and detention laws in India, as Court left that, like many other institution, the detention laws are also a legacy of the British period. The second part focus on TADA, its stated objectives and aims and main provisions as well as its use and abuse that ultimately came under criticism from various Human Rights Organizations, some political parties, academicians and eminent jurists. The third and the last part is an answer to the question,— can terrorism and other such disruptive activities be taken care of under the existing criminal laws or do people another TADA to deal with such situation?

Like the people elsewhere in the colonial world, Indians also struggled hard and fought for their rights and liberties. It was increasingly realized during the course of the freedom struggle that the British Government was denying the basic liberties to the people and the times crushing them completely by resorting to special laws, all in the name of maintaining law and order. As early as 1818, the first Prevention Detention Act, under the name Bengal State Prisoners Regulation Act, 1818 was enacted with the object to provide for personal restraint of individual against whom there might not be sufficient grounds to institute judicial proceeding or when such proceedings might not be feasible, or might for that reason, inadvisable or proper. The individual could be detained on under mentioned grounds.—

(i) Due maintenance for the alliance formed by British Government with foreign power.

(ii) The presentation of tranquility in the territories of native princes entitled to its protection.

(iii) Security of the British Domination from foreign hostility and internal commotion.[82]

Power conferred to enter and search without warrant.— In clause (d) of Section 4 of the Armed Forces (Special Powers) Act, 1958 conferred to enter and search without warrant any premises to make any such arrest as aforesaid or to recover any person believed to be wrongfully restrained or confined or any property reasonable suspected to be stolen property or any arms, ammunition or explosive substances believed to be unlawfully kept in such premises, and the concerned officer may for that purpose use such force as may be necessary. Similar powers of search are conferred on a police officer under Section 47 of Cr. PC. It has been urged that in respect of property or arms, ammunition or explosive substances which are seized during the course of search under clause (d) there is no provision similar to Section 5 requiring the officer exercising the said power to hand over the property and arms, ammunition or explosive substances that are recovered in the search to the officer-in-charge of the nearest police station. It is no doubt true that there is no provision similar to Section 5 of the said Act, requiring the handing over of the property of arms, ammunitions, etc. that are seized during the course of search under Section 4 (c), but since such seized property or material will be required in the proceedings to be initiated against the culprits from whose possession the same was recovered, it is implicit in the power that has been conferred under Section 4 (d) of the said Act, that it should be exercised in accordance with the provisions relating to search and seizure contained in the Criminal Procedure Code and the property or the same, ammunitions, etc. that is seized during the course of search under Section 4(d) of the said Act must be handed over to the officer-in-charge of the nearest police station with the least possible delay together with a report of the circumstances occasioning the search and seizure.[83]

Power of Non-Commissioned Officer in Armed Forces (Special Powers) Act, 1958 on the officers of the armed forces, including a Non-Commissioned Officer are not arbitrary and unreasonable and are not violative of the provisions of Article 14, 19 or 21 of the Constitution.[84]

Power to arrest without warrant.— Under clause © of Section 4 of the Armed Forces (Special Powers) Act, 1958 had been conferred to arrest, without warrant any person who has committed a cognizable offence or against whom a reasonable suspicion exists that he has committed or is about to commit a cognizable offence and the concerned officer is empowered to use such force as may be necessary to effect the arrest. The said power is not very different from the power which has been conferred on a police officer under Section 41, Cr. PC Clause © has to be read with Section 5 of the Armed Forces (Special Powers) Act, 1958 which requires that any person arrested and taken into custody shall be made over to the officer-in-charge of the nearest Police station with the least possible delay, together with a report of the circumstances occasioning the arrest. There is nothing in Section 5 of the said Act to indicate that the officer exercising the power of arrest under Section 4© is obliged to comply with the requirements of clause (1) and (2) of Article 22 of the Constitution. The power conferred under Section 4©, read with Section 5 of the said Act has to be exercised in consonance with the overriding requirements of clauses (1) and (2) of Article 22 of the Constitution which means that the person who is arrested by an officer specified in Section 4 of the said Act has to be mad over to the officer-in-charge of the nearest police station together with a report of the circumstances occasioning the arrest with the least possible delay so that the person arrested can be produced before the nearest Magistrate within a period of twenty-four hours of such arrest excluding the time necessary for the journey from the place of arrest to the Court of the Magistrate and no such person can be detained in custody beyond the said period without the authority of a Magistrate.[85]

Preventive detention and punitive detention.— The special laws gave enormous powers to the executive. The enactment of Rowllet Act,

1918 after the lapse of Defense of India Act was the most in famous and draconian law, which was in fact enacted to scuttle all types of opposition to the British Government. It was rightly dubbed as the "Black law" and vehemently criticized and condemned. Even Government of India Act, 1935 which proposed a federal structure and some decentralization of powers has such provisions which could rob the individual of his basic right to life and liberty under certain circumstances. Then came Rule 26 of the Rules framed by the Defence of India Act, 1939 which authorized the Government to detain a person whenever it was "satisfie with respect to that particular person that such detention was necessary to prevent him from acting in any, manner prejudicial to the defence and safety of the country and the like". This was, of course, a war time measure modeled similar legislation in England during World War II. But even after the cessation of war, preventive detention was continued in India as an instrument to suppress apprehended breach of public order, public safety and the like, by the Provincial Maintenance of Public Order Acts under which there was spate of litigation.

When India got independence and opportunity to taste freedom, it was but natural that the Constitution would provide all those liberties and rights to its citizens, which were denied to them for long by the British Rulers. However the framers of our Constitution simply made it possible for such legislation to be continued under the Constitution subject to certain safeguard laid down therein.[86] Incorporation of a full chapter on Fundamental Rights,— Including Right to Freedom from Article 19 to Article 22,- fulfilled the dream of providing liberties to its citizen. Article 21 of the Indian constitution especially provides that no person shall be deprived of his life or personal liberty except according to procedure establish by law. But ironically the very next Article, Article 22 which gives protection against "arrest and detention" denies this protection to "any person who is arrested under any law providing for preventive detention" Article 22 clause 3(b). This means any detention law passed by the union or the State Government will give the power of "detention or arrest without recourse to law and in such arrests no offence is proved or nor any charge is formulated, justification is just suspension or reasonable probability and not criminal convection which can only be warranted by legal convection".[87] Thus preventive detention means the detention of a person without trial in such circumstances that evidence in possession of the authority is not sufficient to make a legal charge or to secure conviction of the detenue by legal proof, but may still be sufficient to justify his detention. While the object of punitive detention is to punish a person for what he has done, the object of "preventive detention"[88] is to prevent him from doing something which comes within Entry 9 of List I and Entry 3 of List III.[89]

Preventative detention for freedom of country.—The inclusion of the provision for preventative detention was justified by the Founding Fathers of the Indian Constitution on the ground of safeguard the hard won freedom of the country which could be jeopardized by the anti-national and anti-social elements. Dr. B.R. Ambedkar, addressing the Constituent Assembly on September 15, 1949 said that three might be such cases as tempering either with public order or with Defence Services in the country and of people who are "impatient in reaching their objectives and for the purpose resort to unconstitutional methods". He further said: "If all of us follow purely constitutional methods to achive our objective, I think the situation would have been different and probably the necessity of having preventive detention not be there at all." But it is also on record that the inclusion of this provision generated lot of heated debate and criticism in the Constituent Assembly.[90]

Preventive detention for protection.— The twentieth century has witnessed hundreds of nationalist struggles, for protecting the basic liberties in democratic rights all over the globe, particularly in the third world. Indian National Movement, itself, was a continuous and pre-dominantly a non-violent fight against oppression, tyranny and dravonian laws of the colonial rulers. The Universal Declaration of Human Rights, 1948 and the U.N. Charter on Human Rights laid ample emphasis on "life and liberty of all Human beings irrespective of colour, creed or sex. The Indian Constitution ensures liberty to its citizens through Article 19 to Article 22. But simultaneously this liberty has been under threat from many corners. The last two decades, particularly witnessed global rise to terrorism and violence. On the one hand terrorism[91] perpetuated by unmindful groups crushed the basic right of life and liberty of thousands of innocent people, on the other hand[92] the State, in the name of safeguarding "unity and sovereignty" of the nation, acquired stringent and harsh laws in it armory, in addition to the normal laws. In Indian context it may be noted that the special laws, normally known as "Detention Laws", may have helped the State, to some extent, in curbing antinational activities and lately terrorism in some parts of the country. But at what cost? The experience shows that the so-called "special laws" have been, more often than not misused by the Government of the day to curb all sorts of opposition and rob the people of their basic right to life and liberty.[93]

Preventive detention to check communalism and extremist activities.— The Preventive Detention Act, 1950 was originally passed for one year but was periodically extended up to 1969. During this period the Act continued to be challenged in the Supreme Court for its validity and Parliament continued to amend it. Again in 1971, need was felt to frame another Preventive Detention Act with the object to "maintain internal security". And this was the infamous MISA (Maintenance of Internal Security Act, 1971) which was later grossly misused to scuttle all political opposition during emergency (1975-1977). The Act gave extraordinary powers to the executive, the misuse of which was observed by the Supreme Court. "It turned into an engine of oppression posing threat to democratic way of life."[94] The total rout of the Congress Party, during the March 1977 General Election could be taken as a "measure of public resentment against the misuse of MISA". The Janata Party Government fulfilling one of its poll promise repealed MISA on July 3, 1978. Though MISA was gone, yet the Conservation of Foreign Exchange and Prevention of Smuggling Activities Act, 1974 along with Prevention of Black-marketing and Maintenance of Supplies of Essential Commodities Act, 1980 continued. Soon the need was felt to frame another Preventive Detention Act, to tackle communalism and extremist activities. The National Security Act, (NSA) was formulated in 1980 with the object to "cope with situation of communal disharmony, social tensions, extremist activities, industrial unrest and increasing tendency on the part of various interested parties to engineer agitations on different issues.[95]

Production of accused after arrest.— A person arrested and taken into custody in exercise of the power under Section 4 (c) of the Armed Forces (Special Powers) Act, 1958 should be handed over to the officer-in-charge of the nearest police station with least possible delay so that he can be produced before nearest Magistrate within 24 hours of such arrest excluding the time taken for journey from the place of arrest to the Court of Magistrate.[96]

Prosecution not vitiated on error in sanction.— When Parliament enacted the present Code, they advisedly incorporated the words "any error or irregularity in any sanction for the prosecution" in Section 465 of the present Code of 1973 as they wanted to prevent failure of prosecution on the mere ground of any error or irregularity in the sanction for prosecution. An error or irregularity in a sanction may, nevertheless, vitiate the prosecution only if such error or irregularity has occasioned failure of justice.[97]

Recovery on the basic of disclosure statement sufficient for conviction.— It was the prosecution case that the police had information that some terrorists of Punjab were to carry out explosions in various parts of Delhi and, therefore, they were keeping a watch at Vishnu Garden, Rajouri Garden and Tilak Nagar. A watch was also kept on appellant who residing in a house bearing No. F-167, near Vishnu Garden, as some known persons were seen visiting his house. The police party consisting of inspectors and sub-inspectors decided to raid the premises in which they suspected that explosive material was kept. They, therefore, went to the house of the appellant and took him to the office of the Operation cell in Lodhi Colony for interrogation. The appellant made a disclosure statement that 'J' with whom he had good contacts had taken a house on rent bearing No. C-44, near Vishnu Garden and they had kept some explosive material in that room. He then took the police party to that room. It was opened by a key which was with the appellant then pointed out a raxine bag containing on Dalda tin containing 2 kgs. of RDX and one timer device. All these Articles were seized by the police and, after completing the investigation, chare-sheet was filed against the appellant and two others, namely, 'G' and 'J'. As 'J' was not tracted, the trial proceeded against 'M' and 'G'. The Trial Court acquitted 'G' as it was not proved that he had taken that room on lease and was in possession of it. The Trial Court believed the evidence of prosecution witnesses held that the appellant was in conscious possession of the RDX recovered from that room. The Trial Court also believed that the said RDX was recovered on the basis of the disclosure statement made by the appellant. The appellant was, therefore, convicted as stated above.

But, the Court does not see any reason to disbelieve the evidence of the three witnesses who have categorically stated that the key was produced by the appellant and with it the lock of that room was opened. The witnesses have also stated that after opening the room the accused had pointed out the rexine beg containing Dalda tin from which RDX was found. From this evidence, it becomes clear that the appellant was in conscious possession of the said explosive articles.[98]

Sanction not required for other penal offences with TADA.— In Kalpnath Rai's case[99] an FIR was registered under Sections 332, 307 and 427 of the IPC and also under Sections 3 and 4 of the TADA. No prior approval was obtained in that case under Section 20-A (1) and hence, the entire FIR was liable to be quashed. A Bench of two judges of the Apex Court has observed thus:-

"It is of course true that when the above FIR was recorded no prior approval of the Superintendent of Police was obtained as required under Section 20- A (1) but, as noticed above, the FIR was recorded not only for offences under TADA but also for offences under the Indian Penal Code for commission of which the police officer concerned was competent to lodge an FIR without such approval. The absence of approval of District Superintendent of Police as required under Section 20-A (1) of TADA at that Stage only disentitled the investigating agency to investigate into the offences relating to TADA but it had a statutory right to investigate into the other offences alleged in the FIR".

Seizure of arms and ammunition by Armed Forces be submitted to nearest police station.— The property or the arms, ammunitions, etc. seized during the course of search conducted under Section 4(d) of the Armed Forces (Special Powers) Act, 1958 must be handled over to the officer-in-charge of the nearest police station together with a report of the circumstances occasioning such search and seizure.[100]

Some important legal consequences.— It is well known (vide Section 193, Cr PC, 1973) that Sessions judges are not generally empowered to take cognizance unless the case is committed. As TADA judges (and not qua Sessions Judges) they were empowered to take cognizance, as special courts, of TADA offences and together with it, of other offences. Thus if a judge, lacking jurisdiction for the above said reasons, conducts a trial of TADA offence along with, say Arms Act offences and later on TADA is not pressed by prosecution or TADA is not applicable, the remand of such case to the Chief Judicial Magistrate would mean that the charge-sheet has come for the first time before the Chief Judicial Magistrate and power of taking cognizance shall have to be exercised by him under Section 190, Cr PC in respect of the Arms Act and other remaining offences, for the remand not having been done by a competent TADA Court, cognizance by Sessions Judge of Arms Act offences would have been basically untenable.

Under our criminal jurisprudence, the role of Courts is visualized right with the commencement of investigation by police. The moment a case is registered by the police and investigation commences, a person may be arrested and may have to be remanded by a court; a person may choose to surrender before the Court, some seizures may be made and will have to be reported to the Court; bails may have to be heard by Court, prayer for release of articles, search and seizure of places, by order of Courts, and recovery and production of persons unlawful fly confined may have to be made as per order of Court. Investigation might be ideally completed within short time and order on cognizance might have to be passed by court. Existence of a competent court to deal with all these matters simultaneously with the launching of investigation by police seems to be a necessary legal conditions to sustain a lawful investigation. The situation calls for an all the more anxious consideration where some particular offences like those under TADA

Act are triable only by specially designated Judges. It is submitted if not properly constituted special courts are functioning, the registration and investigation of the cases triable by special courts come to function, for criminal jurisprudence may not countenance a situation where a citizen can be proceeded against by police without any competent legal forum existing to hear on remedies.

TADA Act has lapsed. No certificatory notification can be issued. The situations above discussed may be of historical significance generating discussions to avoid identical pit-falls in future.

The existing trials of TADA cases may require an urgent fresh look and may have to be terminated under appropriate judicial power if accused persons have suffered incarceration for long under the aforesaid anomalous situation obtaining in the matter of legal competence of TADA Courts under whose orders incarceration has extended.[101]

State Legislature has executive power.— Under Entry 1 of the State List, the State Legislature has been conferred the exclusive power to enact a law providing for maintenance of public order. This power does not however, extend to the use of armed forces in aid of the Civil Power and that Parliament has been empowered to make a law in that regard and this position has been made explicit by Entry 2-A of the Union List. The submission is that the use of the Armed Forces in aid of the Civil Power contemplates the use of Armed Forces under the control, continuous supervision and direction of the executive power of the State and that Parliament can only provide that whenever the executive authorities of State desire, the use of Armed Forces in aid of the Civil Power would be permissible but the supervision and control over the use of Armed Forces has to be with the civil authorities of the State concerned. The central Act does not make provision for use of Armed Forces in aid of the civil power in this sense and it envisages that as soon as the whole or any part of a State has been declared to be a disturbed area under Section 3 of the Central Act, members of Armed Forces get independent power to act under Section 4 of the Central Act and to exercise the said power for the maintenance of public order independent of the control or supervision of any executive authority of the State. The counsel has submitted that such a course is not permissible inasmuch as it amounts to handing over the maintenance of public order in a State to Armed Forces directly and it contravenes the constitutional restriction of permitting use of Armed Forces, only in aid of civil power. It is further urged that the expression "civil power" in Entry 1 of the State List as well as Entry 2-A of the Union List refers to civil power of the A State Government and not of the Central Government.[102]

State Legislature — Use of Armed Forces — A perusal of Entry 1 of the State List would show that while power to legislate in order to maintain public order has been assigned to the State Legislature, the field encompassing the use of Armed Forces in aid of the civil power has been carved cut from the said Entry and legislative power in respect of that field has been expressly excluded. This means that the "State Legislature does not have any legislative power with respect to the use of the Armed Forces of the Union in aid of the civil power for the purpose of maintaining public order in the State and the competence to make a law to that regard vests exclusively in Parliament. Prior to the Forty-Second Amendment to the Constitution such power could be inferred from Entry 2 of the Union List relating to naval, military and air forces and any other Armed Forces of the Union as well as under Article 248, read with Entry 97 of the Union List. After the Forty-Second Amendment, the legislative power of Parliament in respect of deployment of Armed Forces of the Union or any other force subject to the Union or any contingent or unit thereof in any State in aid of the civil power flows from Entry 2-A of the Union List. The expression "in aid of the civil power" in Entry 1 of the State List and in Entry 2-A of the union List implies that deployment of the Armed Forces of the Union, shall be for the purpose of enabling the civil power in the State to deal with the situation affecting maintenance of public order which has necessitated the deployment of the Armed Forces in the State. the word "aid" postulates the continued existence of the authority to be aided. This would mean that even after deployment of the Armed Forces, the civil power will continue to function. The power to make a law providing for deployment of the Armed Forces of the Union in aid of the civil power in the State does not comprehend the power to enact a law which would enable the Armed Forces of the Union to supplant or act as a substitute for the civil power in the State. During the course of such deployment the supervision and control over the use of Armed Forces has to be with the civil authorities of the State concerned or that the State concerned will have the exclusive power to determine the purpose, the time, period and the areas within which the Armed Forces should be requested to act in aid of civil power. What is contemplated by Entry 2-A of the Union List and Entry 1 of State List is that in the event of deployment of the Armed Forces of the Union in aid of the civil power in a State, the said forces shall operate in the State concerned in co-operation with the civil administration so that the situation which has necessitate the deployment of the Armed Forces is effectively dealt with and normalcy is restored.[103]

TADA a boon or curse.— Though certain credit is being given to

TADA by the power that be, on the grounds that it was with the help of this Act, that terrorism could be neutralized in Punjab and peace returned thereafter seven long years, but it may be argued that it was not TADA alone but a combination of other factors which was responsible for restoration of normalcy in Punjab. Further it may be argued that even when TADA was in force and being energetically used, terrorism erupted in Kashmir Valley. It may be said that law by itself is not deterrent to violent elements. Secondly, if this "draconian law" has done some good by helping to curb terrorism, has it not caused immense harm to our policy, society and human dignity during its sinister life span of ten years? Thus, the early stand of the Union Government and its apologists to defend TADA "as being unavoidable to crush terrorism and related disruptive activities" does not hold valid.[104]

To enact a law in relation to Armed Forces by State.— The expression" or any officer of the Assam Rifles not below the rank of Havildar" occurring in Section 4 of the Armed Forces (Special Powers) Act, 1958 and the expression "or any officer of the Assam Rifles not below the rank of Jamadar" in Section 5 of the Assam Disturbed Areas Act, 19 of 1995 have been rightly held to be unconstitutional by the Delhi High Court, since Assam Riffles are a part of the Armed Forces of the Union and the State Legislature in exercise of its power under Entry I of List II was not competent to enact a law in relation to armed forces of the Union.[105]

Use of Armed Forces to disperse assembly.— (1) If any such assembly cannot be otherwise dispersed, and if it is necessary for the public security that it should be dispersed, the Executive Magistrate of the highest rank who is present may cause it to be dispersed by the Armed Forces.

(2) Such Magistrate may require any officer-in-command of any group of persons belonging to the Armed Forces to disperse the assembly with the help of the Armed Forces under his command, and to arrest and confine such persons forming part of it as the Magistrate may direct, or as it may be necessary to arrest and confine in order to disperse the assembly or to have them punished according to law.

(3) Every such officer of the Armed Forces shall obey such requisition in such manner as he thinks fit, but in so doing he shall use as title force, and to as little injury to person and property, as may be consistent with dispersing the assembly and arresting and detaining such persons.[106]

Use of minimum force in exercise of prohibitory order.— As regards clause (a) of Section 4 of the Armed Forces (Special Powers) Act, 1958, submission is that it empowers any commissioned officer, warrant officer or non-commissioned officer or any other person of equivalent rank in the Armed Forces to fire upon or otherwise use force even to the causing of death against any person who is acting in contravention of any law and order for the time being in force in the disturbed area prohibiting the assembly of five or more person or the carrying of weapons or things capable of being used as weapons or of firearms, ammunition or explosive substances. It has been urged that the conferment of such a wide power is unreasonable and arbitrary. The power under Section 4(a) of the said Act can be exercised only when (a) a prohibitory order of the nature specified in the clause is in force in the disturbed area; (b) the officer exercising those powers forms the opinion that it is necessary to take action for maintenance of public order against the person/persons acting in contravention of such prohibitory order; (c) a due warning as the officer considers necessary is given before taking action. The laying down of these conditions given an indication that while exercising the powers, the officer shall use minimum force required for effective action against the person/persons acting in contravention of the prohibitory order. In the circumstances, it cannot be said that clause (a) of Section 4 of the Armed Forces (Special Powers) Act, 1958 suffers from the vice of arbitrariness or is unreasonable.[107]

References

1. People's Union for Civil Liberties v. Union of India, AIR 2004 SC 456 at 468: 2004 (13) AIC 1(SC).
2. Kartar Singh v. State of Punjab, 1994 (3) SCC 569.
3. State v.Mohd. Afzal, 2004 (1) Crimes 227 at 309, 310.
4. State v. Mohd. Afzal, 2004 (1) Crimes 227 (Del.) (DB).
5. People's Union for Civil Liberties v. Union of India, AIR 2004 SC 456 at 471, 472: 2004 (13) AIC 1 (SC).
6. People's Union for Civil Liberties v. Union of India, AIR 2004 SC 456 at 473: 2004 (13) AIC 1 (SC).
7. People's Union for Civil Liberties v. Union of India, AIR 2004 SC 456 at 473: 2004 (13) AIC 1 (SC).
8. Mohammad Gausuddin v. State of Maharashtra, 2003 Cri LJ 2994 at 3010 (Bom.) (At Nagpur).
9. State v. Mohd. Afzal, 2004 (1) Crimes 227 (Del.) (DB).
10. Mohammad Gausuddin v. State of Maharashtra, 2003 Cri LJ 2994 at 3026 (Bom.) (At Nagpur).
11. People's Union for Civil Liberties v. Union of India, AIR 2004 SC 456 at 478: 2004 (13)AIC 1 (SC).
12. State of Gujarat v. Salimbhai Abdulgaffar Shaikh, 2003 (2) ALD

(Cri.) 774 at 778, 779 780 (SC).

13. Katika Ramesh v. State of A.P. 2003 (1) ALD (Cri) 757 (AP).
14. Mohammed Gausuddin v. State of Maharashtra, 2003 Cri LJ 2994 at 3027 (Bom.) (At Nagpur).
15. Nazir Khan v. State of Delhi, 2003 (2) ALD (Cri) 651 at 664 (SC).
16. State of Tamil Nadu v. Sivarasan, 1997 (1) ALD (Cri.) 631 (SC): (1997) 1 SCC 682.
17. Naga Peoples Movement of Human Rights v. Union of India, AIR 1998 SC 431 at 442, 443.
18. Naga People's Movement of Human Rights v. Union of India, AIR 1998 SC 431 at 440.
19. Naga People's Movement of Human Rights v. Union of India, AIR 1998 SC 431 at 442: 1998 SCC (Cr) 514; (1998) 2 SCC 109; AIR 1998 SCW 8: 1998 SC Cri R 246: (1997) 9 Jt (SC) 431: (1997) 10 Supreme Today 160.
20. Naga People's Movement of Human Rights v. Union of India, AIR 1998 SC 431 at 448.
21. Kalpnath Raj v. State, AIR 1998 SC 202 at 209, 210.
22. Naga People's Movement of Human Rights v. Union of India, AIR 1998 SC 431 at 463: (1998)2 SCC 109: 1998 SCC (Cri) 514.
23. Kalpnath Rai v. State, AIR 1998 SC 202 at 212.
24. Kalpnath Rai v. State, AIR 1998 SC 202 at 212.
25. Naga People's Movement of Human Rights v. Union of India, AIR 1998 SC 431 at 463: (1998)2 SCC 109: 1998 SCC (Cri) 514.
26. Naga People's Movement of Human Rights v. Union of India, AIR 1998 SC 431 at 464: (1998) 2 SCC 109: AIR 1998 SCW 8: 1998 SC Cri R 246: (1997) 9 JT (SC) 431: (1997) 10 Supreme Today 160.
27. Naga People's Movement of Human Rights v. Union of India, AIR 1998 SC 431 at 451, 452 : 1998 SCC (Cri) 514 : (1998) 2 SCC 109: AIR 1998 SCW 8: 1998 SC Cri R 246: (1997) 9 JT (SC) 431: (1997) 10 Supreme Today 160.
28. 1996 Cri LJ, Journal Section 127 at 21.
29. Kartar Singh v. State of Punjab, 1994 Cri LJ 3139 (SC)
30. "Status paper on TADA", prepared by the Union Home Ministry, quoted in Frontline, June, 1995, p. 23.
31. See P.C. Punen, Sanjay is not issue "TADA is", the Tribune, September 3, 1994.

32. See the Tribune, May 7, 1995.
33. See the Tribune and Indian Express, May 1, May 10 and May 17, 1995: 1996 Cri LJ, Journal Section 17 and 20.
34. See 1998 Criminal Law Journal, Journal Section at 168.
35. See 1998 Criminal Law Journal, Journal Section at 168.
36. See 1998 Criminal Law Journal, Journal Section at 168.
37. Naga People's Movement of Human Rights v. Union of India, AIR 1998 SC 431 at 453 : (1998) SCC (Cri) 514 : (1998) 2 SCC 109: AIR 1998 SCW 8: 1998 SC Cri R 246: (1997) 9 JT (SC) 431: (1997) 10 Supreme Today 160.
38. Jaspal Singh v. State of Punjab, (1999) 1 Supreme Reported Judgments 81 at 82: AIR 1999 SC 324.
39. State of Punjab v. Jagga Singh, 1998 Cri LJ 4455 at 4456 (SC.
40. Naga People's Movement of Human Rights v. Union of India, AIR 1998 SC 431 at 447, 448 : 1988 SCC (Cri) 514: (1998) 2 SCC 109: AIR 1998 SCW 8: 1998 SC Cri R 246: (1997) 9 JT (SC) 431: (1997) 10 Supreme Today 160.
41. Naga People's Movement of Human Rights v. Union of India, AIR 1998 SC 431 at 456: (1998)2 SCC 109: 1998 SCC (Cri) 514.
42. Naga People's Movement of Human Rights v. Union of India, AIR 1998 SC 431 at 463: (1998)2 SCC 109: 1998 SCC (Cri) 514.
43. See the Code of Criminal Procedure 1973, Section 129.
44. Naga People's Movement of Human Rights v. Union of India, AIR 1998 SC 431 at 463: (1998) 2 SCC 109: 1998 SCC (Cri) 514 : AIR 1998 SCW 8: 1998 SC Cri R 246: (1997) JT (SC) 431.
45. Naga People's Movement of Human Rights v. Union of India, AIR 1998 SC 431 at 464: (1998)2 SCC 109: 1998 SCC (Cri) 514 : AIR 1998 SCW 8: 1998 SC Cri R 246: (1997) JT (SC) 431.
46. Naga People's Movement of Human Rights v. Union of India, AIR 1998 SC 431 at 453: (1998) 2 SCC 109: 1998 SCC (Cri) 514.
47. Naga People's Movement of Human Rights v. Union of India, AIR 1998 SC 431 at 463: (1998)2 SCC 109: 1998 SCC (Cri) 514 : AIR 1998 SCW 8: 1998 SC Cri R 246: (1997) JT (SC) 431.
48. Naga People's Movement of Human Rights v. Union of India, AIR 1998 SC 431 at 463: (1998)2 SCC 109: 1998 SCC (Cri) 514.

AIR 1998 SCW 8: 1998 SC Cri R 246: (1997) 9 JT (SC) 431.

49. Shaikh Umar Ahmed Shaikh v. State of Maharashta 1998 Cri LJ 2534 at 2537 (SC).
50. Raj Deo Sharma v. State of Bihar, 1998 Cri LJ 4596 at 4602 (SC).
51. Naga People's Movement of Human Rights v. Union of India, AIR 1998 SC 431 at 463: (1998)2 SCC 109: 1998 SCC (Cri) 514.
52. Naga People's Movement of Human Rights v. Union of India, AIR 1998 SC 431 at 452 : 1998 SCC (Cri) 514 : (1998) 2 SCC 109: AIR 1998 SCW 8: 1998 SC Cri 246: (1997) 9 JT (SC) 431: (1997) 10 Supreme Today 160.
53. Naga People's Movement of Human Rights v. Union of India, AIR 1998 SC 431 at 463: (1998)2 SCC 109: 1998 SCC (Cri) 541.
54. State of Gujarat v. Mohammed Atik, 1998 Cri LJ 2252, 2253: AIR 1998 SC 1686.
55. See the Code of Criminal Procedure, 1973, Section 131.
56. Naga People's Movement of Human Rights v. Union of India, AIR 1998 SC 431 at 453: 1998 SCC (Cri) 514: (1998) 2 SCC 109: AIR 1998 SCW 8: 1998 SC Cri 246: (1997) 9 JT (SC) 431: (1997) 10 Supreme Today 160.
57. Naga People's Movement of Human Rights v. Union of India, AIR 1998 SC 431 at 455: (1998) 2 SCC 109 : 1998 SCC (Cri) 514
58. Naga People's Movement of Human Rights v. Union of India, AIR 1998 SC 431 at 463: (1998) 2 SCC 109:1998 SCC (Cri) 514: AIR 1998 SCW 8 : 1998 SC Cri R 246: (1997) 9 JT (SC) 431.
59. Naga People's Movement of Human Rights v. Union of India, AIR 1998 SC 431 at 449, 450 : 1998 SCC (Cri) 514: (1998) 2 SCC 109: AIR 1998 SCW 8: 1998 SC Cri R 246 : (1997) 9 JT (SC) 431: (1997) 10 Supreme Today 160.
60. Durga Shankar Mehta v. Raghuraj Singh, 1955 (1) SCR 267: AIR 1954 SC 520 and later followed in a series of decisions. (Arunachalam v. P.S.R. Sadhanantham, (1979) 2 SCC 197: AIR 1979 SC 1284; Delhi Judicial Service Association v. State of Gujarat, (1991) 4 SCC 406: AIR 1991 SCW 2419.
61. Chandrakant Patil v. State, 1998 Cr. LJ 1613 at 1615, 1616: AIR 1998 SC 1165.
62. Delhi Judicial Service Association v. State of Gujarat, AIR 1991 SCW 2419, as also in Union of Carbide Corporation v. Union of

India, (1991) 5 SCC 584: AIR 1992 SC 248.

63. Mohammed Anis v. Union of India, 1994 Supp (1) SCC 145.
64. E.K. Chandrasenan v. State of Kerala, (1995) 2SCC 99: AIR 1995 SCW 1079.
65. Naga People's Movement of Human Rights v. Union of India, AIR 1998 SC 431 at 462: (1998) 2 SCC 109: 1998 SCC (Cri) 514.
66. Naga People's Movement of Human Rights v. Union of India, AIR 1998 SC 431 at 454: (1998) 2SCC 109:1998 SCC (Cri) 514.
67. State of Maharashtra v. Mayer Hans George, AIR 1965 SC 722; Nathulal v. State of M.P., AIR 1966 SC 43, quoted n Kalpnath Rai v. State, AIR 1998 SC 202 at 212.
68. See Code of Criminal Procedure, 1973, Section 465.
69. Mohammed Zahid V. Govt. of NCT of Delhi, 1998 Cri LJ 2908 at 2910 (SC).
70. Naga People's Movement of Human Rights v. Union of India, AIR 1998 SC 431 at 464: (1998) 2 SCC 109: 1998 SCC (Cri) 514 : AIR 1998 SCW 8 : 1998 SC Cri R 246 : (1997) 9 JT (SC) 431.
71. A.K. Gopalan v. State of Madras, AIR 1950 SC 27: (1950) 51 Cri LJ 1383.
72. Ram Krishna Bhardwaj v. State of Delhi, AIR 1953 SC 318 : 1953 Cri LJ 1241.
73. 1996 Cri LJ, Journal Section 17 at 19.
74. Kalpnath Rai v. State, AIR 1998 SC 202 at 208, 209.
75. 1996 Cri LJ, Journal Section 17 at 19.
76. (Khudeswar Dutta v. State of Assam. 1998 Cri LJ 2274 at 2275 : AIR 1998 SC 1738.
77. Naga People's Movement of Human Rights v. Union of India, AIR 1998 SC 431 at, 450: 1998 SCC (Cri) 514: (1998) 2 SCC 109 : AIR 1998 SCW 8 : 1998 SC Cri R 246: (1997) 9 JT (SC) 431 : (1997) 10 Supreme Today 160.
78. Naga People's Movement of Human Rights v. Union of India, AIR 1998 SC 431 at 463 : (1998) 2 SCC 109 : 1998 SCC (Cri) 514.
79. Naga People's Movement of Human Rights v. Union of India, AIR 1998 SC 431 at 464: (1998) 2 SCC 109: 1998 SCC (Cri) 514 : AIR 1998 SCW 8 : 1998 SC Cri R 246 : (1997) 9 JT (SC) 431.
80. Naga People's Movement of Human Rights v. Union of India, AIR 1998 SC 431 at 463: (1998) 2 SCC 109: 1998 SCC (Cri) 514.

81. Naga People's Movement of Human Rights v. Union of India, AIR 1998 SC 431 at 452: (1998) 2 SCC 109: 1998 SCC (Cri) 514. AIR 1998 SCW 8 : 1998 SC Cri R 246 : (1997) 9 JT (SC) 431 : (1997) 10 Supreme Today 160.
82. 1996 Cri LJ., Journal Section 17 at 18.
83. Naga People's Movement of Human Rights v. Union of India, AIR 1998 SC 431 at 456: (1998) 2 SCC 109: 1998 SCC (Cri) 514.
84. Naga People's Movement of Human Rights v. Union of India, AIR 1998 SC 431 at 463: (1998) 2 SCC 109: 1998 SCC (Cri) 514. AIR 1998 SCW 8 : 1998 SC Cri R 246 : (1997) 9 JT (SC) 431.
85. Naga People's Movement of Human Rights v. Union of India, AIR 1998 SC 431 at 456: (1998) 2 SCC 109: 1998 SCC (Cri) 514.
86. See D.V. Basu, Introduction to the Constitution of India, 14th Edition, New Delhi-1992 at 108, 109.
87. A.K. Gopalan v. State of Madras, AIR 1950 SC 27: (1950) 51 Cri LJ 1383.
88. For detailed account of the provision Preventive Detention. See D.D. Basu, Commentary on the Constitution of India, Vol. II Articles 20 to 117, 5th Edition, Calcutta 1965, at 113 to 142; M.M. Singh, the Constitution of India Student in perspective, the World Press Pvt, Calcutta, 1975, at 423 to 439.
89. 1996 Cri LJ, Journal Section 17 at 18.
90. For Detailed Discussion See, CAD III, 3 468, See also 1996 Cri LJ, Journal, Section 17, at 18, 19.
91. For Violence and Terrorism in Various parts of India. See Rajinder Kaur. "Politics of Secessionism and Violence in India", Mainstream, April 30, 1994, at 9, 10 & 28; P.S. Verma, Jammu Kashmir at the Political Cross Roads, Vikas Publishing House Pvt. Ltd., New Delhi, 1994; Satya Pal Dang, Genesis of Terrorism, Politics of Sikh Homeland, Ajanta Publishing House, New Delhi, 1994. Also see Rajinder Kaur, Sikh Identity and National Integration, Intellectual Publishing House, New Delhi, 1992; Phanjoubm Tarapot, Insurgency Movement in North Eastern India, Vikas Publishing House Pvt. Ltd., New Delhi, 1993.
92. For Terrorism, State Terrorism and Democratic Right, See Randhir Singh, "Terrorism, State Terrorism and Democratic Rights" Mainstream, January 25, 1992 at 29 — 46; Ajit Singh Bains, "State Terrorism and Human Rights", Seminar No. 398,

October 1992 at 36 to 39; and Gopal Singh. "Militancy Terrorism and State Terrorism" (Champ. IV) op. cit at 82-101.

93. 1996 Cri LJ, Journal Section 17.
94. Bankat Lal v. State of Rajasthan AIR 1975 SC 522: 1955 Cri LKJ 439.
95. The National Security Act, 1980 in T.C. Khatri; The National Security Laws, Capital Law House, Delhi, 1984 at 191. Also see 1996 Cri LJ, Journal Section 17 at 19.
96. Naga People's Movement of Human Rights v. Union of India, AIR 1998 431 at 464 (1998) 2 SCC 109 : AIR 1998 SCW 8 : 1998 SC Cri R 246 : (1997) 9 JT (SC) 431.
97. Kalpnath Rai v. State, AIR 1998 SC 202 at 209.
98. Manoranjan Singh v. State of Delhi, 1998 Cri LJ 2062 at 2063 : AIR 1998 SC 2811.
99. In Ahmed Umar Saeed Sheikh v. State of U.P., (1996) 11 SCC 61, quoted in Kalpnath Rai v. State, AIR 1998 SC 202 at 208.
100. Naga People's Movement of Human Rights v. Union of India, AIR 1998 SC 431 at 464: (1998) 2 SCC 109: AIR 1998 SCC (Cri) 514 : AIR 1998 SCW 8 : 1998 SC Cri R 246 : (1997) 9 JT (SC) 431.
101. See 1998 Criminal Law Journal, Journal Section at 181.
102. Naga People's Movement of Human Rights v. Union of India, AIR 1998 SC 431 at 446: 1998 SCC (Cri) 514 : (1998) 2 SCC 109 : AIR 1998 SCW 8 : 1998 SC Cri R 246 : (1997) 9 JT (SC) 431 : (1997) 10 Supreme Today 160.
103. Naga People's Movement of Human Rights v. Union of India, AIR 1998 SC 431 at 446, 447 : 1998 SCC (Cri) 514 : (1998) 2 SCC 109 : AIR 1998 SCW 8 : 1998 SC Cri R 246 : (1997) 9 JT (SC) 431 : (1997) 10 Supreme Today 160.
104. 1996 Cri LJ, Journal Section 17 to 20.
105. Naga People's Movement of Human Rights v. Union of India, AIR 1998 SC 431 at 464: (1998) 2 SCC 109: 1998 SCC (Cri) 514 : AIR 1998 SCW 8 : 1998 SC Cri R 246 : (1997) 9 JT (SC) 431.
106. See Code of Criminal Procedure, 1973, Section 130.
107. Naga People's Movement of Human Rights v. Union of India, AIR 1998 SC 431 at 455: (1998) 2 SCC 109: 1998 SCC (Cri) 514.

5

SOME CASES OF TERRORIST AND DISRUPTIVE ACTIVITIES

September 11, 2001

It was America's darkest day and also her finest hour. As the world watched, jet planes crashed and buildings crumbled and ordinary men and women emerged as true heroes these are some of their stories. With the building in flames, one man needed help. Another man refused to leave him.

DAM MAYBLUM used to enjoy watching as storms lashed the windows of his office. You think that's power Mayblum would scoff. I'm on the 87th floor of the World Trade Center. That's power. The drawstrings on his window shades would appear to sway slightly, but it was an illusion. Although they were 330 meters in the sky, I WTC was quite steady.

When Mayblum felt a devastating rumble on that September morning, he glanced at the drawstrings. They were careening wildly, a meter in either direction.

Mayblum would be one of thousands cast into an extraordinary purgatory that morning. While as many as 25,000 would find their way safety, 5000 would not.

For some, it was a matter of geography — nor just which tower they worked in or on which floor, but in which corner of the building.

For some, the choices were as basic as which staircase to use. Others faced the ultimate moral dilemma: Save yourself, or save another.

The confusion inside Adam Mayblum's office at May Davis, a financial-services firm, lusted just seconds. He knew he needed to get out. He ripped his T-shirt into pieces. Soaked the pieces in water and gave them to colleagues to cover their faces. Among them: Harry Ramous, head trader at May Davis. Mayblum had worked with Ramous off and for 14 years.

Sparks bit at Mayblum's ankles as he raced for the stairs. He bolted down two flights before realizing that his trading partner. Hong Zhu, had been left behind. He went back upstairs, the whole area now filled with smoke and burning jet fuel.

There was no sign of Hong, Mayblum hurried down again and made it to the 78th floor, a transfer lobby where one set of elevators and stairs ended and another began. He saw a reassuring sight, Ramous had waded into the pandemonium to help panicked workers into a stairwell.

Mayblum continued his descent, the muscles in his calves contracting in spasma. On the 53rd floor, he came across a heavyset man whose legs just wouldn't move anymore.

"Do you want to come or do you want us to send help" Mayblum shouted.

The man asked him to send help. Adam said he would.

In noise, smoke and sparks, Mayblum didn't realize that his friend Hong Zhue was behind him in the stairwell the whole time. When Hong got to the 53rd floor, he came across Harry Ramos. Ramos had stopped to help the heavyset man Mayblum had seen earlier: "I'II give you a hand," Hong said.

Together Ramos and Hong helped the man down more flight to an elevator.

"Don't take it" an official screamed.

Hong and Ramos tried to send a magazine down in the elevator to test its safety. But when they pressed the "down" button, the doors wouldn't close. So Hong decided that he would be guinea pig instead. He stepped inside, and the doors shut behind him.

Hong took the elevator down to the 44th floor, the next transfer lobby. So far, so good. He pressed "52", want back up and collected Ramos and the heavy set man.

On 44, Hong and Ramos helped the man towards the last bank of elevators that would take them all the way down.

Hong pressed the "down" button again. Nothing. They would have to take the stairs.

Ramos and Hong tried to support the man. "One step at a time," Hong said.

They had been trying to get out for an hour and five minutes. They were on 36 when they felt the south tower collapse.

"We really have no move," Hong said.

The rumbles of the collapsing tower next door seemed to sap the heavyset man of his last gasps of energy. "I can't do it anymore." He said, sitting down.

Hong and Ramos tried to persuade him to continue. "You don't have to move your legs" Hong shouted. "Just move your butt. Let's go "But the man couldn't go on."

A fireman ran up to them. Hong expected that he would join in to get the heavy man to move. Instead the fireman turned to Hong

"Who are you, screaming at him to get out" the fireman shouted." "You get out".

Hong looked at Ramos, who was still standing with the heavyset man.

"I'm coming down with you," Ramos told the man. "I'm not going to leave."

"I left," Hong says sorrowfully. "Alone."

The next day, Adam Mayblum sent an e-mail describing his experience to friends and relatives, who sent it to still others. The e-mail was read by some one in San Francisco who knew a woman in New York named Rebecca. Her husband, Victor, a heavyset man, was missing.

On Saturday, September 15, May Davi's chairman had a gathering at his New Jersey home. Adam Mayblum was there. So was Hong zhu. Rebecca was also there. Learning how her husband, Victor, had been comforted in his last moments, how Harry Ramos had refused to leave him behind.

Ramos's wife, Micky, was there too. She kept asking Mayblum and Hong where her husband was, convinced that somehow, harry–the only May Davis employee still missing–was alive.

Piece by piece, she developed a picture of his escape:

Harry was on 87 when the plane hit. He stopped to help on 78. He met up with Hong on 53. But as hard as she tried, many question as she asked, the picture to fade on the 36th floor.

Five thousand people were heading straight for disaster. Then came the call that would save them.

VICTORIA CROSS KELLY was at a breakfast meeting in the world Trade Centre when she heard a commotion and saw people running. The Deputy Director of the Port Authority Trans-Hudson, or PATH, train system, which transports commuters between New York and New Jersey, hurried to the street to investingate. By then, she said, "Paper was running down".

It was 8:52 a.m., six minutes after the first tower was hit. Kelly didn't know yet what had happen. But she knew that on a typical day thousands of people would pass through the World Trade Centre station. Immediately, she phoned Richie Moran, PATH'S train master on duty. No more passengers were to be discharged at that station, Kelly instructed.

Two trains, however, were already approaching the station. Moran ordered the conductors to make an announcement: all passengers should remain on board.

Trains leaving New Jersey were sent back or diverted to stations north of the area.

At 9:06 a.m., a recue train swept through, collecting the last of the PATH workers and a homeless man, who had to be coaxed on.

When that train left, says Moran, "there was nobody left in the station.' It was the last train ever to enter the World Trade Center. By 10:29 a.m., both towers had collapsed.

Had Kelly been wrong, she admits, "a heck of a lot of people would have been annoyed. "In the end, says Moran, anywhere from 3000 to 5000 people were saved.

The building was collapsing Jarrell Henson was pinned.

Should his cries for help be heard ?

Shattering explosion.

Flames. Agonized cries.

Hijacked American Airlines Flight 77 had just slammed into the Pentagon. Jarrell Henson, a 64-years old retired naval officer, was instantly entombed in rubble. He felt the searing heat of fire and thought. You have five minutes to live.

Meanwhile, two naval officers, Captain David Thomas and Lieutenant Commander David Tarantino a doctor, had rushed to the smoldering crash site. After crawling through holes in the wreckage, Thomas turned a fire extinguisher on erupting flames. Then he saw Jerry Henson's bleeding head protruding from the rubble.

As Thomas struggled to free Henson, Tarantino appeared at his side. Already to free Henson was close to losing consciousness. Tarantino lay on his back, placed his feet against the desk next to Henson's chair and pushed with all his strength. The imprisoning pile shifted a bit.

"Move" Tarantino yelled at Henson. "It's now or never." Henson managed to squeeze free, and his rescuers led him out of the blazing room. As all three-crawled back through the holes. Tarantino heard the rumble of explosions. Within minutes the room collapsed behind them.

While Henson's life was spared, many other were not so lucky. One hundred and eighty-nine people died in the Pentagon attack.

Passengers staged a mutiny that thwarted an evil plan.

Long before setting off across the country on United Airlines Flight

93 to move in with her daughter in California, 79-years-old Hilda Marcin had given folders to her family with an accounting of her assets and prepared obituary. Unfailingly organized and considerate, the widow and had wanted to ease her family's ordeal should something happen to her.

As Marchin boarded the Boeing 757 in New York, bound for San Francisco, those folders were in the hands of her daughters in New Jersey and California. Marchin took her seat on a jetliner that was practically empty. Just 37 passengers had tickets on a plane that could hold almost 200.

At least four of those on board would soon seek to dictate the destinies of their fellow passengers and seven crewmembers. The other fliers brought together by chance, would try to wrest control of their fate.

The first 45 minutes of the flight seemed uneventful as the jet headed west and climbed to about 11,000 meters, breakfast was served.

From phone made to relatives on the ground, passengers learnt that two planes had hit New York's World Trade Center at about 8:45 and a few minutes after 9 that morning. But around the time a third plane smashed into the Pentagon, Flight 93 suddenly made a U-turn.

Air-traffic control had picked up, a transmission from Flight 93 as it neared Cleveland. A stuck microphone revealed something was wrong in cockpit. Controllers heard the words "Get out of here" and sounds of an apparent scuffle.

Soon a man speaking in broken English announced: "There is a bomb board. This is captain speaking. Remain in your seat. Stay quit. We are meeting with their demands. We are returning to the airport."

Passengers had already started calling the outside world to tell authorities and family members of unfolding terror.

Thirty-eight-year-old Tom Burnett, in New York on business was supported to flown out that afternoon, but switched to Flight 93 to get home earlier. Using his cell phone, he called his wife, Deena, who was getting their daughters ready for school at their home in California.

Burnett spoke quickly but quietly, "I'm on the plane, he said. They have already knifed a guy. Please call the authorities," Deena dialed 911 and was patched through to the FBI. A few minutes later, Tom's second call came through.

"They are talking about flying the plane into the ground," Burnett informed his wife. He asked Deena several questions; then, suddenly, he had to go.

Minutes later Tom called back to tell her the man who had been stabbed was dead.

Deena, a former flight attendant, remembered her own training and urged Tom to keep a low profile. "Please don't call attention to yourself" she begged.

He refused. In his final call, he told her that he and several others passengers had decided to act rather than passively face death. "we are going to try to do something," he said.

Meanwhile, Jeremy Glick, 31, a New Jersey resident who worked for an Internet company, called his wife, Lyzbeth. She and their three-month-old daughter. Emerson, were visiting her parents in New York. In their 20 minute conversation, Glick and his wife tried to stay calm, with Jeremy joking that he and fellow passengers might assault the hijackers with butter knives from the in flight breakfast.

Lyzbeth's mother, Jo Anne Makely, got on the cell phone with 911, and with state troopers taking down information, Glick described the four hijackers. They wore red headbands and held a red box they said contained a bomb. The call ended when the six-foot-one Glick told his wife about the passengers plan to "jump the hijackers".

About the same time, Todd Beamer was one of the plane's phones, speaking to a phone company supervisor Lisa Jefferson. He told her that, he along with many other passengers and crewmember or two, had been herded to the back of the plain. The remaining passengers were in first-class, the pilot and copilot nowhere to be seen. Todd remarked that he thought the plane was going down, but then he said it was turning.

A man who appeared to have explosive strapped to his midsection was guarding beamer's group. Beamer, a basketball and basket ball player in college and take charge guy, said he thought that he and the other passengers could "jump the terrorist with the bomb".

In the background, Lisa Jefferson could hear screaming, but Beamer's voice never wavered. He asked the supervisor to recite the Lord's Prayer with him. And he made her promise she would call his prayer with him and he made her promise she would call his pregnant wife and his Sons Andrew, one and David, three, to tell them he loved them dearly.

Then Beamer apparently dropped the phone and said: "God help me. Jesus helps me. Are you ready let's roll".

At her parent's house, Lyzbeth Glick couldn't stand it any more and handed the telephone to her father. After a silence that lasted two minutes, there was screaming. More silence, followed by more screams. Finally there was a Mechanical sound, followed by nothing. It was around 10 a.m. the family held the phone line open for two hours.

Shortly after 10 a.m., workers on farms in Somerser Country, Pennsylvania, looked up to see an aircraft flying low and erratically. Bob Blair was driving on the high way when he saw the jet plummer "straight down". Barn windowpanes for almost a kilometer around shattered as the jet dived into an old strip mine and exploded.

"I just watched with my mouth open as this yellow mush room cloud rose up like an atomic bomb over the hill were I like to go hunting," said 72 years old John Walsh. Bare foot and in his bathrobe, he drove up the mud road to rescue any one he could find. There would be nothing he could do.

Debris, including photographs and papers that survived the fireball, was strewn over a waddle area. The local residents would spend days collecting the material.

Among the remnants were Hilda Marcin's treasured Family photos, including a picture of her father, a German immigrant, which her daughter had asked her to bring on the trip. Marcin had carefully swathed them with clothes in her luggage.

After her husband's last call, Deena Burnett stayed in her house and sent her girls to school with a friend. She believed Tom could no fail, that he would be home.

Later, when Deena learned of her husband's faith, she had one of the hardest jobs any mother can have explaining to her children that their father was dead. "Where is he now?" asked one of their daughters.

"Is he in heaven?"

"Yes," she said.

"Can we call him on the cell phone?"

Deena explained that was not possible.

"I am going to miss Dad's silly faces."

"He is smiling down on you."

On Clifford was on his way to meet a client at the New York Marriott. Arriving early, the Sales Director for a California based high-tech company wandered over it investigate the hotel's connection to the World Trade Center and then returned to wait in the hotel lobby.

Within three or four minutes, Clifford recalls, "there was an almighty explosion. I saw this woman standing out side in the haze, and she was very, very badly burned. She stumbled in side. It was bed lama lot of debris flying I ran into the bathroom and got a plastic bag full of water and poured it over her.

Clifford knelt with the woman and talked to her and prayed with her. A hotel manager brought a first aid kit and oxygen. Clifford wrote down the woman's personal information so he could call her family. Her name was Jennie Ann Maffeo.

And then the other plane hit.

"A whirlwind of debris came through the building,"

Clifford says. "I knew we had to get out of there".

An emergency worker and the manager helped to get Maffeo through the crowd and outside.

"When I looked around, my God. The carriage was unreal", says Clifford. "Cars were on fire, pieces of building and metal were falling on the street.

The three rescuers struggled across the roadway and delivered Maffeo to a parked ambulance. Before heading home, Clifford called his wife to tell her that he was alive.

"I thought when I got home, I was home free" says this Irish American. I was so delighted to see my wife, my 11 years old. It was her birthday. And then I got a call from my family."

In one of the crueler twists of the World Trade Center tragedy, Clifford learnt that his sister, Ruth Mc Court, had been on United Airlines Flight 175, the plane that slammed into WTC Tower Two. Shed and her four years old daughter, Juliana, were traveling to California for a vacation.

Days earlier, Clifford says, he had talked with his sister on the phone. He had a very important meeting set for September 11. She'd advised him on "what to wear a sharp suit and a bright tie. That's the kind of girl she was, he says. Always so concerned about me."

Clifford received another call in those dark days from the family of Jenieann Maffeo. With burns over 90 per cent of her body, she was in critical condition. Despite spending long hours at the hospital, her family phoned to thank him."

"But you know what" says Clifford. "I thanked her. Unless I had someone to help get out of therein think I still be there. The truth is, she saved my life.

Robart Doremus, carpenter was on a New York street when the terrorist attack began. He walked over eight kilometer, to the World Trade Center, where he had once worked building an offence.

Doremus waded into the still flaming wreckage and began helping the ironworker. All night he carried oxygen and gas tanks and hauled hoses that brought fuel to their blowtorches.

"We built this city, you know," said Doremus.

"And we're going to build it back again too," added fellow carpenter Tom Killacky. "Watch."

MY WIFE and I were near 2 WTC when it imploded. A Cop raised his arms to shield us from the mushrooming clouds of rubber. We ran away. He did not.

A doorman at a nearly apartment waved us unto his building, then advised us to get out when the basement in which he'd sheltered us became chocked with concrete dust. Ankle deep in lava like power, we staggered along.

At another building, the Regatta, a worker flung open the doors in welcome. A doorman brought water to wash out stinging corneas. The supervisor gave out water bottles. Some one handed us the only working phone to call loved ones. Residents offered juice, curds, and tissues. New arrivals, dozens of them, got the same embracing treatment. Before long, a plush lobby was a bustling bomb shelter smoky and scary, yet life affirming.

Then WTC burst apart Day became pitch black night. When light slowly returned, I be held one of the greatest sights on earth — the men and women of the New York Police Department coming to the rescue.

Officers had hacked through a locked gate at the Hudsan River esplanade so evacuation vessels could berth. They led us an old lady, her husband in a wheel chair, couples with babies, a pregnant woman, a gasping asthmatic- to a police to take us out of town.

"Don't look back," a harbor Cop said, as we steamed across the Hudson. But of course we did at a city of lame. And we'll look back as we live at the wonders performed by the unknown angels who guided us out of the cataclysm.

FIREMEN

From where we stood on the 78th floor building, the explosion was metallic and deafening. And then the smell of jet fuel filled the air, I went to the window and looked up just above us was a roar of orange light, black smoke and multicolored papers flying.

I turned to my colleague Mike Hingson and shouted, "We have to get out now" I grabbed my computer bag and portfolio. Mike reached for his beautiful yellow Labrador guide dog, Roselle.

We decided to take stairs, Mike got in front of me, Roselle, to his left. The first 20 or so floors went smoothly. No one in front of us just a few behind. They were patient, but obviously we slowed them down, so we let them pass.

Somewhere around the 50th floor, we hit a traffic jam of people. I looked down. Hundreds of heads not moving. Several people, clearly panicked were sobbing. Others saw Mike and Roselle and began to call for those below us to "move right," to make room for us to come down.

As we dropped a few floors lower, the fumes of jet fuel got so intense I thought we might pass out, Roselle was panting heavily.

It was then that we ran into our first real hero: a New York fireman.

He was walking up from the lobby, clothed in a heavy, fire-retardant jacket, pants and heavy gloves. Others followed, 35 or 40, carrying an unbelievable array of equipment: axes, picks, shovels, fire hoses and compressed air tanks.

They were perspiring profusely, exhausted and they had to go all the way to the 90s-straight into hell. This was not lost on the crowd. We all broke out into applause. The firemen were extremely polite, constantly inquiring about our welfare.

"Are you all right?" they asked Mike.

"I am fine. Thank you," he told them.

Then to me; "Are you with this guy?"

"Yes, I am with Mike and we are okay, thank you," I said.

We had this conversation with almost every one of the 35 to 40 firemen who passed us.

They are all gone now

Brothers.

Usman Farman, a 22 years old Muslim of Pakistani decent, worked in Building 7 of the World Trade Centre. His office was literally a stone's throw from the 'Twin Towers'. After the second plane hit, Farman made his way down 27 flights of stairs to the street. He had walked past several buildings when the first tower collapsed.

"The next thing I remember," he says, "Is that a dark cloud of debris about 50 storey's high came tumbling towards us. I ran as fast as possible, but fell down trying to get away. I was on my back, facing this massive cloud that must have been 200 meters off. And then help came from the least expected place.

"I wear a pendent around my neck, inscribed with an Arabic prayer for safety," says Farman. "A Jewish man came up to me and held the pendent in his hand. He read the Arabic aloud". Then he said, "Brother, if you don't mind, there is a cloud of glass coming at us. Grab my hand and let's get hell out of here".

MUSICIAN

Yestarday I had the most incredible experience of my life. Students at the Julliard College, where I am a first year student organized a Quarter to play at the 69th Regiment Armory. This is a huge military building in New York where families of people missing from the World Trade Centre disaster waited for news of their loved ones.

I found my Julliard buddies, and for two hours we sight-read quarters. At 7 p.m., the other players had to leave—they had been playing for 6 hours by then—but I volunteered to stay and play solo violin.

A man in fatigues who introduced himself as Sergeant Major Miguel Cruzado asked if I'd mind playing for his soldiers as they came back from digging through the rubble at Ground Zero. I played everything I could from memory: Tchaikovsky's violin concerto, Paganini's Caprices 1 and 17 Vivaldi's "Winter" and "Spring", "Meditation" from Thais, "Amazing Grace" and "Turkey in the Straw".

Never have I played for a more grateful audience. Somehow it did not matter that by the end, my intonation was poor and I had no bow control. The men would remove their helmets, look at me, and smile.

Just before midnight, I asked Sergeant Major Curzado if it would be appropriate if I played the US national anthem. He called his soldiers to attention, and as I played, the 350 men of the Fighting 69th saluted an invisible flag.

Never have I played for a more grateful audience. Somehow it did not matter that by the end, my intonation was poor and I had no bow control. The men would remove their helmets, look at me, and smile.

Just before midnight, I asked Sergeant Major Curzado if it would be appropriate if I played the US national anthem. He called his soldiers to attention, and as I played, the 350 men of the Fighting 69th saluted an invisible flag.

In the office where I work, one of my colleagues said, "Yesterday my three-year old grand son was stacking up his Legos. And then he pretended that he crashed a plastic plane into the little building he had just constructed."

How do we, as adults, explain to children the images of evil they have been seeing these past months?

Perhaps by doing what we have done since the beginning of our human existence: by telling stories. Stories of courage and dignity in the face of all that has been lost help us to maintain our sense of hope and goodness in the grip of adversity.

Many years from now, children will be studying the events of September 11, 2001. Let them read about a young fireman rushing up the stairs of the World Trade Centre because he thought he might be able to save someone.

Let them hear about the suburban couple who, after learning of the need for equipment at Ground Zero, bought $700 worth of shovels and drove through the night to New York city to deliver them to rescue workers, in the hopes that this small act might difference in someone's life.

Above all, teach the children the story of Jeremy Glick, who helped overpower the terrorists on Flight 93. Speaking to his wife by phone, he told her, "Do not be sad."

We will all go to our deaths with lives lived, with regrets and joys, with sorrows and victories. So what do we say to those we love when our lives are done?

We say to our children. "Do not be sad" those are the words of a human and spiritual hope that there is a place of joy either in the memories of a life well lived, or in the promise of a life still to come.

Let's teach the children to remember the words of William Faulkner, one of America's greatest storytellers: "I believe that man will not merely endure: he will prevail. He is immortal, not because he alone among creatures has an in exhaustible voice, but because he has a soul, a spirit capable of compassion and sacrifice and endurance."

Do not be sad.

MIND OF A MONSTER

The twisted world of Saddam Hussein:

The Tyrant must steal sleep. He moves from secret bed, to secret bed, varying the locations a and times. It is too dangerous to be predictable, and whenever he shuts his eyes, his iron grip slackens. Plots congeal in the shadows. For those hours, he must trust someone, and nothing is more dangerous to the tyrant than trust.

Saddam Hussein, President of Iraq, field marshal of its armies and Great Uncle to all its peoples, rises at about 3 a.m. 'after only five or six hours' sleep. When he rises, he swims. His scores of palaces all have pools. Water is a symbol of wealth and power in desert country, and Saddam splashes it everywhere — fountains, pools and indoors streams.

Swimming keeps him trim and fit. This satisfies his vanity, which is epic, but fitness is crucial for other reasons. He is now 65, but because his power is grounded in fear, he cannot afford to become stooped, frail and grey.

Weakness invites challenge, coup d' etat. One can imagine Saddam urging himself through a fixed number of laps each morning. He dyes his gray hair black and won't use his reading glasses in public. And because a bad back forces him to limp, he avoids being seen walking more than a few steps.

Fresh food is flown in for him twice a week — lobster, shrimp, and lean meat and diary products. The shipments are sent to his nuclear scientists, who X-ray and test them for radiation and poison. European trained chefs under the supervision of al-Himaya, Saddam's personal bodyguards, then prepare the food.

He likes wine with his meals, but he is careful not to let anyone outside his trusted circle of family and sides see him drinking. Islam forbids Alchol, and in public Saddam is dutiful son of the faith.

The president - for life reads voraciously and has a particular passion for books about military history and great men, specifically Winston Churchill. He spends long hours every day in whichever office he and his security minders select. A loner by nature, power has isolated his further.

Walled in by palaces and ministers who rarely dare to tell him what he doesn't wish to hear, he has become ignorant of his land and his people. He exists only to preserve his wealth and power. Survival is his overriding passion.

GAINING POWER

Saddam grew up in a poor village in north central Iraq, a member of a clan known for being violent and clever. In the late 1950s he joined the Baath Socialist Party. Its goals were to rebuild the entire Arab region, sharing property and wealth, seeking a better life for all.

To fellow revolutionaries, Saddam was an impressive combination: a tough who was also well read, articulate and seemingly open-minded a natural leader who could steer Iraq into a new era.

When the Baath party seized control of the government in 1968, Saddam became the real power behind the new Revolutionary Command Council. Through the '70s-a-relatively good period for Iraq-Saddam served as vice-chairman of the council. He orchestrated a nationwide literacy project, and built schools, roads, public housing and hospitals.

Saddam had always planned to take formal control of top position in the country. Some of the party leadership had other ideas: Rather than just hand him the reins, they had begun advocating a party election. So Saddam took action, staging his ascendancy like theatre.

On July 22, 1979, he invited council members and hundreds of party leaders to a conference hall in Baghdad. Wearing his military uniform, he walked slowly to the lectern. There had been a betrayal, he said, a Syrian plot. There were traitors among them.

Then Muhyi Abdul Hussain Mushhadi, the council's secretary-general appeared and confessed his own involvement. Arrested and tortured days before, he now started naming names. As he fingered members of the audience one by one, armed guards grabbed more than

60 "traitors" and escorted them from the hall. When one man shouted he was innocent, Saddam shouted back, "Itla Get Out" (Saddam later had the mouths of the accused taped shut so they could utter no trouble some last words before their firing squads.) Of those singled out that night, 22 were executed including Mashhadi. Films of the purge were shown throughout the country.

This chilling performance had the desired effect. Every one in the hall understood that one man now controlled the destiny of their nation.

Within two years of his seizing full power, Saddam's ambitions turned to conquest. From exile, his old party allies now see his support for the social-welfare programmed as an elaborate deception.

"In the beginning," says Hamid.

TOXIC GENECIDE

Would Saddam think twice about attacking his enemies with weapons of mass destruction? Consider the fact that the Iraqi dictator has already done just that to his own people. The there-day attack took place in March 1988 in the northern town of Halabja. Clouds of poisonous gases killed as many as 5000 Kurds. Many were struck down where they stood. Dead children littered the streets like discarded dolls. The Kurds' offence: siding with neighboring Iran during the Iran-Iraq war.

"Saddam used a cocktail of chemicals-mustered gas, a known carcinogen, and nerve agents sarin, tabun and VX," says Dr. Christine Gosden, professor of medical genetics at the University of Liverpool, UK". Horrible agents. These chemical affect virtually every system of the body." Even 14 years later.

Gosden, who visited the toxic area in 1998, says the chemicals caused unsightly and "virtually untreatable" genetic changes in skin cells. Half the population has respiratory complaints. On an average day, there are no normal birth defects and mental retardation. Doctors report a high incidence of cancer in children who were not even born at the time of the attack. "This indicates that there is a genetic damage" says Gosen. "Their DNA is permanently and irreversibly changed."

The mustard gas also had a devastating effect on the environment. Deadly toxins-some from victims' bodies-seeped into the earth and the water table. This land, once the most fertile in the area, looks like a nuclear wilderness.[13]

Al-Jubouri, former acting secretary general of the Command Council, who lives in London' "Saddam was charming and impressive. He took all of us in. But he was hiding his real self, building his power quietly. He has a great ability to hide his intentions - may be his greatest skill."

VANITY

The root of Saddam's bloody, signal minded pursuit of power appears to be simply vanity. He most wants to be admired, remembered and revered. A 19 volume official biography is mandatory reading for Iraq government officials. Saddam told his biographer he wasn't interested in what people think of him today - only in what they will think of him in 500 years.

Saad al-Bazzaz, once general director of Iraqi TV and Broadcasting Establishment, was summoned to meet with Saddam got to the point. It was the practice for poems and songs written in praises of him to aired daily on TV. Most of the work was amateurish-ridiculous doggerel written by unskilled poets. In recent weeks, al Bazzaz had urged his producers to be more selective.

"I understand" Saddam said, that you are not allowing some songs that carry my name to be broadcast."

Al-Bazzaz was stunned and suddenly frightened. "Mr. President", he said, we still broadcast the songs, but I have stopped some of them because they are so poorly written."

"Look," Saddam snapped, "you are not a Judge. How can you prevent people from expressing their feelings towards me?"

Al-Bazzaz feared he was going to be taken away and shot. His heart pounded heavily.

"Now it is all clear to you?" Saddam asked.

"Yes, sir".

With that Saddam dismissed the terrified Al-Bazzaz. That evening, a full broadcast of the tributes dedicated to Saddam resumed.

CRUELTY

Saddam studies and embraces cruelty. Ultimately, guilt or innocence don't matter, because there is no law or value beyond the tyrant's will; if he wants someone arrested, tortured, tried and executed, that is sufficient. Compassion fairness concerns for due process of the law are all signs of weakness. Cruelty asserts strength.

In the early 1980s, several bureaucrats in the Housing Ministry were accused of accepting bribes. They were sentenced to die.

"All of us in the office were ordered to attend the hanging," says a former mid level bureaucrat, who now lives in London. He and his colleagues were led into a prison courtyard, where their friends were marched out with sacks tied over their heads. They watched and listened as the accused begged, wept and protested their innocence. One by one they were hanged. According to one estimate, more than 3000 Iraqis were executed in.

HIDDEN ARSENAL

So what is Saddam sitting on? Since he ousted UN weapons inspectors from Iraq in 1998, it has been tough for US intelligence analysts to size up his stockpile. We know he has potent conventional weapons: Soviet -designed T-72 tanks, helicopter, gunship and surface to air missiles. But Iraq is also equipped with short range cruise and tactical missiles-particularly troubling because they can potentially deliver weapons of mass destruction.

This chart shows some of Saddam's biological and chemical weaponry, along with the amounts of each agent that Iraq admitted to producing by the end of the Gulf War. Moreover, while Saddam claims to have destroyed all equipments and facilities that could be used to develop nuclear weapons, virtually no one believes him. Almost certainly Iraqi scientists are forging ahead with a nuclear weapons programme.

1981 and 1982. But lost among Saddam's most outrageous atrocities are smaller acts that shed light on his personality.

Lieutenant General Omar Al-Hazzaa was verheard-speaking ill of the great Uncle in 1990. He was not just sentenced to death Saddam ordered that prior to his execution his tongue be cut out. For good measures, he also executed al-Hazzaa's son and bulldozed Al-Hazzaa's homes, leaving his wife and other children on the street.

BLUNDER

By 1990, the horrific eight years war with Iran had left lakhs of Iranians and Iraqui dead and cost Iraq billions. Despite the huge losses, Saddam was flushed with victory.

Emboldened by his military might, he planned to over run neighboring Kuwait, with its rich oil deposits. He gambled the world would not care. It was one of the great military miscalculations of modern history. The United States and its allies began assembling one of the largest military forces ever in the region.

It was apparent to everyone in the Iraqi military that they could not stand up against the United States. Saddam, however, to be intimidated. His plan was to capture US soldiers and tie them up around Iraqi tanks, using them as human shields. "The Americans will never fire on their own soldiers", he declared. Then his troops would roll unopposed into eastern Saudi Arabia, forcing the allies to back down.

Biological	Description	Declared
Anthrax	Bacteria cause fever, septic Shock, difficulty breathing, death in 24-72 hours.	87,007 litres
Botulinum Toxin	Toxin causes blurred vision, difficulty swallowing, paralysis, Respiratory failure, death in as few as 24 hours.	380,030 liters
Aflaxtoxin Gas	A mould toxin; can cause hemorrhage, convulsions, coma, liver cancer, death Bacterial	2195 litres
Gangrene	infection can cause tissue death, shock, and kindney failure, coma, often death.	3407 litres

Chemical	Description	Declared
VX Merve Gas	Disrupts nervous system, causes convulsions, respiratory paralysis, death.	4 tonnes (Intelligence estimate: over 200 tonnes)
Saqrin	Attack nervous system paralyses muscles used for breathing: can cause death within minutes.	100 to 150 tonnes; (Intelligence estimate : upto 350 tonnes)
Mustard Gas	As liquid causes skin and eye burns and blisters, Inhaled, can cause long term respiratory disease Cancer.	00 to 600 tonnes: (Intelligence estimate : upto 800 tonnes).

Wafic Samarai, Iraqi's chief of military intelligence, knew Saddam's plan was preposterous. At a meeting in Saddam's office, Samarai swallowed hand and delivered his grim assessment, backed up with photographs, news reports and statistics. The Iraqis could expect nothing more than swift defeat, he said.

Saddam listened to his assessment and then said confidently," I will now tell you my opinion. Our forces will put up more of a flight than you think. They will fight for a long time, and there will be many casualties, the Americans would not accept the losses of large numbers of their soldiers. The American people are weak." Samarai was flabbergasted.

Heavy aerial attacks began three days later. Five weeks after that, the ground offensive began, and Saddam's troops surrendered or fled. Thousands were killed. The war unfolded just as Samarai had predicted.

Since the, Saddam has responded with even wilder schemes, Predicting victory in what he refers to as the "Mother of All Battles," a show down with the United States. To that end, he started secret Programmes to develop nuclear, chemical and biological weapons (see "Hidden Arsenal" on page 133).

DESTINY

Over the years, Saddam has escaped death on numerous occasions, each time strengthening his conviction that his path is divinely inspired and that greatness is his destiny. He has ordered genealogists to construct a plausible family tree linking him to Fatima, daughter of Prophet Mohammad.

If Saddam has a religion, it is a belief in the superiority of Arab history and culture, a tradition he is notion of history has nothing to do with progress, the advance of knowledge, the evolution of individual rights and liberties, the things that matter most to civilized people. It has to do simply with power. To Saddam, the present global domination by the west is just a historical quirk, a consequence of its having acquired technological advantages. It cannot endure.

When-Arabia-the wellspring of civilization - rises again, Saddam believes he will be judged a great natural leader, the likes of which his world has not seen in 13 centuries.

"His aim is to be leader of Iraq for as long as he lives," says Samarai. "This is difficult, even without the United States targeting you. The Iraqis are a divided and ruthless people. To accomplish his rule, Saddam has shed too much blood."

He wants to be leader of Iraq
for as long as he lives
Difficult even without the US targeting you.

This, ultimately, is why Saddam will fail. His cruelty has created waves of hatred and fear. His speeches no longer resonate even in the Arab world, where he is despised by secular liberals and Muslim conservatives a like. The loyalty of those who protect him is based on fear and self-interest, and will tilt decisively if and when an alternative appears. Saddam's enemies are numerous, strong and determined. His dreams of pan Arabia and his historical role in it grow ever more fanciful. Any man who reads as much as he does and who studies the dictators of modern history must be aware that in the end, they are disdained and toppled.

As Saddam retreats to his secret bed each night, he must it will end badly for him.

INTO THE MIND OF TERROR

Through out his capture and conviction, Oklohma City Timonthy MCVeigh maintained a stony silence. What drove him to commit an act of such unspeakable cruelty? Now reporters unmask the man whose face became syrionmous with evil.

WHEN A BOMB BLEW UP a government building in Oklahoma City, USA everyone wanted to know: who was Timothy Mc Veigh and why would any one do such a thing?

Veteran newsman Lou Michel and Dan Herbeck started digging for answers-and ended up in their own yards. Tim Mc Veigh had grown up in his father's house about 20 minutes away from where Lou Michel lived. Capitalizing on local contacts as well as their best investigate instincts, Michel and Herback were able to get to Mc Veigh's father, and then to Timothy Mc Veigh himself-who, from his death-row cell, divulged what was going through his murderous mind that fateful day.

NO MERCY

DAWN, April 19, 1995.

He woke with the sun on this Wednesday, yawning and stretching in the cab of the truck. He'd slept like a body in the rented truck, less than a meter in front of a 3000-kilo bomb.

The padded seat in the big yellow truck had been like a fine hotel had compared with many of the places he'd slept in recent years, in Army, he'd learned how to sleep without being comfortable.

He had also learned how crucial rest was when you were preparing for action, and there would be plenty of action today. Timothy Mc Veigh was going to teach the American government a lesson. He intended to strike back for Waco, for Ruby Ridge, for high taxes, for gun laws and a host of other grievances he'd been amassing for years.

He reached below the cost and pulled out an envelope made of thick brown plastic. He peeled open the wrapping, pulled out a food packet and tore it open. This was breakfast, a spaghetti MRE or meal-ready-to-eat. High in calories and carbohydrates, it was specially formulated for soldiers on the move. Energy food. He would need every bit of it to steal himself for what was to come.

After finishing his meal. Mc Veigh got out and thoroughly examined his truck, checking the tyres, making sure that the rear and side doors to the cargo box were securely locked.

All this came naturally to him. He was a detail man meticulous and tireless. He was not, those who knew him would agree, an overtly violent or nasty person. Yet here he was, four days shy of his 27th birthday, preparing to use a truck bomb to destroy an office building filled with people he had never met-a mission he considered an act of war.

Mc Veigh checked the gun he carried close to his heart, in a leather holster across his chest. It could fire 16 bullets without reloading, and he was prepared to use it to kill anyone who interfered with his task.

He was dressed in faded black jeans and Army boots with a windbreaker over his favorite T-shirt, worn as a token of his defiance. On the front was a drawing of Abraham Lincoln. Underneath was the Latin refrain that John Wilkes Booth screamed after he assassinated Lincoln-Sic Semper tyrannies ("Thus ever to Tyrants").

On the back of the shirt was a picture of a tree dripping blood, bearing a quotation from 19th century US President Thomas Jefferson: "The tree of liberty must be refreshed from time to time with the blood of patriots and tyrants."

A lot of blood will be shed today, Mc Veigh thought. Innocent people will suffer. But there is no other way.

He found the truck to be in good running order. He'd checked all the fluid levels the night before when he stopped for petrol.

Timothy Mc Veigh turned the key in the ignition, threw the truck into gear and headed for Oklahoma City.

CALCULATIONS

As he drove down the high way, Mc Veigh carefully obeyed the speed limit. With 3000 kilos of explosives behind him, he could hardly afford a traffic accident. But he had another tactical reason for taking his time. He had planned the bombing for 9 a.m. he did not want tc get there too early before the Alfred P. Murrah government building in Oklahoma City filled up with people. He wanted his body count.

At least two of the agencies he most despised- the Bureau of Alcohol, Tobacco and Firearms (A T F), and the Drug Enforcement Administration had offices in the Murrah building, as did the secret service. The other agencies housed there were all part of a government Mc Veigh regarded as evil and out of control.

Both fuses burning and his fingers tight on the steering wheel, Mc Veigh willed the red light to change.

To justify what he was about to do, he summoned up a favorite movie from childhood; Star Wars. Mc Veigh likened himself to Luke Sky walker, the heroic Jedi knight whose attack on the Death Star is the climax of the film. Mc Veigh dismissed the killing of secretaries. receptionists and other personnel with the same cold blood calculation. They were all part of an evil empire.

Mc Veigh had carefully scouted every aspect of his plan. On a previous trip to Oklahoma City he had worked out the exact route he would take, looking fir speed traps high way construction, possible road hazards and especially, under passes too low for the truck.

About 8:50 a.m. Mc Veigh entered Oklahoma City the weather was warm and sunny, the sky a brilliant blue. Most people were just setting into what promised to be an ordinary workday.

Mc Veigh wore no expression as he sat at the wheel of the truck. He drives on, scanning his surroundings and reviewing every contingency he might face in the moments ahead.

Expecting to be either captured or killed after the bombing, he had filled a plain white envelope with articles explaining his antigovernment ideology. No matter how things turned out, he counted on the police getting hold of the documents and leaking them to the news media.

At a stoplight he took a moment to cram a pair of green foam earplugs into his ears. As the rented vehicle rumbled along, nobody thought any think of it. Such trucks drove through the city all the time.

He was surprised at how little traffic there was, keeping his eyes peeled for on lookers, Mc Veigh pulled to the side of the road just long enough to take out a lighter and ignite the five-minute fuse to his bomb.

Soon the truck cab filled with the acrid smell of burning gunpowder. As Mc Veigh continued along, he rolled down both windows to let out some of the smoke.

Near the target, he stopped for a traffic light. Now he lit a second, shorter fuse-the one he had measured at approximately minutes. For 30 seconds, Mc Veigh sat watching the red light. With both fuses burning and his fingers tight on the stearing wheel, he glared at the light, willing it to change.

When it finally turned green. Mc Veigh made sure to ease away from the inter section. No stamping on the accelerator. No trantric movements.

Approaching the building, he spot red the location he had chosen for bomb a drop off point, several car lengths long, cut into the pavement on the north side of the structure.

No other vehicle was there when he arrived. Mc Veigh breathed a sigh of relief. If the drop off spot had been filled, he had planned to drive on to the pavement and crash his truck into the building. That would not be necessary now.

As calmly as any ordinary deliveryman, Mc Veigh parked his vehicle. He was right below the tinted windows of a day care center on the first floor.

He looked over his creation one last time. The fuses were burning. The vehicle was exactly where he wanted it, its back close to the building. He grabbed the envelope full of anti government articles, locked the truck and walked away.

Mc Veigh counted off the seconds to himself as he headed north into an alley. He was about 150 meters from ground zero when he broke into a jog.

That bomb should have blown by now, he thought. For an instant he wondered if some thing might have gone wrong. Then he heard the roar. And felt it.

DEVASTATING BLAST

When the Murrah building exploded, it lifted Tim Mc Veigh nearly three centimeters off the ground. Even muffled by earplugs, the sound was deafening. The blast rocked hundreds of building in the area.

Looking up, Mc Veigh could see the buildings near him wobbling from to side, plate glass showering down into the street. He felt the confusion buffeting his cheeks. A live power line snapped and whipped towards Mc Veigh. Some falling bricks struck him in the leg, but he was able to hop out of the way of the power of the line. Smoke and dust billowed high into the air. Fires erupted.

Just like at Waco, thought Mc Veigh. Reap what you sow. He reached his get away car. It was still in a car park some distance from the blast site. He had placed a "Do Not Tow" sign in the windshield. It was still there. No one, it seemed, had interfered with it.

But when Mc Veigh got behind the wheel, the car did not start. He tried several times, the engine would not turn over.

He stamped the accelerator to the floor. Finally the engine coughed to life. Tires squealed as he shot out of the car park.

I do not want to get caught in Oklahoma City, he thought. The automatic transmission was slipping badly as Mc Veigh headed north. By 9:10 am eight minutes after the bombing, he was heading out of the city, driving carefully under the speed limit.

An observer watching the scene from a helicopter would have seen many people rushing towards the crippled building. They would have seen drivers abandoning cars and running to the blast scene. They would have seen the flashing emergency lights on police cars, fire engines and ambulances, all heading towards the rising dust and smoke.

Mc Veigh's bomb killed 167 people, including 19 children aged five and younger, 163 of the victims had been inside the building, 168th victims dies while assisting in rescue efforts. Over half the dead worked for the government. The others did not. Many of the dead would not be positively identified for several days.

In the chaos, few would have noticed an old yellow car. Though he was not exactly eager to get caught, there was a part of him that was curious to see how things would play out if he did.

He'd put his future in the hands of fate by leaving the license plate off his car. Ultimately, he figured, some officer would pull him over for the missing plate, but he hopped it would happen in another state. He was counting on the cops being to busy with the bombing to bother with anything else.

Mc Veigh rolled on through the countryside. Nearly a hundred kilometers north of Oklahoma City, he saw a high way patrol car by the roadside. A trooper stood outside the vehicle, looking over a van. Probably speeding arrest, Mc Veigh thought.

About 20 minutes later Mc Veigh saw what looked like the same trooper in his rear view mirror. The cop was in the passing lane, roaring up a long side Mc Veigh.

The Car was almost past him when Mc Veigh noticed the front end dip slightly. The police cruiser slowed down and fell along side Mc Veigh's car. The trooper at the wheel was Charles Hanger, a 19 years police veteran.

For Hanger, the morning had already been hectic. Shortly after the bombing, he and other troopers had been directed to hurry to the command post in Oklahoma City. But the order was soon cancelled. They already had enough help at the post.

Hanger was indeed the trooper Mc Veigh had seen by the roadside. He had been helping two women get assistance for their disable van. Then, as Hanger headed back north, he saw Mc Veigh's car without the license plate.

As he drove wheel to wheel with the other car, Hanger glanced over and nodded Mc Veigh nodded back. The trooper then fell behind him and turned on his emergency flasher, directing him to stop.

Mc Veigh complied, easing the right tires of his car onto the grass. It was decision time. He considered pulling out his gun and killing the trooper. It had a Black Talon bullet, known for expanding with lethal effect on contact, ready in the chamber.

If I want him, I can take him Mc Veigh thought.

MINOR CRIMES

As Hanger stepped out of his car, Mc Veigh emerged from his as well. He sized up the trooper. If he drew on him, he figured the element of surprise plus his expertise, as a former Army marksman would put the officer at a servere disadvantage.

Then Mc Veigh thought again: No. If Hanger had been working for the US government, Mc Veigh would have probably started shooting. But he had a grudging respect for local and state cops and their right to do their jobs. He would not draw his gun on this officer of the law.

For his part, Hanger wondered what Mc Veigh was up to as he watched the younger man step out. Most people just sat in their cars, nervously waiting for the trooper to approach. Hanger stood behind his open car door, watching Mc Veigh's hands closely as he came forward.

Cautiously, the trooper began walking towards the other man. He looked at Mc Veigh's car. "You don't have a license plate," Hanger said.

Mc Veigh glanced at the rear bumper of car "Eh. No," he said.

The trooper kept a wary eye on him. "Do you have insurance?"

"No, I just bought the car."

"Have you a registration? Do you have a bill of sale?"

"Not yet, but I have a license.

Mc Veigh pulled out his wallet. As he look out his driver's license, Hanger noticed a bulge under Mc Veigh's windbreaker "What's that?" he asked.

"I have a gun," Mc Veigh replied calmly. Hanger felt for the gun. Then he pulled out his own gun and pointed it a Mc Veigh "Move your hands away, slowly," he instructed. "Get both hands up in the air."

The trooper pointed his gun at Mc Veigh's head and reached around to remove the other gun from its shoulder holster.

"My gun is loaded," he warned the officer.

"So is mine," Hanger said and directed Mc Veigh to put his hands on the boot of the car and spread his legs.

Mc Veigh told the officer that he would find a clip of ammunition and knife attached to his belt. Hanger removed them and the gun and tossed them away. He then hand cuffed Mc Veigh's hands and asked why he was carrying a weapon.

It was his legal right to carry it, Mc Veigh insisted. "You know when you carry a gun around like that, one wrong move could get you shot," the trooper told him.

"Possible", Mc Veigh said.

Hanger marched his hand cuffed prisoner to the police car. He then radioed headquarters to run a computer check on Mc Veigh. The report came back quickly. Timothy Mc Veigh had never been arrested in his life.

Hanger also asked for a check on Mc Veigh's gun. The gun was not stolen.

The trooper then searched Mc Veigh's car but noted nothing unusual except for a scaled white envelope in the front seat. Soon they were heading towards jail.

When they got there. Mc Veigh took off his jacket and Hanger got his first look at the odd T-shirt that his prisoner was wearing. The trooper had never seen one like it, with its picture of Lincoln on the front and an illustration of a tree on the back. But he did not really read the slogans.

Marsha Moritz, the jailor, booked Mc Veigh on four changes: transporting a loaded firearm in a motor vehicle, unlawfully carrying a weapon, failing to display a license plate, and failing to maintain proof of insurance.

The booking process went routinely until Moritz Told Mc Veigh she needed to know his next of kin. After an awkward silence, he gave the name of James Nichols. Mc Veigh's driver's license listened Nichols farm as his home address.

"You carry a gun around, one wrong move could get you shot," The trooper said. "Possible," Mc Veigh answered.

Moritz took the prisoner's mug shot. In his thick- soled combat boots, Mc Veigh was well over six foot two. He seemed surprisingly relaxed for a man being arrested. As Moritz prepared to finger print him, he was asked to wipe the perspiration off his hands, as prisoners tend to sweat from nervousness.

"No problem," Mc Veigh said. "My hands are dry."

The two chatted briefly, Mc Veigh even kidding around with Moritz a little.

But the light mood did not last long. A TV set was in the office, and the on going board cast about the bombing cast a pall over everyone in the jail. Mc Veigh, pretending to be paying little attention, was watching and listening to every word.

His initial reaction to what his bomb had done was disappointment. Danaher though. The building did not come down. Mc Veigh then heard someone in the jail office mention how horrible it was that the blast had destroyed a day care center in the building, killing a group of children. This news stopped him, he had not planned for children to be among his victims. Then a more cold-blooded reaction kicked in. The deaths innocent children would over shadow his political message. In the court of public opinion, this would be a disaster for his cause. The media's going to latch to that, he thought.

Everyone in the office listened closely as a TV reporter gave the first sketchy descriptions of a possible suspect: white male, somewhere between five foot nine and six foot one. A police man eyeballed Mc Veigh."Hey, you are a recent arrival," he said.

"That's not me," said Mc Veigh, laughing off the suggestion.

Rescuers were still pulling bodies out of the building. Everyone- both jailers and prisoners alike-watched in stunned disbelief. How did this happen? Who would do such a thing? They wondered.

Mc Veigh concentrated, maintaining his poker face. More than anyone, he knew that the answers were elusive. As a psychiatrist would later suggest, the path he had traveled to this point stretched back through his unsettled life the breakup of his persons, his Gulf War experience, and the tragedy at Waco.

AN UNSATISFACTORY REALITY

In many ways Timothy Mc Veigh was like millions of young, middle-class American man. He had grown up the son of a factory worker, in love with TV, movies and the outdoors. He liked football and comic books about super heroes.

Mc Veigh's mother, Mickey, was boisterous and enjoyed exchanging stories and jokes with friends. In contrast, Mc Veigh's father, Bill, was shy and quiet, homebody.

Small and scrawny for his age, Timothy Mc Veigh was ten when another boy while playing baseball him walloped him.

Stunned, the youngster ran to his father's car, hid in the back seat and cried. He was scared and embarrassed the men of the Mc Veigh family were not supposed to shed tears. Now here he was bawling his dyes out.

Indeed, Timothy Mc Veigh felt like a failure in the eyes of his father. He lacked the aggressive mentality, the muscle coordination and the size to be a star athlete.

By adolescence, size and coordination caught up with Tim. But his humiliation at the hands of the bully on the baseball field was something he remembered forever. Over time, he developed a see thing hatred of bullies of any person or institution that he perceived to be picking on the weak.

The fundamental differences between Bill Mc Veigh and his wife finally became too much. In December 1979 the couple separated, letting the children decide where they wanted to live.

Their two daughters, Patty and Jennifer, wanted to stay together with their mother. But Tim cast his lot with his father. "I don't want Dad to be alone," he said.

The real problem, Tim Mc Veigh said latter, was that he never really fell close to his parsents. With both of them working full time, he never had an adult to talk with when he came home from school.

Even when Tim's mother returned to try to work out her differences with Bill. It didn't bring the boy any closer to his family. The only persons he would actually and unabashedly say he loved was his paternal grandfather, Ed Mc Veigh.

Tim was developed to the graying and is spectacled older man and his feelings were met with unconditional love. Their relationship revolved around a common interest: guns. On regular outing the two would walk to a ravine where they practiced target shooting with a rifle. Their Grandpa Mc Veigh would offer bits of wisdom.

"When you're carrying a gun on the road, the ammunition is always sin your back pocket," Ed would say.

"When you're shooting, make sure you have something behind you and consider the possibility of a bullet ricocheting."

Again and again Tim saw things in his grandpa that he wished he could see in his dad. The words I love you never rolled easily off shy Bill Mc Veigh's tongue. As long as he provided the necessities- a good home, food and a few extra bills felt his actions are spoke love.

Blessed with a high lQ, Tim stayed out of trouble in school. He became a devotee of action heroes and filled his bedroom with boxes of super hero comics. These fantasy adventures were a welcome distraction from the furious words he heard more and more often coming from his parents; bedroom. Some nights he lay in bed frightened at times his parents seemed so angry he feared they might kill each other.

Looking increasingly to escape, Tim took refuge in imaginary games. One neighbour, Liz Mc Dermott, recalled that when the youngster came over, he'd transformed the house into a battleground field with toy soldiers. Tim also engineered elaborate catching games with torches. He would draw down the shades and turn off the lights, and then he'd move through the house trying to catch the others with the torch beam. "We'd fall on the floor and freeze for a while," his younger sister, Jennifer, recalled.

But his super hero imagining were only temporary, and Tim would always find himself once more facing an unsatisfactory reality.

SOMETHING MISSING

When the Mc Veigh's marriage ended for good in 1986, Tim was in his final year in high school. It was during this year that he found Sarah, his first real girl friend.

For six months they were very close. But then Tim abruptly broke off the relationship. "I'm not ready to get serious," he explained.

Soon after passing out from school, Tim opted to work. For self-education he read gun magazines and ordered books. One title that captivated him was To Ride, Shoot Strait, and Speak the Truth by Jeff — Cooper, an expert on self-defense and firearms. A sort of training manual, the books broader messages resonated in Tim's fertile young mind. He liked the idea of going through life in a combat mind-set, aware of his surrounding at all times.

The Turner Diaries was another book that hit a never. This 1978 novel by whiter supremeist William Pierce told the story of Earl Turner, a gun enthusiast who reacts to tighter firearms laws by making a truck bomb and destroying the FBI's headquarters in Washington.

The possibility that the government might take guns away from law-abiding citizens seemed a very real threat to Tim. He decided to start collecting his own firearms. To finance his appetite, he become an armed security guard.

Tim enjoyed his guns and newfound independence, but he still fell something was missing from his life. When a family friend suggested he enlist in the military, he listened carefully. By May 1988 he had made up this mind.

Mc Veigh threw himself into Army life. He enjoyed it all the 5 a.m. wake-ups, crude jokes, even the uniform inspections. Mostly he loved anything to do with firearms.

William David Dilly, his room mate for over a year noticed the attention Mc Veigh paid to detail, and his desire to perform his duties better than any one else. Mc Veigh reveled in long marches in the scorching sun, crawling on his belly under the barbed wire. What Tim really loved was night guard duty, when he could be alone with nature, gazing in silence at a sky so rich and black that he could see the outlines of the Milky Way.

Mc Veigh also formed a powerful bond with Terry Lynn Nichols the oldest recruit in the company. An intense, compelling man, Nichols had a number of jobs before the army, and made it clear he deeply disliked the government.

With his spectacles and slight build, he was not imposing, but he tried himself with an air of maturity that made Mc Veigh and others look up to him.

After basic training Mc Veigh was posted to the First Infantry Division. Joining him were Nichols and another soldier, Michel Fortier, who shared many of Mc Veigh's political views?

At his new posting, Mc Veigh was devoted to becoming the best soldier on the base. He even went to the expense of keeping a separate uniform, specially starched and dry cleaned, and buying an extra pair of boots and additional gear just so he could have them in immaculate condition for his follow soldiers noticed he kept dozens of books and magazines on firearms stacked next to his bunk.

Though not particularly talkative, whenever the subject of gun rights came up, Mc Veigh's blue eyes would flesh in anger. He would then launch into intense speeches about guns and men who stood for liberty and freedom from Government, no matter what the cost.

Determined to be the top gunner in his unit, Mc Veigh trained hard. Eventually, he got a perfect of 1000 the best in his Battalion.

His sterling record resulted in his receiving orders to try out for the Army's elite Special Forces. But before he could report, Saddam Hussain invaded Kuwait and Mc Veigh's company was told to prepare for combat duty in the Persian Gulf.

The young soldier did not like too seeing the United States meddling in the affairs of smaller nations. At the same time, Saddam appeared to be the kind of leader he hated most- a bully, brutally attacking a smaller and weaker neighbor. Someone had to stand up to him.

Mc Veigh arrived in Saudi Arabia in January 1991, part an enormous Allied force. On February 24 a huge explosion in the pre-dawn hours told Mc Veigh that he was about to get his chance to fight.

On the second day of the ground war, his crew spotted a dug-in-enemy machine gun nest nearly two kilometers away. Mc Veigh's platoon leader ordered him to fire.

Pressing his forehead against the viewfinder, Sergeant Mc Veigh zeroed in on the target. An Iraqi soldier popped his head up for a second. Mc Veigh fired, and everything above the Soldier's shoulders disappeared. The same shot, a 25 mm high explosive round, killed another Iraqi soldier standing a meter or so away.

"Did you see that?" a fellow gunner exclaimed. "Great shot."

Yet Mc Veigh was emotionally torn about what he had done. This was the first time he had fired at a human being. In a way, it had been a great thrill, putting his skills to the test and succeeding. But later, Mc Veigh found this first test of killing made him angry and uncomfortable.

The carnage he saw in the war left him with a feeling of sorrow. Beating the Iraqis was almost too easy. It rankled Mc Veigh further to be part of a United Nations force that, he feared, was eventually planning to take over the world.

In late March 1991 Mc Veigh got good news he was ordered back to the United States, to the Special Forces Selection and Assessment Course. His future was brimming with promise.

RUDE AWAKENING

Since the day he'd joined the Army, Mc Veigh had been hoping for a chance to join one of its special units. But when he reported for duty, he quickly realized he wasn't ready.

The three months he spent in the Persian Gulf had broken him down, physically and emotionally. The commanding officers recognized this difficulty, and they called all the Gulf War veterans together, inviting them to defer their tryouts.

An Iraqi popped his head up for a second. Mc Veigh fired. Everything above the soldier's shoulders disappeared.

"No," one of the proud Desert Storm veterans yelled out. "We're ready".

Peer pressure took hold. Asking to delay the tryout might be seen as a sign of weakness, Mc Veigh thought. He decided to go ahead.

It was a mistake- and a critical one. The grueling 24-day programme was designed to push the soldiers much further than anything they had seen in basic training. Just two days into the assessment programme, Mc Veigh surrendered. Though still a couple of weeks short of his 23rd birthday, he felt like a tired old man.

"I just can't do it" Mc Veigh told the commanding officer. His three years in the military had been one success after another, but now his star was falling. By late 1991, tired and disillusioned, he decided to leave the Army altogether.

When he returned home, Mc Veigh still had high expectations for his future. After all, he had gone off to war and come back with chestful medals. But he didn't work out that way. A disappointed Mc Veigh found himself trading in his crisp Green army uniform for the dull shirt and slacks of a security guard.

He made the best of it, but the demanding schedule-80 hours some weeks took a toll. Becoming angry and sullen, he began to request posts giving him the least possible exposure to the public.

During this time, McVeigh was staying with his father. Even just three people linving there- Bill, Tim and Jennifer, who had rejoined her father- the little house felt crowded. Tim Mc Veigh was unable to get enough rest, and he grew increasingly irritable. A disheartening realization finally hit hum: I don't fit in here any more.

DOWNWARD SPIN

Less than three months after returning from the Army, Mc Veigh hurried out of his father's house one snowy day in a state of panic. He had to get away, but where? He climbed into his car and drove over to his grandfather's home. Tears streaming down his face, Mc Veigh knocked on the door.

"Timmy, what are you doing? Said Ed Mc Veigh ushering him inside. He saw the tears. "Tim," Ed said. "What's wrong?"

"Grandpa……I can't tell you," Mc Veigh answered.

Ed suggested his grandson come in and lie down for a while. As Tim lay there, he was overcome by dark thoughts he even considered killing himself, but stopped because he knew how much it would hurt his grandfather. Finally his anxiety subsiding, he fell into a deep sleep.

Later Tim would come to believe he had suffered from post-traumatic stress disorder brought on by the gulf war whatever the cause of his depression, he began reading more anti government books and sharing them with his inquisitive younger sister. Some of the literature struck Jennifer as bizarre, but she looked up to her older brother and was flattered he would share his political views with her.

In the summer of 1992 Mc Veigh pointed to the events of Ruby Ridge as proof that his theories were correct. On August 21 Central government agents got into a shoot out at the Cabin of Randy Weaver, a white separatist accused of selling illegal shotguns to a government informant. By the time Weaver was finally arrested his wife and son, and a government official had been killed.

Ruby Ridge reinforced Mc Veigh's belief that America was becoming a police state. Whenever Tim saw a newscast detailing some inept government operation, or any example of faltering leadership, he'd shout and throw things at the TV.

Frustrated and restless, Tim Mc Veigh felt he had to make a change he told his dad he was leaving to search for a place where he could find more personal freedom. Tim spent the next 26 months traveling, mostly from gun show to gun show, selling books and survival items.

During this time something happened that would galvanize him in February 1993 US government agents raided the home and church of a religious group known as the Branch Davidians in Waco, Texas, Agents arrived to execute a search warrant for illegal weapons. A shootout erupted, taking the lives of four agents and injuring more than a dozen. On the Branch Davidian side, six people died and more were wounded, including David Koresh, their strange and charismatic leader.

The agents then retreated, Koresh and his followers remained inside their compound.

Nobody in America followed the stand off closer than Mc Veigh Day after day he devoured every articles and broadcast account he could find. Finally, he decided he had to go to see for himself. He packed up his car with a supply of antigovernment materials and headed for Waco.

When he arrived, he was stopped at a checkpoint nearly six kilometers from the compound.

As Mc Veigh reluctantly turned his car around, he watched the agents gathered in a circle. His mind swung into military mode. I could take them all out with one hand grenade, he thought.

Mc Veigh left Waco after a few days. He attended a gun show and finally found his way to the farm of Army Bundy Terry Nichols, who lived with his mother. With the help of Terry and his brother James, Mc Veigh hoped to learn how to live self sufficiently off the land.

On the afternoon of April 19, 1993, as Mc Veigh was changing the oil in his car, a voice shouted from inside the farmhouse, "Tim it's on fire".

Mc Veigh raced inside. On the TV the Branch Davidian complex was burning. He stood, transfixed, watching the flames and the armored vehicles ramming the walls.

The blaze in Waco, more than any single event, was a turning point in Mc Veigh's life. He felt it epitomized the arrogance of central government law enforcement agents in dealing with the public-everything that was wrong with intrusive government.

LAST, THIN THREAD

A month later Mc Veigh visited his old friend Michael Fortier. His hatred for the government had taken on a sharp new edge and he angrily shared his views with his friend.

Mc Veigh continued to bounce one gun show to the next. He was still seething about Waco when news arrived in September 1994 that a new assault-weapons ban was becoming law.

To Mc Veigh, his heritage, his income and perhaps his very life were threatened. It was time to take action.

Mc Veigh revealed to Michael Fortier that he was going to blow up a government building and he asked Fortier to join him.

"No," his friend answered. "I would never do anything like that, unless, there was a tank in my front yard."

Undoubted on October 4, 1994, Mc Veigh rented a storage locker. Soon afterwards, Mc Veigh appeared at Fortier's home and told Michael he wanted to show him something. Frothier came outside and found Terry Nichols waiting for them in his truck. They drove to the storage locker, where Mc Veigh pulled back a blanket covering a stack of boxes. Fortier saw that the top box contained explosives.

Mc Veigh said the explosives had come from a quarry near where Nichols was now living. He described how, a few nights earlier, he and Nichols had robbed it.

Mc Veigh checked the boxes carefully, looking for the freshest explosives.

"Like shopping for milk," he thought.

It was drizzling when the two men arrived at the quarry. Mc Veigh walked around each of the lockers to make sure there weren't any burglar alarms. He drilled out the padlocks and the door swung open. His torch shone on crates of Tovex, a high-explosive gel shaped like 40-centimeter long sausages.

Mc Veigh carefully examined each 30-kilo box, checking the dates. He knows the older the material, the less effective it was. He grabbed seven of the fresher boxes. Like shopping for milk, he thought.

Mc Veigh had already managed to assemble 1800 kilos of ammonium nitrate and was now eager to conduct a test of the ingredients he planned to use in his bomb's main charge. He loaded the materials in a truck and invited Fortier to watch the detonation. Fortier refused, commenting, "It looks like a lot of trouble." So Mc Veigh himself exploded the bomb out in the desert.

Later, alone with Fortier and his wife, Lori, Mc Veigh told them that he had figured out how to convert a truck into a bomb. He had also chosen a target the Alfred P. Murrah government building in Oklahoma City. They explosion would occur on the second anniversary of Waco April 19, 1995.

"What about all the people?" Fortier asked. "Think about the people as if they were storm troopers in Star Wars," Mc Veigh answered. "They may be individually innocent, but they are guilty because they work for the evil Empire".

Mc Veigh had chosen the Murrah Building for several reasons. The front of the structure was made of glass, which would shatter from the explosion. The car park across the street would minimize collateral damage deaths and injuries to the people in nearby non-government buildings. This was something; Mc Veigh claimed, he was genuinely concerned about.

But another colder calculation influenced his final choice the photo opportunities. He wanted a site with open space around it, to allow for the best possible news photos and television footage. He wanted to create a stark, horrifying image that would make everyone who saw it stop and take notice.

In late October, Mc Veigh's plans were disrupted when he got the news that his grandfather, Ed, had died. Mc Veigh returned home to help his father. In a sense, his grandfather's death freed him. He no longer had to worry about him ever finding out about his grandson's involvement in the bombing. Mc Veigh knew the crime would have emotionally destroyed Ed, but now that thin thread of restraint was gone.

A FRIGHTENING RAGE

On Friday, April 14, Mc Veigh registered at a motel called Dreamland giving the Nichols farm as his address. The next morning he finalized the rental of a six-meter tuck, using the name Robert D. Kling. On Easter Sunday, Mc Veigh arranged to meet Terry Nichols at a cafe. But Nichols failed to show up.

In the last few weeks Mc Veigh had begun to suspect that his friend's enthusiasm for the bombing was waning. As he waited impatiently, his anger grew.

Infuriated, Mc Veigh finally called him. When he answered, Mc Veigh let loose, screaming so loud that Nichols's son, Josh, could hear his voice through the phone three meters away. Mc Veigh cursed Nichols, threatening him and his family. "Get in your truck," he screamed now. This is for keeps.

Finally Nichols gave in perhaps afraid that Mc Veigh would make good his threats.

The men arrived in Oklahoma City in the evening. Mc Veigh parked his yellow get away car, at some distance away from the Murrah Building. He placed a note on the windshield: Not Abandoned. Please do not Tow. Will Move by April 23 (Needs Battery & Cable).

The next day Mc Veigh got the truck, and the following morning he and Nichols headed for a lake. There, Mc Veigh later said, the two men went to work in the back of the truck. Mc Veigh combined nitro methane fluids with ammonium nitrate Fertilizer. It was a big job. The thirteen 210-Litres drums were each large enough to hold several bags of fertilizer and a bought 50 kilos of liquid fuel.

As work continued, the barrels were roughly arranged to form a letter T, with the top flush against front of the cargo bay wall closest to the truck's cab. The 3000 kilos needs to be equally distributed or the truck might flip over.

He then set up the dual ignition system he had designed. There would be a two-minute fuse as well as a second, five-minute fuse, which would serves as a back up.

The job of mixing the bomb completed, Mc Veigh wiped the inside of the truck's cab for fingerprints. Then he changed into a fresh set of clothes, put on a pair of gloves and climbed back into the cab. More three hours had passed since he and Nichols had started building the bomb. Now they would see each other as free, unshackled men.

WE FOUND HIM

Waking up in his cell on the morning of April 21, two days after the bombing, Mc Veigh wondered why agents hadn't come for him yet. Hadn't they discovered that staff in his get away car?

He would soon find out. Hundreds of agents and police officers had begun chasing leads all across the United States, hoping for a break that would lead them to the Murrah building bomber.

To many observers the obvious assumption was that foreign terrorists were responsible, However, the FBI's Clinton Van Zandt was offering a different opinion. Asked to put together a psychological profile of the Oklahoma bomber, Van Zandt said immediately that the date-April 19, the anniversary of the death at Waco was the key.

"You're going to have a white male, acting alone or with one other person," Van Zandt told colleagues. "He'll be in his mid-20s. He'll have military experience and be a fringe member of some militia group. He'll be angry at the government for what happened at Ruby Ridge and Waco."

The first break was recovering the trunck's 110-kilo rear axle. Agents found a confidential vehicle identification number stamped on it. Later, policeman digging through the rubble found the rear bumper from the same truck, its license plate intact.

A series of computer checks showed that someone had rented the truck two days earlier, named Robert Kling. Less than eight hours after the bombing, agents were on their way to the shop where the truck had been rented. The next morning, using information from workers who had seen Robert Kling an FBI artist drew up composite sketches of both him and another man who was in the shop.

Agents spent the day taking the sketches door to door through out the area. On Thursday, April 20, the evening after the bombing, they hit pay dirt at the Dreamland Motel. The manger recognized one of the suspects as a recent guest. But she didn't know him as Robert Kling. She knew him as Timothy Mc Veigh.

And yes, she recalled, she saw him in big yellow truck. And he had an old yellow car too. The authorities had their suspect.

And soon they had another lead. When he registered for his motel room, Mc Veigh had listed his residence as the Nichols family farm. Before long, investigators would be looking in the direction of his old Army buddy, Terry Nichols.

Mc Veigh was now the subject of an intense manhunt. A huge task force of investigators began making phone calls. May be, the investigators thought, this guy was already sitting in a jail somewhere.

And sure enough, within two days of the bombing Mc Veigh was located. When the news came, several task-force agents bolted from the room for a waiting helicopter. Meanwhile others started typing an arrest warrant. Later one would also be drawn up for Nichols.

Mc Veigh knew nothing of this as he sat in his cell on April 21, waiting to appear before a judge. The appearance was expected to be brief.

More than likely, the judge would release Mc Veigh on minimal bail. The matter was about as routine as it could get.

The prosecutor was standing in the courtroom, waiting for the session to begin, when he was given a note.

"This guy, Mc Veigh is the one FBI has been looking for in the bombing case." the note said. "We need to keep him in custody."

There was a prickly new vibration in the jail and Mc Veigh instantly picked it up. He could sense a change in the demean our of the employees and the other prisoners as well.

The people around him, he noticed, were giving him sideways glances.

"Mc Veigh," a policeman said, "there are some government agents here. They want to talk with you."

Mc Veigh agreed to see the agents, he wanted to find out what the government was up to. Two FBI men from the bombing task force, Special Agents Floyd Zimms and James Norman, Jr, were waiting in a room for him.

"Any idea why the FBI wants to talk to you?" Zimms asked Mc Veigh.

"That thing in Oklahoma City, I guess", Mc Veigh said.

"Exactly right," Zimms replied. "Our investigation has showed you may have information about the bombing."

By 5 p.m., 56 hours after the bombing, as team of agents had arrived, with orders to bring Mc Veigh back to Oklahoma City. Another team had already secured his get away car, which had been left by the high way, completely unattended, for more than two days.

A convoy of vehicles pulled up outside the courthouse to await the prisoner's emergence. Mc Veigh was still wearing the orange jail jump suit as he left the courthouse. The news photos and videos sent around the globe by satellite showed the prisoner; tall, wiry and grim, his eyes cold and narrow.

As cameras whirred, Mc Veigh squinted into the sun. He heard the screams of the crowd as he made his way towards a van, his shackled feet unable to move quickly. Mc Veigh did not turn his head, nor hunch his shoulders. He walked.

VISIONS OF VIOLENCE

After Mc Veigh's arrest, Dr John Smith was the court appointed psychiatrist assigned to examine him. Smith found the prisoner very intelligent; with an lQ of 126. As Mc Veigh calmly explained how he designed, built and delivered his bomb, the psychiatrist saw no signs of remorse. He talks about this crime like it's some kind of successful science project, he thought.

According to Smith, as a boy, Mc Veigh had been so upset by his parents; fighting that he invented a fantasy world." He created this super hero role for himself," Smith said. "He fantasized all these monsters, which he fought."

As an adult, Mc Veigh came top see the American government as the ultimate monster. The psychiatrist concluded Mc Veigh was not delusional that he knew exactly what he did.

After the trial, a fellow prisoner poured his heart out to Mc Veigh during a recreation period, telling him erect. He and a team of agents got into the van and left.

GUILTY AS CHARGED

Judge Ronald Howland called the hearing to order at 8.30 p.m. on April 21, almost 60 hours after the bombing. How his life had gone wrong?

When he finished, the inmate looked at Mc Veigh and asked, "Tim where did you go wrong?"

"I did not go wrong," Mc Veigh said.

Prosecution introduced the FBI arrest warrant accusing Mc Veigh of using an explosive device to "maliciously damage or destroy" the Murrah Building.

Mc Veigh sat ramrod straight, looking forward most of the time. With his court appointed defense lawyers beside him, the accused bomber told the judge that he understood the charges.

Afterwards marshals took Mc Veigh to a nearby medium security prison.

Mc Veigh's new court appointed attorney, Stephen Jones, brought in a psychiatrist to help determine whether Mc Veigh was competent to stand trial.

The doctor talked with the prisoner for nearly 25 hours, but found no signs of remorse as Mc Veigh dispassionately discussed the bombing.

"I expect to be convicted and expect to receive the death penalty", Mc Veigh told the psychiatrist.

He was right. In June 1997 a jury found him guilty and a few days later, sentenced him to death.

His fellow conspirator, Terry Nichols, would be sentenced to life in prison. Nichols continues to proclaim his innocence even as he faces murder. Michael Fortier later received 12 years for crimes including failing to warn the government of the bormbing.[15]

Timothy Mc Veigh was executed by lethal injection on the morning of June 11, 2001.

THE ALMOST PERFECT MURDER

Christine Elkins hesitates in the dark doorway.

Tony Emery, a muscular 34 year old, is urging her to strip inside the shadows, past the strip or dusty floor and onto the braided rug. Elkina had sold met amphetamine for Emery in this small town of Missouri. But now she is an informant for the police and knows this meeting could be dangerous.

Elkins plants her feet and refuses to budge. Emery's powerful arms push here and she stumbles through the doorway...

On Monday August 6, 1990, special Agent Michael Schimitz, 28, arrive early at the Kansas City office of the Bureau pf Alcohol, Tobacco and Firearms (ATF). After ten tough weeks at the Bureau's National Academy, Schmitz is finally an agent. And he can't wait to get started.

While he was at the academy, he was kept a breast of the Emery case by his mentor, Special Agent Mark James, a maverick ATF agent know for cracking a high percentage of cases. Duane Nichols, 47, reversed by lawmen throughout the region for his no nonsense leadership, is their supervising agent.

According to investigators, Tony Emery controlled met amphetamine sales in the north - west corner of Missouri. People were scared of him and for good reason. When a prosecutor started pursuing an assault case against a friend of Emery's bullets blasted into the wall above the bed of the prosecutor's young daughter. Emery was never charged with this, though he was a suspect.

Government agents had just got a woman inside Emery's empire Christine Elkins, 32, a recovering meth addict and mother of two. But after cops arrested her in December 1989 she said she'd help them get Emery. But she had her kids to thank about, so the agreed to do what no one else would.

On July 26, 1990, Special Agent James had met Elkins at a small airport in Maryville. He handed her a micro cassette recorded, which she slipped into the waistband of her jeans.

She left the airport in her maroon car. James and a trooper pulled their unmarked vehicle into a car park, from which they could see Emery's house. Fifteen minutes later Emery walked towards their car, starting straight at James. We're burned James thought. How did he know we were here? The officers pulled out of the car park, realizing their surveillance was blown.

Back at the airport 45 minutes later, Elkins's maroon car came screeching up to them. "He saw you" Elkins screamed.

Sobbing and shaking, she explained that Emery had taken her to a dark, deserted house. He'd run his hands by her sides, looking for a wire.

Emery didn't find it, she said, but he told her he'd seen the cops. "If you assist law enforcement," he said, "I'll kill you."

After calming her down, James told Elkins to stay away for Emery. She promised she would. But now, during Schmitz's first week on the job, James is worried. He hasn't heard from Elkins for several days. Is she still alive?

As the summer of 1990 wanes, Elkins misses work something she isn't known to do. Also, she hasn't spoken to her mother at all and the two are close. James's instinct is telling him that Christine Elkins is probably dead.

Adding to James's fore bedding is a conversation he would have with Jerry Moser, a friend of Elkins's, which indicates that she'd met one last time with Emery.

It was late on the night of August 4 when Elkins showed up at Moser's door with her younger son." Can you watch (my son) for ten minutes? She'd asked. "I've got to go get some money." Then she added, "If you don't see me in ten minutes, you'll see me in the morgue."

Sinister, but there is no evidence of a murder, no blood, no witnesses. On top of that, her maroon car with Missouri plate number B6E-652 has also vanished, so she might have just taken off.

In September 1990, Colorado drug dealer James Witt is driving about when he hears a small airplane behind him. I'm being tailed, he thinks. He knows he is looking at an arrest may be ten years in prison.

He contacts the local police department to make a deal, offering some attractive bait to lesson the charges against him. It seems he has something on a couple of guys in a drug operation two men named Emery. "I might know of a murder that happened," he tells the police. There was a girl missing in Maryville, Missouri, he says. Some guys killed her over something to do with drugs.

At 5 p.m. on December 18, 1990, Witt watches Tug Emery, Tony's cousin, pull into the parking lot of a restaurant. Witt, now a wired government, motions for Tug to get in. Their conversation is to be transmitted to a nearby van.

Witt broaches the topic of murder.by mentioning that he has a man he needs to "do". He adds,"But I don't know what to do with the body".

Tug's advice: "A mineshaft is what you need, but if he's" driving something you've to get rid of it too."

But how do you get a body out of a house? Witt asks.

"Wrap him in the rug. You can't tell what's in there." Tug, not often in a position to play the wise professional, has an answer for every concern.

Without referring to Elkins by name, Witt asks, "Was there a lot of blood?"

"A little, She went."

How do you hold down the pedal to sink the car? Witt asks.

"Put a stick in there," Tug says.

From the taps, James and Schmitz. deduce that Elkins has been murdered. But her name never came up and Tug didn't really confess to a murder so much as describe a hypothetical crime. They still have no case against Tony.

Eight months after Elkins disappeared, Tony Emery pleads guilty to conspiracy to possess with intent to distribute met amphetamine. He is sentence to 110 months in jail on the drug charges, but federal agents aren't stopping there.

Prosecutors ask them whether it is wise to pursue a murder charge that still has no body, no weapon, no witnesses, no blood. But supervising agent Nichols has no intention of letting a killer go free. "If you don't have a case now," he says,"we work until we build one."

Schmitz and James interview everyone believed to be connected to Emery's drug organization. The interviews yield little. "Look, you can send me to in jail," they are told time after time. "But if Tony finds out that I talked to you, I'm Dead."

"We can protect you."

"Is that what you told Christine?"

In January 1992, the police department promotes a cop named Randy Strong to investigator and assigns him to the Elkins case. He is awe. Here he is, a wet behind the ears local policeman, working on a profile murder case with experienced agents. "What do they need with me?" he wonders. The answer, he decides, is effort. He studies every detail of the case, looking for a crack.

During the summer of 1995, Assistant US Attorney Mike Green offers immunity from prosecution to a man named Bobby Miller, a friend of Tug Emery's, Miller, it seems. Was around for the planning of the murder and he heard screams coming from the house. But he claims panicked and bolted from the scene, never saw a body, didn't see a killing.

Still, with the tape recording of Tug Emery that was enough to make a case against Tug. If Tug is facing life without parole, he might give us Tony, Green thinks.

On November 20, 1996, Mark James carries a sheet of papers and a photo into a Colorado detention center interview room. Tug Emery, serving time for the same drug bust that imprisoned Tony, is seated at a table.

James walks to the table and lays down the papers. Emery's eyes only needed a few seconds to tell him the papers are an indictment against him for the, murder of Elkins. Next to the indictment, James places a photo of Elkins. Emery looks briefly at it and then jerks his head away.

"This woman was a mother of couple of young boys. She was a daughter," James says. "There are people who need closure and she deserves a decent burial."

With that, James leaves.

Every phone call from Leavenworth is taped. Inmates know, however, that with hundreds of calls each day, the volume of recordings can be impossible for investigators to sort through. So some times crimes are discussed, even if only in code.

It is this knowledge that repeatedly brings Schmitz and Strong to the

Leavenworth tapes. Finally, in early December 1996, they discovered a conversation. From prison, Tony Emery calls his mother for the holiday.

Mother: "You know what's going on? Nationwide news. Tug.

Tony: "Oh, no."

Mother: "That's right. First-degree murder charges. Something to do with a person being missed. You know what I am saying."

Tony: "Yeah."

As he listens to the conversation, a groin spreads across Sehmitz's face. For six years Emery has been smug confident he would get away with murder. New for the first time. Schmitz can hear panic setting in.

Tony "Somebody needs to tell him to stand his ground." Schmitz and Strong slap hands

"He's feeling the pressure," "Schmitz says. Without referring to Elkins by name, Witt asks, "Was there a lot of blood?"

Schmitz and Strong vow to re-check every detail of the case. In June 1997 they show up at the farmhouse of Dana Clizer, who is among the more than 200 people connected to Tony Emery who have been investigated. The brother of Tony's ex. girl friend, he was interviewed the first time only because he bought a car from Emery.

After about half an hour of talking with Clizer on the front porch, the conversation seems to be going nowhere. Strong prepares to leave. But Clizer's next words freeze him. Clizer says he has a good story about Tony, if they want to hear it.

At 12:51 p.m. the diver emerges holding a muddy Missouri License plate.

"Yes, we do," Schmitz, says.

Clizer explains that it was back in 1990, right before the time he laid some carpet for Tony in of his houses.

"We were getting ready to got to bed. I saw headlights. Tony pulling in my farm."

Clizer said Tony told him he had to get rid of the car. "He wanted me to show him the fastest way to where I put my boat in the river, and stay off the highway as much as I could." Schmitz and Strong spit out questions: "Did he tell you what was in the car?"

"No".

"What model of car?"

"Later model, G.M. car."

Elkins vanished. She must have been in the truck.

Several days later, at the Amazonian boat ramp, Schmitz stares at the muddy water of the Missouri River. He's been warned that the chances of finding the car in the murky depths are slim.

On July 26 and 27, 1997 the search team trolls more than a kilometer's stretch of the river. At the end of the second day, they hand Schmitz a map. "We'd say you should start your search here," One man says. He points to a slight bend in the river, not 200 meters from the boat ramp.

The next morning, Schmitz and Strong watch as a diver jumps into the river and descends to the riverbed.

At 12:51 p.m. the diver emerges holding a Missouri license plate above his head. It's muddy, but white numbers shine through: B6E-652. "That's the car" some one shouts.

Nobody speaks much as a tow truck drags the car into a circle of cops who've waited seven years to jammed behind the accelerator and in the truck they find rolled up carpet padding. Soon they discover Elkin's skull, which has a soup can sized hole on the right side.

In July 1988, a Kansas City jury listens as Tug Emery tells how Elkins died. Tony wanted Elkins dead, he says, convinced a drug case against him would vanish if she was not around to testify.

Tony lured Elkins to the house on August 4, 1990, telling her he was going to give her money to start a new life. Tug was hiding inside, waiting to hit her and wrap her up in a rug. Miller was outside, ready to haul away the body.

When Tony pushed Elkins inside, Tug slammed a blackjack down on her head. But it didn't knock her out. Elkins fought back, so he struck her again and again. But the plan was not working — they were now fighting. Tug took another swing and Elkins managed to grip the blackjack. As she wrested it away, steps. Tony told Tug, "Get a pipe and finish her off. I've got to get rid of her car." Then Tony walked away from the house.

Tug headed from the house and asked Miller to help him. Miller refused, saying. "I am not a killer". The two decided to leave the scene.

The next afternoon, Tug told Tony why he fled. "It was better that way," Tony said. "I took care of the dirty laundry."

Later, Tony told Tug how he'd returned to the house with a friend and struck Elkins one more time with a flash light evidently, they wrapped her up in some carpet padding, carried her to the car and stuffed her in then trunk. Then they dumped the car in the river.

The judge announces a sentence of life in prison without chance for parole.

Schmitz, James and other agents gather in a conference room. They shake hands and exchange hugs. ATF supervisor Nichols steps forward. The room quiets as he starts to speak. "You have no idea how much this means to me," he says, his eyes filling with tears. I am announcing my retirement today. I put it off to see this case closed to see that no matter how corrupt this world might look, in the end, justice will prevail.

"And, gentlemen, justice did prevail."

PROTECT YOUR CHILD FROM CRIME

An unidentified man asked a seven-year old girl to get into his car. She refused. He got out of the car and grabbed her arm. The girl managed to break free and run for home.

From Ladies Home Journal

Although kidnapping by stranger is a relatively rare crime it's one of the most frightening. More frequent crimes against children include theft and robbery. And these can happen anywhere.

It is clear though, that when children know what to do they have a much better chance of staying safe than those who don't. Teaching them basic crime prevention techniques at an early age. says American social psychologist Jerry Simmons, "can significantly reduce their chance of being victimized".

While that sounds simple enough, how do you do it without making your child fearful or paranoid? Simmons suggests parents emphasize what kids do to protect themselves — making a game out of role playing different situation and acting out the best response.

TEACH THE BASICS

There are certain things your child must learn as early as possible.

His or her full name, address and phone number, including area code.

Tell your child to immediately surrender money or any item that a mugger demands.

Both parent's first and last names.

Where to go for help. "Safe places include a trusted friend's house, the police station, busy stores, restaurants, the school or other public places," says Steven Anderson a senior police officer. Accompany your child along his route to school, for example and show exactly which places are safe to go to, in case of an emergency.

How to say no? It's imperative for your child to understand that he has right to protest if someone's touch makes him uncomfortable. If accosted by a stranger, he should yell, "This person is not my father" (or mother). Kids who simply struggle and scream may appear to be having a tantrum.

Be streetwise. Teach your child to play with a friend or in a group whenever possible. When walking to and from school, friend's house or parks, kids should avoid dark, isolated areas.

If your child senses that some one in a car is following him as he walks along a street, he should turn around and hide in the opposite direction. The driver is not likely to attract attention to himself by also turning around. Tell your child stay at least five to six meters from the door of a vehicle if someone stops to talk or ask directions. (Demonstrate this distance.) Emphasize that it's okay to say "I don't know" and walk away.

Caution your child to stay alert, walk confidently and pay attention to his surroundings. Criminals are expert at spotting easy victims — kids who look lost, confused, sad or upset.

"On the bus" says New York City detective Jose E. Santiago, "your child should know his stop. He should stay alert and avoid burying his head in a book, wearing headphones or sleeping."

It's common sense that children avoid wearing expensive jewellery or watches. Tell your child to immediately surrender money or any other item that a mugger demands. He should not try to argue. The thief may have a weapon.

Be school-smart while the situation at your child's school may not seem dangerous, don't assume that he is safe there.

Attend school board meetings, join important, talk to your child. Is he fearful of school or certain students? Why? Follow up on his comments. If he really doesn't feel safe, consider changing schools.

If that's out of the question, talk to the principal. Try to get both sides of the story before demanding any action.

Finally, talk frankly with your child about avoiding students who use drugs, carry weapons or seem to be involved in frequent fights.

Be neighbourhood safe:- "Teach your child to keep you informed of his whereabouts, even if he's just going across the street to a friend's", says Anderson. He advises that you should also know your child's friends, including their parent's full names and where they live.

Sometimes safety- or the lack of it is a question of locking out for one another's children. Ask neighbors to call you or the police if they see anything unusual.

Finally, teach your child basic home security rules, such as looking doors. If a youngster must be home alone, instruct him never to say so over the phone. Tell the child to take a message and that you will call back. Hands-on practice will reinforce good security habits.[17]

MISSISSIPPI JUSTICE

Moved by a widow's plea, a young prosecutor sets out to solve a 26-year-old murder. In the process, he puts his career and life at risk and forces a community to revisit its darkest moment.

PROLOGUE

It has just after midnight on a warm June evening in Jacksion, Mississippi USA. A full moon illuminated the driveway of house number 2322 Guyanes Street as a powder blue car pulled in.

Inside the house, a woman and three young children heard the familiar sound of the motor.

"There's Daddy," the youngster said. They had waited up for him long past their bedtime.

Just then, the peace of the night was shattered by a terrible blast. The two eldest children grabbed their little brother, dropping to the floor as their father had taught them to do. The woman ran to the door, flung it open and found her husband lying before the steps with his keys in his hand, blood everywhere.

She screamed uncontrollably, as the children, rushing up behind her, called out to their mortally wounded father.

Strewn around the fallen man and clutched in his hand were T-shirts that bore the words "Jim Crow Must Go."

Neighbors soon arrived on the scene. Some of them put the wounded man on a mattress and a station wagon to take him to the hospital.

Other well-meaning friends restrained the victim's wife from going with her husband. If was something she would never get over that she did not make that last journey with him.

Someone called the victim's physician, Dr. A.B. Britton, who rushed to the emergency room.

"When I first came in," he recalled later, some of them spent a little time trying to prevent me from getting in. This was 1963 and all of the hospital doctors were white males. So, naturally, it was a common reaction to want to know what in the world l, a black man, was going in there.

"One of the physicians recognized me and said," come on, Doctor, we're trying to get a drip started.

As Dr. Britton pushed down on the dressing on the wounded man's chest to try to stop the flow of blood, he spoke to him: "This is Dr. Britton. Do you know who shot you?"

But all the other man said was, "Oh, Doc, Doc, oh...."

Then he expired.

Medgar Evers, civil rights pioneer, husband and father, was dead on the other side of town, in a white neighborhood, a nine-year-old boy slept, unaware of the assassination and of how his life would be profoundly affected by it 26 years later.

I was that boy.

MAKING HEADLINES

On the morning of October 1, 1989 clad in dressing-gown and slippers, I made my way out by the front door and picked up the Clarion Ledger, our local Jackson newspaper. Back in side, I settled on the couch in the early morning quiet, My wife Dixie wasn't at home. She was gone a lot since taking a job in the clarion Ledger's circulation department.

That morning it was up to me to rouse our three kids. Burt, ten, Claire, six and Drew four. I usually couldn't linger long reading the papers, but today the front page headline caught my eye: "State Checked Possible Jurors in Evers Slaying". The reporter, Jerry Mitchell, whom I knew well, had obtained access to some revealing record. These implied the Sovereignty Commission government body established in the 1950s to promote racial segregation, had, in 1964, run secret background checks on the jury during the second trial of Byron De La Beckwith for the murder of Medgar Evers.

I had been too young to remember much of those events from my early boyhood. Beckwith, a slight, unprepossessing man in his mid-40s, seemed an unlikely player for so large a drama. But he was an unrepentant racist, consumed with his own importance and eager to share his views. On his way to and from court day, he would smile and joke with reporters, acting, more like a movie star than an alleged murderer.

I vaguely recalled my parents' friends talking about him during the first trial. Some one said he was guilty, but state could not prove it.

Sure enough, the trial resulted in a hung jury and so did a subsequent one. Though he'd have another brush with the law, Beckwith was never again tried for the murder. And for the last 25 years, he had openly mocked law enforcement for its futile efforts to pin the crime on him.

I did not think much about the Clarion-Ledger's article- I was an assistant District Attorney for Hinds County, Mississippi and in the middle of another prosecution. But Tuesday morning, I unfurled the paper and saw that Jerry written a follow up piece. This one said that Myrlie Evers, widow of the slain civil rights leader, wanted the case reopened.

I went to talk to Ed Patters, my boss. The District Attorney (DA) for the past 17 years, Ed was tall, lanky and known for his formidable presence in the courtroom. His drawl and pleasant manner have lured defendants into carefully laid traps during cross-examination.

When I asked him for his response to the article about Myrlie Evers, he was typically direct. Without new evidence there was no constitutional way to reopen the case.

Made sense to me. After all, it had been 26 years since the Evers murder and the Mississippi Supreme Court had reversed verdicts in criminal cases prosecuted after delays of only a few years.

There was no way we'd be allowed to go to trial again unless there was new and dramatic evidence. The flurry of renewed interest in the Evers murder will just go away, we thought.

We couldn't have been more wrong.

DREAM OF JUSTICE

To my surprise, public reaction to the articles was immediate and divisive. For our reluctance to rush out and reindict Beckwith, Ed Peters and I were labeled by some as resists. Conversely, I received calls and letters from people who fervently hoped we were not considering reopening the matter. "The case is too old," they said. "It will cost too much money." It will open up an old wound".

To this group, Beckwith's guilt was not an issue. I was repeatedly told, "We know he's guilty, everybody knows that, but that's not the point."

As misguided as that feeling was, it was there. After some 25 years of integration some people couldn't get beyond race and harbored a subterranean rage I could only try to imagine. But I didn't find a way to deal with it, there was no hope of ever winning over a jury that included people like this.

In the end, Ed asked me to look into the allegation of misconduct concerning the jury. Unfortunately, I couldn't go to the file room and pull out a folder bearing Beckwith's name. Our records went back only as far as 1972. We had no court minutes, no case files, no crime scene photos, and no exhibits. We had Zilch.

As I shook hands with Myrlie Evers, her eyes drew my attention. They were haunted and sad, but hopeful.

However, I was able to find out the names of the original jurors and began to set up interviews. Tentatively, I made a beginning.

Part of my effort consisted of sending a letter to Myrlie Evers asking if it would be possible for us to meet in our office and talk about what we planned to do, as well as to receive feed back and information from her.

I didn't really believe Mrs. Evers could come to us. But on the morning of December 4, I was in the office pouring coffee when Ed approached me. "Myrlie Evers is coming here in about an hour."

"Today?" I asked, spilling hot coffee over my hand and the floor. Great. Just great, I thought. I pictured an in-your face confrontation and dreaded the prospect. I expected Mrs. Evers to hammer us for not going after Beckwith, notwithstanding that we had no evidence.

I felt about the coming meeting much the same way I imagined a condemned prisoner would prepare for a firing squad. All I could think was let's get this over with.

At the appointed time I was summoned to Ed's office and introduced to Myrlie Evers. As we shook hands, her eyes drew my attention. They were haunted and sad, but hopeful.

Clearly she was still free and De La Beckwith was still free and continued to boast of his freedom to whoever would listen.

Unfortunately, Ed did not have good news for her. The accounts from the jurors we had interviewed fell far short of proving jury tampering or any misconduct.

"Mrs. Evers, there is no case," Ed told her. "We have no physical evidence from the 1964 trials: no gun, no bullet, no photographs. Lord knows where the witnesses have scattered to, if they are still alive. And there's the problem posed by the constitutional guarantee of a speedy trial. There is nothing speedy about twenty-six years".

I has expected Myrlie Evers, political activist, to speak. Instead, I heard Myrlie Evers, wife and mother, tell us of her dream that in a day the coward who had killed her unarmed husband would be brought to justice.

There was strength in her, but not only in her words. Listened, mesmerized, as she told her story. I opened the door and saw Medgar lying in a pool of blood, pulling himself across the floor towards the door.

"The children had got to the door by that time and were crying. Daddy, get up, get up". She described the events of that dreadful June night, with her children wailing as they watched their father dying and images of my own children flashed through my mind. Wouldn't any one want the same thing the Evers family wanted?

I knew that after the murder, Myrlie Evers had refused to succumb to despair. She had taken her kids to California, finished her education and through hard work had become a Commissioner of the public works department in Los Angeles.

She raised all three children into find adults. All outward appearances suggested they had not merely survived but had overcome their tragedy.

But what about inside? I sensed the pain in Myrlie Ever's eyes would not recede until justice was done.

After our meeting ended, I saw her to the elevator. She turned, grasped my hand and said "Mr De-Laughter, please keep me informed."

That night, after I tucked my kids into bed, I sat down with the lights out except for the warm glow in the fireplace.

I recalled Mrs. Ever's stating in the police report that when the first shot rang out, her children hit the floor and lay still for a moment, just as their Daddy had taught them to do. Baseball, dolls, fishing and cartoons-those are the things that should occupy youngster's minds, not what to do when gunfire erupts.

I was also thinking about something Mrs. Evers had said earlier that day. Mississippi needed justice in this case as much as her family did.

I love my state. My roots run deep here and I have never planned on living anywhere else. I wanted Mississippi to be known as a place where law-abiding people no matter what race live and raise their families in peace and safety that was the legacy I wanted to leave to my children.

CRUCIAL CLUES

I knew that involving my self in this politically hot, divisive case might jeopardize my hoped-for career in public office. I knew, too, that larger issues than my career prospects were at stake if we moved forward.

My mother expressed her apprehension one day when the kids and I were at her house for dinner.

For your sake and the children's, I would just as soon that nothing comes of this Beckwith thing, Mama said. "There are all kinds of crazy people out there, and Beckwith is one of the craziest."

I promised to be careful.

Dixie also seemed less than happy about my work on the case. Some people had made derisive comments about my involvement with it. I attributed her apparent uneasiness to embarrassment, but in my gut I sensed that there was some deeper reason though I wasn't sure what.

"There are all kinds of crazy people out there". Mama warned me, "and Beckwith is one of the creasiest" I promised to be carful.

Despite my own and family's reservations, I knew I couldn't look myself in the mirror if I knowingly let a man get away with murder. So I pressed on. In the process I learned a lot about Medgar Evers.

Back in 1954, when the US Supreme Court Ruled that schools could no longer be racially segregated, Evers was working as an insurance salesman in Mississippi.

A young war veteran and graduate of Alcorn A&M College (where he's met Myrlie), he traveled the area's back roads, seeing firsthand the desperate living images from his mind or his heart.

Ever's resolve to make a difference only deepened after he was denied admission to Law College at the University of Mississippi. In time, he became the first field secretary of the National Association for the Advancement of Colored People (NAACP) in the state.

As the struggle for equal rights intensified, Evers became the point man on the NAACP team- and a lightening rod for segregationists.

Immediately, the family began receiving threatening phone calls, forcing them to get an unlisted number.

Asked once about threats to his life, Evers said he could not be swayed from his fight for racial equality. "If I die, it will be good cause. I've been fighting for America just as much as the soldiers in Vietnam. I'm determined (that) we be accepted as human beings with dignity."

By the time of his murder, Evers had become the leading civil activist in Mississippi.

Reading the Jackson Police Department's report on the case, I knew the officers fully appreciated the political powder keg they were sitting on. If the assassin weren't caught, it wouldn't be because of lack of effort on their part.

The evidence they had gathered against Beckwith was strong. They found the murder weapon, a 1917-30-06 Enfield rifle, hidden in a thicket in a semi-wooded area near the Evers house. Analysis revealed a fingerprint on its scope.

A young planter named Thorn McIntyre, who saw a picture of the weapon in the local paper, contacted the police. He told them that he had traded a 1917-30-06 Enfield rifle about three years earlier to a man named "Mr. De La Beckwith of Greenwood Missssippi."[18]

According to the police report, McIntyre said that Beckwith "is very radical problem and this problem and he (McIntyre) would not be surprised as to what this man might do".

An employee of a hangout called Joe's Drive-In, which adjoined area where the gun had been found, told detectives that around 8:30 on the night of the murder, white car had pulled into the car park. She remembered it had a long, whip like aerial on the back. Backwith had a car like that.

CONCLUSION

That, the Terrorists are the Enemy of the Society, due to frustration, due to any other reason they are killing the innocent persons, actually they are not concerned with any offence of any else. We can take example of Saddam Hussain of Iraq, he was thinking as a Superman of his country and his behavior was so cruel due to which common people of Iraq could not tolerate such cruelty and then cruelty and that United Nations Organization had taken cognizance and through United States had taken action against the Saddam and he was arrested, some type of Hitler and other Kings of the world harassed the public at large, in India even British Region also played same tactics and Nationalist were crushed in "Jalianwala Bag" even. Now similer Terrorist activities are going in Indonesia, Malaesia, Pakistan and in India especially in Kashmir area. We must find out the reasons behind such Terrorist activities. Government Servant and also public are responsible for such corruption. And specially, in courts the Judges always administering the oath to witness". Taking oath of God", but generally Government want the Nation is secular; they cannot understand the meaning of Secularism, Secularism not Restraining the faith of God, when there are no faith on the God then why oath of God administered to the witness. All those activities are going on far restraining the leadership; they are not faithful to Nation and now even poor, man cannot get any relief without corruption, and due to these real offences of corruption it is too difficult to check Terrorism in the country and in the world. Even Government Machinery, including Mantralaya it is too difficult to get relief of any problem without corruption, unemployed persons cannot get employment without corruption, due to heavy corruption, business man with the help of corruption are adultering the foods, patrol, poor man's kerosene only corruption are giving shelter to rich persons and rich persons are getting maximum benefits, including contracts etc. Terrorism is nothing but one step of revolution. Naxalites are doing the same activities; we must strictly check the corruption. Then only there will be check of Terrorist activities, now seems the person those who are fighting for the bread are ready to accept any work after getting money from the politicians and Dadas political persons wants to continue. Terrorism activities for their ultimate aim of getting chairs in Government and their selfish gain. Now in democracy elected persons are using all the methods to elect including corruption and Terrorist activities even example is of Bihar State there are several-elected M.P.s. and M.L.A.'s are in power. Police are their private servants; hence there are heavy Terrorist Activities. This is important to note that Supreme Court and High Courts also are continuously directing to restrain such Bahubalis and they should be arrested and detained in the prisons, but Government is of Bahubalis who will control them.

Now prices of essential commodities are going up day to day and now VAT addition tax is including, how a poor man and cultivator will survive when the children of the poor person are crying for the bread and whole family are fighting for the bread, then naturally will be increase in Terrorism Activities. For Ration card there is Corruption, police, court clerks and some cases of Judicial corruption, everywhere there is corruption then there will be increase of corruption, firstly it is necessary to check the corruption. Freedom fighters are fighting for the pension, they have no money then they cannot get freedom fighters pension etc.

The mounting toll of criminally and alarming rise in juvenile delinquency has become a problem of national concern all over the world. Most counties now recognize that prevention of crime and treatment of offenders is not an isolated problem; that social defense and correction cannot be considered as unrelated to the total culture and the social and economic fabric of society.[19] This is evident from the fact that "Battle against crime does not end at the court-room door but continues through imprisonment to release and beyond." Despite improved correctional methods and recent innovation in criminal procedure and sentencing law the problem of crime and criminal continues as a challenge to "new era of penology."[20]

With the changing trends in penology the old penal philosophy, which rejected any intervention by the behavioral sciences, stands completely discarded. The old belief that harsh and lengthy punishments are necessary for the security of the community has become obsolete in the present context.

Currently, our approach to crime prevention centers round four major considerations, namely:

(i) The offender is essentially a human being.

(ii) The object of imprisonment is to bring about prisoner's reconciliation through the process of rehabilitation.

(iii) There is greater need for legislative participation in the shaping of correctional policy and subjection of correctional theory and practice to rule of law in the administration of criminal justice.[21]

(iv) Control of delinquency implies ecological interpretation of sociological problems. Therefore in order to hold in check the incidence of crime, the conditions conducive to it must also be, kept under control.

Twentieth century pragmatism has brought in its wake a new wave of reformation in the era of penal justice and correctional services. The shift of emphasis from "crime" to "criminal", that is, from the criminal act of the offender to his personality has brought about revolutionary changes in the field of penology and criminal science. The modern system of probation, parole, reformatories and open institutions have proved potentially helpful in elimination of isolationism from which preventive and correctional schemes have suffered so far. New scientific methods are now used for crime detection and apprehension of criminals. The working of prison institutions has been remodeled to suit the modern corrective methods of treatment of offenders. All these measures speak for the growing concern of modern penologists for crime prevention.

The development of penal science in different parts of the world has been more or less on a uniform pattern. The old brutal and barbarous methods of punishment are abandoned in favor of modern correctional measures. Sentencing procedures have been radically changed to suit the requirements of the individual offender. As rightly pointed out of Justice Theodore Levin,[22] the "courts in sentencing of convicted persons must be something more then mechanical instruments of punishment." The judge should not lose sight of the fact that it is the human being who stands before him as a criminal. Thus the modern law administrators are not relieved of their responsibility merely by sentencing and sending the convicted person to prison or a similar institution; but they have an active role to play in making the rehabilitation of the offender possible through institutional methods.

Reviewing the progress of sentencing procedures in context with prevention of crime Curtis Book suggests that we are presently passing through the fourth phase of criminological development.[23] The earlier three phases according to him are:

The first phase covering the period of seventeenth century and the first half of the eighteenth century when punishments were general brutal, barbarous and harsh.

The second phase which covered the period of latter half of the eighteenth century and early decades of nineteenth century is remarkable in the history of penal science because emphasis shifted from to criminal and individualization of offender because the cardinal principal of penal reforms.

The third phase of criminological development covers the period of past one hundred years when 'treatment" and not "punishment" became the guiding principal for all penological reforms creator emphasis was on the treatment of offenders through clinical methods rather than confining them inside the closed prisons. A number of minimum-security

institutions such as open-air camps, prison-farms, etc. were e
for the rehabilitation of offenders.

Unprecedented rise in recidivism is perhaps the most
problem in relation to crime prevention these days. The
of recidivism has always been discussed in the recent inte
conferences on prevention of crime and treatment of offender
been generally accepted that recidivists and hardened crimina
be punished with long-term sentences to ensure their eliminatio
society. There are, however certain penal reformists who firmly b
that correctional programme can be equally effective in case of recid
as in case of other offenders. In their opinion the reformation offe
must be sought within the society itself. Significantly, the working of
jails for the rehabilitation of dacoits from Chambal and Bundelkh
regions of Madhya Pradesh has established beyond doubt that even
most hardened and dangerous criminals can be corrected and redeem
to society as law abiding citizens if they are properly treated throug
correctional institutions.

Another cause so often attributed to rise in crime rate is the wide spreac discrimination in the treatment of person's accused of crime on grounds of social position and financial status. The criminal law procedure should be so amended as to eliminate needless arrest and detention of suspected offenders. Persons should be detained in custody only when absolutely necessary. Uniformity of sentence for similar offenders should be the guiding principle of the Criminal law should not allow any disparity in trial or sentencing on the basis of social status of the offender.[24]

The law should be flexible so as to adapt itself to the changing socio-economic needs of society.[25]

Recent trends in correctional measures have proved beyond doubt that only one-fourth of the total population of criminals consists of incorrigible offenders while the majority of them are corrigible and respond favorable to the treatment methods. It must be reiterated that treatment of offenders through modern clinical methods symbolizes society's preparedness to accept delinquents as trustworthy citizens. The concept of individualized treatment through correctional measures presupposes that offender is a deviant, who can be redeemed to normal society if adequate opportunities for rehabilitation are offered to him. The system of parole, probation, in determinate sentence and open prisons are some of the rehabilitation devices which find place in the modern penal programme of most countries of the world. Needless to say that these measures are intended to remove or reduce offender's disposition to repeat the offence or break the criminal law in any way.[26]

The corrective techniques inter alia includes:

(i) Custodial measures, which deprive the offender of his liberty and test his responsiveness to self-control, discipline etc. within the institutional life help him to live as a law abiding citizen after his release.

(ii) Semi-detention method is intended to restrict liberty without completely separating the offender from his occupation or family.

(iii) Reformative measure such as probation and people enable the offender to rehabitate himself within the society.

The constantly mounting toll of juvenile delinquency is presenting a major threat to problem of crime prevention in modern times. Commenting upon the problem of juvenal offenders that F brown observed that the crime problem of the day is to a large extent a problem of youthful offenders.[27]

From the foregoing discussion it is evident that penal laws have a close bearing on the problem of crime prevention. Again crime being a relative term the concept of "criminal" also varies from place to place depending upon the provisions of criminal law. Thus conceptual differences arise from variation in legal definitions. For example, murder under the Indian Penal Code is more or less similar to that of manslaughter under the American Criminal law. Therefore amending substantive law of crime according to needs of the time would indirectly help in reducing the number of crimes at a given place. It is from this point of view the American Law institute prepared a Draft of Model Penal Code in 1965. The Republic of Germany also prepared its retribution oriented Draft Penal Code in 1962. The New Swedish Penal Code, which came into effect from January 1965, lays greater emphasis on rehabilitation rather than retribution or deterrence. It must be stated that there is an urgent need for re-statement of Indian Panal Law and the law of evidence, which are more than a hundred years old[28] and are hardly to the present needs of the country. The ultimate object of criminal law should be to create conditions, which are conducive to progress, and prosperity of the community and afford "Good Life" to people in general.[29]

From the point of view of social forces and suppression of criminality, following changes in the Indian criminal law and procedure may be suggested to make it consonant with the needs of the time:-

The existing law does not provide for reparation or Compensation to victims of the crime for the injuries caused or loss suffered by them due to the offender's Criminal act. Punishment of the accused may offer consolation to the person affected by the Offender's act but it offers no pecuniary satisfaction. It is therefore desired that compensation be awarded to the injured parties particularly, in cases of crimes relating to property. The payments of compensation may be made from the money recovered by the State from the offender by way of fine. It is further suggested that imposition of heavy fines instead of imprisonment in case of crimes relating to property seems to be a rational policy in the present context of penological of development. The existence of double sets of law for certain offences present difficulties for the magistracy to determine punishment for offenders in such cases. To take a concrete illustration, the law relating to bribery India is governed by two different sets of laws, namely, Section 161 of the Indian Penal Code and the Prevention of Corruption Act,[30] 1947. So is the case with regard to offences relating to trafficking in girls and minors for immoral and illegal purposes.[31] It is therefore desired that duplicity of legal provisions for the same offence should be avoided to make sentencing more definite and effective.

In view of the changed socio-economic conditions of the present time there is an urgent need to reclassify the offences contained in the Indian Penal Code. With the growing political indiscipline in the country it has become necessary that political offences be included in the Penal Code under a separate chapter. The cases of defections, resort to corrupt practices during election campaigns and such other offences should be made punishable under the Penal Code itself.

Crimes relating to person should be punishable with a term of imprisonment while those relating to property should be punished with fine or reparation of damages to the effected parties Unnecessarily long terms of sentences should be avoided to make rehabilitation of the offender possible after his release. Likewise, too short sentence will also defeat the object of punishment. A rational policy in this regard will be to determine the term of sentence according to the gravity of crime sociology of the offender and his psychological traits. As to the retention or abolition of capital punishment the generally accepted view is that its abolition should not be over emphasized. The retention of death sentence undoubtedly serves as an efficient deterrent for recidivists and hardened criminals. The retention of this penalty in the statute book is further justified on the ground of protection of society from dangerous and incorrigible offenders. It would therefore be expedient to retain death penalty though in practice it may be sparingly used[32] in rarest of rare cases. This contention also finds support in the report of the Law Commission of India.

The modern western trend favors deletion of all such offences from the penal code, which are solely dependent on moral considerations. Thus in England home sexuality is no longer an offence if committed at non-public place. Likewise in India many States did not introduce prohibition law because they were convinced that it is difficult to put a check on liquor habits of people by imposing external legal restrictions unless of course, the liquor addicts themselves begin to realize that drinking is an evil and must be given up. So is the case with gambling and "satta" etc. that have become a common menace these days. It is true that there are many offences, which cannot be suppressed by legal penalties alone unless the members of society voluntarily begin to think that what they are doing is morally wrong and against social interest.[33] But keeping in view the India taboos it is difficult to agree with the western view that most sex-offences should be deleted from the statute book because they largely depend on moral precepts. Unquestionably, this cannot be recommended as an effective measure to reduce sex crimes in India.

The misused and abuse of the law of Preventive Detention such as MISA, COFEPOSA etc. in recent years particularly during emergency period have led to serious rethinking to repeal those statutes. In most of the cases the final authority for detention is the officer in charge of the police station whose report is generally rubber stamped in turn by Superintendent of Police or the District Magistrate. The law relating to Preventive detention therefore needs to be modified so as to prevent its abuse and misuse. The system of collection of intelligence and reporting should be over hauled so that facts are reported correctly. Many people, from even had motives such as spite, jealously; anger and self-interest do not hesitate to set the law in motion against their enemies or rivals. Therefore, if the intelligence and police personnel perform their duty honestly and are not under so obligation to any party or politics, then and then only morality and common decency and conventional respect for government can be ensured.

Frequent interference in investigation of cases by politicians or politically motivated prosecuting machinery headed by politician lawyers who are more interested in party in power have destroyed the image of criminal law administering agencies, particularly the police.

Crime reporting in India continues to be faulty even to this day. As a result of this, crimes are suppressed, minimized or not reported. The reporting procedure therefore needs to be over hauled.

An objective evaluation of crime prevention programme further suggests that there is a growing need for enhancing the existing powers of the police relating to arrest, interrogation and search of suspected persons. Police officials should be empowered to arrest a suspected offender even without a warrant. Experience has shown that much time is lost in observing the procedural formalities of law, which afford sufficient opportunity for the offender to escape. Moreover, it is quite often noticed that proceedings against the apprehended person are dropped on flimsy grounds of procedural irregularity. In result many offenders go unpunished due to procedural flaws in the system of arrest, detention, interrogation and search, which certainly threatens the security of society. That apart, the police in India is looked with distrust and bias. They are generally accused of misuse of power. In situations warranting stern action the police is often criticized for atrocities and excess. Public criticism has a demoralizing effect on police officials and they find it difficult to perform their law enforcement duties with confidence without an active support from the public. The lack of public police co-operation is therefore a contributing factor for failure of efforts to cope with the rising incidence of crime and delinquency.

Another important aspect of crime problem relates to certain new offences such as bank robberies,[34] forgery, counterfeiting causing death by slow poisoning.

Utilization of the services of 'police dogs' in spotting out criminals is one of the most significant development in them area of crime-detection in recent times. The device it extensively being used in tracing out the offenders and detecting crimes which are committed under mysterious circumstances.[35] It is significant to not that in cases where the services of with the expansion of banking in rural areas Bank robberies in India have become a common occurrence police dog are utilized for the detection of crime it is necessary to ensure that the place of its occurrence must be left completely untempered. The police dog must be brought to the place of crime within forty-eight hours of its occurrence. There is again a controversy about the evidentiary value of the detections made with the assistance of police dogs. The American Courts accept police dog as a valid piece of evidence against the accused provided it corroborates with other evidence in the case. But if other evidence does not corroborate this evidence, and then in that case it cannot be accepted as a significant evidence to warrant conviction of the accused. The Indian law also takes the same stand in this regard. The reasons advanced for the necessity of corroboration of police dog's evidence is that these trained dogs may err in tracking out of the offenders correctly.[36] Moreover, they being animals can neither speak nor be subjected to cross-examination.

Crime control essentially involves the services of well trained personel that possess adequate knowledge about different kinds of offences and the related statistical data about crime and criminals. It must be remembered that crime statistics do not present a true picture of crime incidence because many crimes go undetected and many more unreported. Moreover, statistics being the measuring rod for gauging efficiency the institutions connected with crime and criminals, such as, police, courts and prisons, may be inclined to furnish cooked figures about their performance. Despite this fact the importance of statistics cannot be over emphasized. Rise in crime statistics of a particular area draws the attention of law administrators to locate the cause of mounting criminality in that region and suggest measures to combat it. Crime statistics therefore provide necessary guidance and clue to those who are concerned with the prevention of crime Computerization of statistics now seems inevitable.

The increasing role of psychology and psychiatry in the field of penology has helped in understanding the problem of crime and criminal to a considerable extent. Criminality is now attributed to psychiatric defects in the offender. It is now universally accepted that infliction of pain and suffering through imprisonment serves no useful purpose for the rehabilitation of offenders. The basic philosophy that underlies the modern clinic methods is that the offenders should be treated and not punished. It is because of this fundamental assumption that the importance of prisons is resending day-by-day and correctional measures such as probation, parole, open champs and reformatories are being extensively used for the rehabilitation of offenders. The modern clinic measures stress on the need for a deeper insight into the human nature and psychology working behind the offender. The goal of modern penology is to bring about a change in the mentality of the criminal thought a process of moral education and social reformation.[37] It must be recognized that crime is not a unitary phenomenon but a composite reaction of multiple factors.[38] Therefore no single theory can provide a satisfactory explanation for the varieties of the behavior involved[39] in the criminal act. Reformation of the offender should be brought about within the community itself through the process of rehabilitation.

According to Nigel Walker one of the indirect techniques of crime detection is reduction of opportunities. This includes control over the sale of firearms, explosives, poisons etc. and restrictions on holding public meeting, prohibiting illegal entry and adequate lighting of public laces and roads. This shall make the task of opportunity-seeker criminals difficult.

Adequate education and intensive propaganda against the conduct involving law, violations can also contribute to reduce crimes considerably. An effective censorship on the media of entertainment shall help in inuleating a sense of morality amount youngsters and the public. Mass media, which depicts violence and undesirable behavior, is bound to add to the crime problem.

Despite legal, social, psychological and penal measures for combating crime the problem still persist in alarming dimensions. With the passage of time new crimes are coming up and the older ones are vanishing. The advancement in knowledge of human behaviour and growth of commerce and industries has brought in their wake new complexities in life. These complexities lead to criminality. It is therefore, apparent that crime, though an evil, is and inevitable phenomenon of a progressive society. There is no reason to be upset with the present increase in crime rate. Nor should it create a misleading impression that the penal programmes are faulty or ineffective. It must be admitted that criminality in India is much less than in many other countries of the world. The reason being that Indian society still retains the virtues of tolerance, mutual respect and co-existence through its social institutions such as religion, family and parental control etc. in common man's distrust for law, justice, police, prosecutors and the members of the bar. Instances are not wanting when people watch a crime being committed in their presence but never report it to the police either because of the fear of culprit or possible harassment from the police or the court. A commoner always prefers to avoid police or law court even at the cost of suffering a little harm or injury. He refrains from instituting criminal proceedings against the offender to avoid the botheration of contacting police or visiting law courts. This apathy of people towards law enforcement agencies provides futile ground for offenders to carry on their criminal activities, which hinders the cause of crime prevention. It must be accepted that there is a great divergence in practice and precepts so far working of police and law courts is concerned the problem of the day therefore is to revive confidence among the public for these agencies of justice through an extensive propaganda and convince them that these institutions are meant to help and not to harass them. Prevention of crime should be treated as everyone's concern[40] unless this broader outlook is developed among the members of the society; elimination of crimes seems to be impossibility. The traditional outlook that crime prevention is solely a concern of law enforcement agencies must be changed and it should be treated as a social cause necessitating Involvement of every citizen. Then only the crusade against crime prevention can succeed and public tranquility prevails in the community.

Terrorism means acts of terror and whoever with intent to overdue the government as by law established or strike terror in the people or any section of the people or to alienate any section of the people or to adversely affect the harmony amongst the different sections of the people does any act or thing by using bombs, dynamite and or other explosive substances or lethal weapons or poisons or noxious gases or other chemicals or any other substances (without biological or otherwise) of a hazardous nature in such a manner, as to cause or as is likely to cause 'death of, or injuries to, any person or persons or damage to or destruction of, property or disruption of any supplies or service essential to the life of the community, commit a terrorist acts. Terrorist means persons' using violence fear threats etc. And terrorism means some section of society or a group of persons creates terror to satisfy their demand with the help of violence fear threats etc. And terrorism means some section of society or a group of persons creates terror to satisfy their demand with the help of violence.

Now in the society maximum elements in the society is to get their interest by way of creating terror in the society.

For example a person wants to get something he will create terror in the society to satisfy their demand. Suppose a person of the community wants to marry with some girl and her father or relative don't like such marriage, then such person using acid or petrol to finish the girl or to kidnap her and after birth of child they are openly coming before the society.

Now a days in India and abroad even there are several legislation passed by the Parliament and state legislatures to curb the mentalist of terrorism. We will have to consider why such terrorism is increased in the terrorism. There are several aspects behind it. Some of those are as under:-

1. Public wants easy money.
2. Cinemas are also equally responsible for such terror in the society.
3. Political atmosphere.
4. Communal Riots.
5. Immoral Mentality.
6. Election system.
7. Heavy corruption.
8. Ineffective Police Machinery.
9. Lack of knowledge of laws.
10. Corruption in judiciary.
11. Corruption in police.
12. Corruption in Public Service Commissions.
13. Lack of proper training to the younger lawyers, shortage funds for Library.

14. Defective Legislation.
15. Training to the elected legislatures.
16. Duties by Police Officer and Magistrates must be clear and breach of it there must be punishment.

Sir Mathew Hale drawn some Rules for the junior Magistrates:-

1. In the Administration of justice and interested in God.
2. That is to be done.
   (a) Uprightly
   (b) Deliberately
   (c) Resolutely
3. That I rest not upon my own understand upon, the directions and strength of God.
4. That in the Execution of Justice, I don't give way to them, however crooked.
5. That I be wholly intent upon the business, I'm about, all others cares and though as unreasonable and interruptions.
6. That I suffer not myself to be proposed with my judgment at all till the whole business and both parties have been heard.
7. That I never engage myself in the beginning any cause. But reserve myself unprejudiced till the whole be heard.
8. That in the business capital though my natures prompt me to pity, yet to consider there is a pity also due to the country.
9. That, I be not too rigid in the matters purely conscious, when the harm is diversity of judgment.
10. That I be not biased with compassion to the poor or favor to the rich, in point of justice.
11. That popular or court applause or mistake have no influence in anything I do in point of distribution of justice.
12. Not to be solicitous what men will say think so long I keep myself exactly according to Rules and Rules of Justice.
13. If in criminals it be measuring cast, to incline to mercy and acquittal.
14. In criminals that consists mercy in words, where no harm ensures moderation is no injustice.
15. To abhor all private solicitations of what kind so ever and by whom so ever, in matter depending. These principals if six Mathew's must be followed. In the same way there must be strict rules of conduct in respect of police persons, if the Police persons by corrupt means or any other reasons disobeyed the provisions of law then they must be punished.

Now a days terrorism continuously increasing the world and particular in India. For example in Kashmir or Bhandara or in Nizamabad etc. all Terrorist activities increased at Kashmir Laskar a Toyaba, in Gulbarga or in Andhara Pradesh Naxalwadi movement committing Terrorist activities.

And in the world just for example World Trade Center in America or in Seria and Iraq and Iran even Terrorists activities increased, in India, Pakistan is sending continuously Terrorist and killing pilgrim and innocent persons in huge numbers. Some time Terrorist sabotage Railway and some time sensitive industries and some time Military and Police persons killed by Bomb blasting it is necessary to maintain and preserve confidence in the administration of justice.

Magistrate to conduct themselves properly in court when the Magistrate is interested or witnesses or party to the proceeding are related with the Magistrate then it will be proper to write order "Not before me and matter be transferred to any other court."

Primary functions of the police are prevention of crimes and also detection of crime maintenance of law and order. The apprehension of offenders but now the police are not friends of honest citizens and law abiding citizens but the police are the friends of offenders, in several instances police asked the culprits to commit offence like theft and dacoit etc. and taking shares from the stolen property. In and several cases police themselves committed offence by snatching the pockets of common man. And further some police persons are taking caution that there should not be injury to them, these are the reasons of increasing terrorism in India.

Under Section 4 of the Bombay Police Act (XXII of 1951) the Superintendent of Police Force throughout the State vests with the Government, due to this reasons the police persons cannot work properly.

Now there is one more Example of Bihar State there is no law and order, terrorist killing several innocent persons those are not concerned with any affairs. There is Bomb blast in Cinema Theatre, Religious Yatra and markets in New Delhi, in which common man killed in heavy number.

I had taken this subject of terrorism in India and abroad because to find out the problem behind terrorism. visited the jails, I recorded the statements of convicted terrorist, and I also recorded the statements of police persons and also judicial officers including High Court judges. I will read books on the topic from libraries of different universities. Example, Delhi University, Nagpur University, Hyderabad University, Madras University, Calcutta University etc. and also I visited America and libraries, including Indian Law Institute Delhi.

I will try to find out reasons of terrorism and to suggest the solutions to prevent such heinous crime.

Hence this is the conclusion.

US REPORT ON TERROR GIVIN SOFT BURIAL

The Document was Flayed for Under Reporting Last Year:

New Delhi: The U.S. has killed its annual report on global terrorism. The U.S. state department's "Global patterns of terrorism" will now be replaced by a simpler "Country reports on global terrorism". The "Global patterns….." report was generally regarded as the Last word on trends in global terrorism, listing and prescribing terrorist groups from around the world. It was one U.S. report that the Indian Government eagerly waited every year. It served as a vindication for the kind of terrorism that India regularly faces.

The new report, said U.S. officials at the embassy here, would be submitted to the U.S. senate on April 30, but significantly. It will be devoid of any data." The statistical appendix will not be there," said a spokesperson of the U.S. embassy. However, he said, the report will have several new element like a list of "umbrella terrorist groups and one on "global Jihadi networks". According to sources, the decision to kill the report was taken by the new U.S. secretary of state Condoleezza Rice, shortly after she took over.

In 2004, the U.S. administration suffered a huge humiliation of having to retract this report after it become clear that it had under reported the number of terrorist attacks, which was a central plank for U.S. Presiding George Bush's claim that the U.S. was winning the war on terrorism. According to Larry Johnson, a former CIA official writing in a counter terrorism blog, if the number of significant attacks in 2003 was 172, 2004, they had jumped to 655, the highest since 1985. Of these, 300 attacks happened in Jammu and Kashmir alone, particularly in a year when the India-Pakistan peace process was on. The figures, which he says, came from the newly created National Counter Terrorism Centre, did not include the attacks in Iraq.

The all important statistics are excepted to be released by the National Counter Terrorism Centre, though no dates for that have been set. For India, it is a loss of sorts, because for years, New Delhi had lobbied with the U.S. government to prescribe Pakistan groups like Lashkar-e-Toiba and Jaish-e-Mohammed in this report.'

The Terrorists are the enemy of the society, due to frustration and due to any other reason they are killing the innocent persons, and actually they are not concerned with any offence of any else. We can take example of Saddam Hussain of Iraq. He was thinking as a supreme of his country and his behavior was so cruel due to which common people of Iraq could not tolerate such cruelty and then United Nations Organization had taken cognizance and through United States had taken action against the Saddam and he was arrested. Same type of Hitler and other Kings of the world harassed the public at large. In India even British Reign played same tactics and Nationalist were crushed in "Jalianwala Bagh" even. Now similar terrorist activities are going in Indonesia, Maleayasia, Pakistan and in India especially in Kashmir area, we must find out the reasons behind such Terrorist Activities. I think some of these are corruption is the basis cause of such Terrorist activities Government servants and also public are responsible for such corruption. And specially, in courts the judges always administering the oath to the witnesses "Taking oath of God", but generally Government want the Nation is secular, they cannot understand the meaning of secularism, secularism not Restraining the faith of God, when there is no faith on the God then why oath of God administered to the witness.

All those activities are going on for retaining the leadership, they are not faithful to Nation and now even poor man cannot get any relief without corruption, and due to these real offences of corruption it is too difficult to check terrorism in the country and in the world. Even Government Machinery, including Mantralaya it is too difficult to get relief of any problem without corruption. Due to heavy corruption, businessman with the help of corruption are adulating the foods, petrol, poor man's kerosene only corruptions are giving shelter to rich persons and rich persons are getting maximum benefits, including contracts etc. Terrorism is nothing but one step of Revolution; Nexalities are doing the same activities. We must strictly check the corruption. The only there will be check of terrorist activities. Now it seems the persons those who are fighting for the bread are ready to accept any work after getting money from the politicians and Dadas. Political persons want to continue terrorism activities for their ultimate aim of getting Chairs in Government and their selfish gain. Now in Democracy Elected persons are using all the methods to elect including corruption and terrorist activities even. Example is of Bihar State, there are several elected M.Ps. and M.L.As. are in power polices are their private servants. Hence there are heavy terrorist activities.

This is important to note that Supreme Court and High Courts also are continuously directing to restrain such Bahubalis and they should be arrested and detained in the prison, but government is of Bahubalis who will control them.

Now the prices of essential commodities are going up day-to-day and now VAT additional tax is included. How a poor man and cultivator will survive, when the children of the poor persons crying for the bread and whole family are fighting for the bread, then naturally there will be increase in terrorism activities, for Ration Card there is corruption. Police, Court clerks are some cases of judicial corruption: Everywhere there is corruption then there will be increase of corruption. Firstly it is necessary to check the corruption. Freedom Fighters are fighting for the pension. They have no money then they cannot get Freedom Fighters pension etc.

References

(1) Scott gold in los Angeles times.
(2) ROBERT SCHWAN EBERG in New York, NJ, Star-Ledger.
(3) RALPH KINNY BENNETT.
(4) JAXON VAN DERBEKEN in San Francisco.
(5) JOHN CHIPMAN in National Post (Canada).
(6) SALLY JENKINS in Washington Post.
(7) DOUGLAS PEIDEN in New York Daily News.
(8) DAVID FRANK.
(9) Adapted from e-mail.
(10) WILLIAM HARVERY in Salon COM.
(11) WILLIAM HARVEY in Salon COM.
(12) CHRISTOPHER DE VINCK in the Record (Bergen County. NJ).
(13) ED BRADLEY on "60 minutes".
(14) Adopted by ANTHONY H. CORDESMAN, Center for Strategic and International Studies from material provided by the National Security Council Staff Research.
(15) By Lou Michel and Dan Herbeck.
(16) BY MATHEW SCHOFIELD FROM KANAS CITY STAR.
(17) BY SHARLENE KING JHONSON.
(18) By Bobby De Laughter From "NEVER TOO LATE".
(19) Perlman & Allington: The Tesks of Penology (Third Reprint 1970), p. 4.
(20) Bid Preface.
(21) Silving: "Rule of law in Criminal Justice" in ESSAYS IN CRIMINAL SCIENCE (1961 Ed.) Chap. 5.

(22) Theodore Levin was the Chief Judge of the United States District Court for the Eastern District of Michigam.

(23) Curtis Book: Problems in Criminal Law. (1952) p.58.

(24) Priopr to 1975 a number of notorious smugglers who were detained under rule 127. D.I.R. procured their release on bail. Now with the government of India Notification, dated October 23, 1975, this is not possible.

(25) The third United Nations Congress on the Prevention of Crime and Treatment of offenders, Agenda item (1965).

(26) Nigal Walker: Sentencing in A Rational Society (1972) p. 98.

(27) Thad F. Brown's article entitled Crime Prevention and Youthful Offenders. Published in the Police Year Book, 1957 pp. 77-80.

(28) The New Code of Criminal Procedure, 19073, has already repealed the old Criminal Procedure Code of 1898.

(29) Hall Jerome: Studies in Jurisprudence and Criminal Theory, p. 253.

(30) Modified by Anti-corruption Laws (Amendment) Act, 1964.

(31) The relevant provisions are contained in section 372 of the Indian Penal Code and there is also a Special enactment of 1956 prohibiting trafficking in minors and girls for immoral purposes.

(32) Supra Chapter XV.

(33) Dowry is another illustration on the point. Despite stringent provisions of the Dowry Prohibition (Amendment) Act, 1985, doubts are being expressed about the actual abolition of dowry in practice.

(34) With the expansion of Banking in Rural Areas Bank Robberies in India have become a common occurrence.

(35) The Sanyal murder case of Delhi (1972).

(36) India has not progressed much in training police dogs for crime detection. There are at present only two institutions functioning to train dogs for this job, one is at Madras and the other in Himachal Pradesh. There is a need for a Central Training Institute, which may train dogs for crime detection and procure their breeds.

(37) Carrel Alexis: Man the Unknown, pp. 240-241.

(38) Sutherland and Cressy: the principles of Criminology, 6th Ed. P. 391.

(39) Vold. G.B.: Theoretical Criminology, p. 314.

(40) Ressler: reading in Criminology and Penology (Second Reprint) p. 650.

BIBLIOGRAPHY

Barness, Teeters : New Horizons in Criminology (Third ed.) 1966.

Bonger William A. : Criminality and Economic Conditions, (1916) Little Brown & Co., Boston.

Burt Cyril : The Young Delinquent (1st Ed. 1938) London.

Caldwell Robert G. : Criminology (New York, Ronald, 1956).

Cavan, Cavan : Delinuquancy and Crime.

Clellan M.C. : Crimes without Punishment.

Cohen Frank J. : Youth and Crimes (New York 1957)

Cross, Jones : Introduction to Criminal Law (Fourth Ed.)

Courtis Book : Problems in Criminal Law (1955).

Deb, R. : Principles of Criminology, Criminal Law and Investigation Vol. I & II (Second Ed. 1968).

Donald Taft, Raiph W. England : Criminology (Fourth Ed.).

Don. C. Gibbons : Delinquent Behaviour (1970).

Dressler David : Readings in Criminology (1966 Ed.).

Durkheim Emile : Crime as a Normal Phenomenon.

Edward Sagarin (Edited) : Criminaology New Concerns (New York) (1979).

Fitegera P.J. : Criminal Law and Punishment (Oxford 1962 Ed.).

Fransis Allen : Boarderland of Criminal Justice (1964 Ed.).

Garofalo Raffaele : Criminology (1970) Little Brown & Co., Boston.

Gault R.H. : Criminology (Boston, Health, 1932).

Gilbert Geis (Edited) : White Collar Theory and Ressearch Sage Publications California (1980).

Gillin John L. : Criminology and Penology (Third Ed.).

Glonville Williams : The Criminal Law (Second Ed.).

Glanville Willams : The proof of Guilt.
Gluck Sheldon : The problem Delinquency (Boston, 1959).
Gois : White Collar Crime.
Hart : Morality of the Criminal Law.
Heinrich Oppenheimer : The Rational of Punishment (1913).
Howard John : The State of Prisons.
Howard Jones : Crime and the Penal System (London University Press, 1956).
I.P.P.F. Publication : Studies in Penology (1964 Ed.).
Kenny : Lutlines of Criminal Law (17th Ed.).
Lionel Fox, Sir : The English Prison & Borstal System (1952).
Mannheim Harmann : Comparative Criminology, (1965) London.
Martin J.P. : After Care in Transition (1964).
Nigel Walker : Crime and Punishment in Britain.
Nigel Walker : Sentencing in a Rational Society (Second Ed.) 1972 (A Penguin Book).
Osmania University Publication : Police in a Developing Society (1972).
Oughton : Fraud and White Collar Crime.
Partipurnand Varma : Crime, criminal and Convict (1965 Ed.).
Periman Harvey : The Tasks of
& Thomas Allington : Penology (3rd Ed.) 1970.
Thomas Allington
Petric Police : Crime and Society.
Pillai K.S. : Theories of Criminology.
Quinney Richard : The Problem of Crime (New York, 1970).
Radzinowicz L. : Cambridge Studies in Criminology Vol. XII (1960).
Reiss Ira : Pre Marital Sexual Standard in America.
Rubin Sol : Crime and Juvenile Delinquency (New York) (1958).
Sen P.K. : Penology: Old and New (1943 Ed.)
Sethna M.J. : Society and the Criminal (2nd Ed.) 1964.
Shah Jyotsna, H. Dr. : Studies in Criminology- Probation Services in India (1973 N.M. Tripathy Pvt. Ltd.).
Sather land and Cressey : The principles of Crimionology (7th Ed.). 1966.
Tappen Paul W. : Crime, Justice and Correction (1960 Ed.)
Taylor Jan, Paul Walton
& Jack Young : The New Criminology; For a Social Theory

of Deviance (2nd Ed. London 1973).

Varma : Pathology of Crime and Delinquency (1972).

Velder and Kay : Penology Realistic Approach.

Vold G.B. : Theoretical Criminology (1958) Oxford University Press.

Walter C. Reckless : The Crime Problem (1967).

Winfield A. Elkin : The English Penal Syatem.

Mohomad Sugal Esa Manasan Rais Allah v. King, 287
Moolraj v. State, 73, 81
Moore v. State, 396
Maqbooluddin v. Rex, 262
More's In re, 376
M.P. Sharma v. Satish Chandra, 175, 178
M. Rangaraulu Naidu, In re, 507
Nadir Ali Baqz Zaidi v. State of U.P., 369
Ngarali Nazarali, In re, 309
Nag Shawe Bwin In re, 408
Nandi Singh v. Sita Ram, 13
Nandlal Singh v. Crown, 431
Nandlal Srivastava v. Rex, 234, 235
Nanhu Prasad Singh v. State of Bihar, 56, 278
Nani Gopal Mitra v. State of Bihar, 145, 147
Naravan v. State, 39, 46, 78, 88, 89, 242
Narayanan v. State of Kerala, 118
Narayan Swami Naidu v. Rangaswami Naidu, 5, 6
Narayan Lal Bansi Lal v. Maneck Phiroze Mistry, 170, 178
Narayan Prasad Tiwari v. State of Orissa, 545
Narendra Kumar v. State, 16
Narsingdas Lakhotia v. State, 541
Nathilal v. Emperor, 226
Nathu v. State of Uttar Pradesh, 524
Nathuni Sao v. Md. Bashir, 390.
People v. George, 395
People v. Gilbert, 395
People v. Harvey, 395
People v. Hemrich, 395
People v. Hickman, 390, 397
People v. Huff, 397
People v. Kathan, 391
People v. Langit, 393, 394, 395, 396, 397
Qasin Rizvi v. State of Hyderabad, 300
Qazi Rahimullah v. Emperor, 338
Queen v. Ahmad, 19
Queen v. Coote, 171
Queen v. Hussun Ali, 111
Queen v. Madhub Chundra, 19
Queen v. Nimchand Mookarjee, 431
Queen v. Nibokisto, 19

INDEX

P

R

S